BACKWARDNESS IN READING

BACKWARDNESS IN READING

A
STUDY OF ITS NATURE AND ORIGIN

BY

M. D. VERNON, M.A., Sc.D.

*Professor of Psychology in the
University of Reading*

CAMBRIDGE
AT THE UNIVERSITY PRESS
1960

CAMBRIDGE
UNIVERSITY PRESS

University Printing House, Cambridge CB2 8BS, United Kingdom

Cambridge University Press is part of the University of Cambridge.

It furthers the University's mission by disseminating knowledge in the pursuit of education, learning and research at the highest international levels of excellence.

www.cambridge.org
Information on this title: www.cambridge.org/9781316603642

© Cambridge University Press 1960

First printed 1957
Reprinted 1960
First paperback edition 2016

A catalogue record for this publication is available from the British Library

ISBN 978-1-316-60364-2 Paperback

CONTENTS

CONTENTS

ILLUSTRATIONS

ACKNOWLEDGEMENTS

I wish to acknowledge with thanks the help which has been given me in studying the problem of reading backwardness: by Mrs Scott Blair, who drew my attention to the urgency of the problem, and assisted me in testing backward readers and in obtaining supplementary information about them; by the Chief Education Officer of Reading County Borough, who gave me permission to work in a Reading school; by the Head Teacher of the school, who was so helpful in making the necessary arrangements; by the staff of the Berkshire Child Guidance Clinic, who also gave me facilities for testing; and by the children themselves, who were always co-operative and willing. I should also like to thank Professor Zangwill for advising me and discussing the problem with me.

Acknowledgement for permission to reproduce figures is made to the following: Dr Lauretta Bender, the American Orthopsychiatric Association and the George Benda Publishing Company for Fig. 1; *Archives de Psychologie* for Fig. 2; the *Journal of Educational Psychology* for Figs. 3 and 5; the Journal Press for Fig. 4; Mrs E. Newson for Fig. 6; the *American Journal of Psychology* for Fig. 9.

Acknowledgement is also made for the tabular data quoted in the book.

CHAPTER I

INTRODUCTION

When adults study and assess children's ability to read, they are apt to consider this ability as a single homogeneous entity. This is not unnatural, for in educated adults reading has become a firmly established habitual activity which they perform with great ease and speed. Consequently they are unaware of the various processes which they themselves must carry out in reading. And they do not recognize that children who are in the early stages of reading may utilize procedures which are quite different from those employed by adults. In such children, reading is not a well-organized system of habits. A child must go laboriously through a number of inter-related activities before he can fully understand the meaning of printed words and sentences. He may stumble or break down at any stage in the proceedings. Such a failure may interfere badly with the whole process of reading, and the child will appear to be a backward reader or even an illiterate.

It is important therefore before we begin to investigate the causes of backwardness in reading to attempt a rough classification of the various stages in reading, and the failures that may occur at these stages. A more detailed analysis of the psychological processes taking place at some of these stages will be given later.

There seem to be few if any recorded cases of adults, or even of older children, who have passed through the educational mill without learning to read anything at all, apart from those of low intelligence or with organic brain defect or injury. The illiterate adult can usually recognize a few words which he has memorized— for instance, the words which he frequently sees on advertisements and public notices. The illiterate child often knows his letters, and can pick out a few simple words in a story book, especially if these are accompanied by appropriate pictures. But he cannot read consecutively, nor recognize words other than the few he has memorized.

At the next stage, we have the individual who reads with great difficulty; the adult or the child who can stumble through an easy story book with a simple vocabulary, or can read the remarks in a 'comic'. When he encounters a word he cannot recognize, he may guess at it, or he may try with greater or less success to work it out by sounding the letters or groups of letters in the word. At a rather higher stage are the children who, when asked to read aloud, do what has been called 'barking' at the print. They may be said to have mastered the 'mechanics' of reading, in that they are able to analyse the printed words into their constituent units, give these their correct phonetic sounds, blend these sounds together and enunciate the whole words more or less accurately. But they do this slowly and with difficulty, and their attention is concentrated to such an extent upon enunciation that they do not take in the meanings of the words. Thus they cannot remember what they have been reading about, nor answer questions on it. These individuals, once they have reached a certain age, are usually classed as semi-literates.

Among those who can read with some understanding, there are all degrees and varieties. There are those who can understand only short sentences and newspaper headlines; those who can read simple stories, but slowly and laboriously, perhaps studying almost every word in the text. These individuals may have learnt to read very late, and their disability may still appear in their wildly incorrect spelling. Finally, there is the highly educated adult who can skim rapidly through even a difficult book, extracting what interests him and disregarding the rest. There are even geniuses such as Carlyle who, we are told, could 'read' a whole page at a single glance. But their mental processes are quite outside our purview.

Now it seems clear that in any study of backwardness in reading we should be clear as to which of these stages we are investigating. The difficulties encountered in the illiterates, those who have failed to learn the mechanics of reading, and the underlying causes of these difficulties, may very well be different from those of less backward readers. As we shall see, the former appear to be similar

2

to those of the child who is just beginning to read. But the condition, in older children and adults, is so severe as to put them in a class apart from those who are merely backward; and it may well be termed a specific 'disability'.[1] The problem it presents is one of unusual interest to the psychologist. It is also of considerable importance to the teacher, who finds that an illiterate child of eight or nine and upwards is often excessively resistant to remedial teaching.

In the very extensive investigations which have been carried out into the incidence and causes of backwardness in reading, the distinction between the illiterate and the semi-literate has too often been overlooked. Frequently, large groups of children have been tested with standardized reading tests, which give the children scores in terms of the average performance of children of a given chronological or mental age. Individual cases are then classified as backward readers when their test performances—or 'reading ages'—are retarded by one year, two years, three years, and so on, below the average performance for their chronological or mental age. This practice is convenient from the point of view of the teacher who has to classify and teach the children. But it does not reveal the manner in which they attempt to read, nor their difficulties in doing so. A more detailed study of these difficulties is necessary before it is possible to gain a psychological understanding of their disability.

Fortunately the number of illiterates in the general population is small in comparison with the number of semi-literates. In the investigation described in the Ministry of Education's pamphlet, *Reading Ability* (1950), 'illiterates' among older children, aged 15–18, were defined as those with reading ages below 7 years; that is to say, they could probably guess a few simple words at sight, but had not grasped the mechanics of reading, and could not be

---

[1] In recent years the term 'dyslexic' has been applied to children of normal intelligence with marked specific disability in reading. Apparently this term has been adopted in order to indicate that these cases are comparable with those of 'alexia' produced by cortical injury. For reasons described in chapter v, this hypothesis cannot at present be accepted. Therefore the term 'dyslexic' will not be employed in this book.

I-2

said to read in any real sense of the word. They constituted 1·4% of the 15-year-olds and 1·0% of the 18-year-olds. Among the 11-year-olds the term 'illiterate' was used in rather a different sense. But 4·2 per cent of this group had a reading age under 7 years. A further 20·3% of the 11-year-olds, 4·3% of the 15-year-olds and 2·6% of the 18-year-olds had reading ages of 7 years or over, but under 9 years. They probably formed a somewhat heterogeneous group, who had acquired the bare mechanics of reading, so that they knew how to analyse words into their constituent letter groups, and thus were able to tackle new and unfamiliar words. But their reading was stumbling and halting; they read one word at a time, and hence reading was of little pleasure to them because comprehension was so slow.

A more recent study of a sample of 11-year-olds in London schools (Child, 1955) showed the proportion with a reading age below 7 years had dropped to about 1·0%. But the proportion of backward readers with reading ages between 7 and 9 years had not decreased, and might even have increased. Another recent study was made in Middlesbrough (1953) in which the complete 11-year-old age group of about 2000 children was tested with the Burt Graded Word Reading Test. It was found that 3·9% of the boys and 1·3% of the girls had a reading age of 7 or less—that is to say, they were illiterate in the sense of the word used above. This figure is lower than that of the Ministry of Education pamphlet, but above that of Child. Hence a certain fluctuation may be expected from time to time and in different parts of the country. It is doubtful if the figure would ever fall to zero, but it should not rise above 4% if teaching conditions are adequate (see also Appendix II).

The main study of this book will centre upon the illiterates—those who for some reason or other are unable to master even the simpler mechanics of reading. From the vast literature on the subject, we shall endeavour to select experimental and clinical studies of such cases, and differentiate them from those who have some grasp of the mechanics of reading, but are failing in other ways—for instance, in understanding what they can enunciate. The latter form an ill-defined group to whom little systematic study has been devoted. It may be that in general they are in a transitional stage, and that a continuance of adequate teaching will enable them to learn to read successfully, provided that they have sufficient intelligence and interest. We know, however, that real illiterates, even those of good intelligence, require special teaching, and even to this they are often extremely resistant. They are unlikely to surmount their difficulties at all without such special attention. It is also interesting to compare them with older children who have managed to learn to read, but are utterly incapable of learning to spell correctly. Their difficulties may be due to the same factors as cause complete illiteracy.

It seems fairly clear that many of these illiterates, and especially the older ones, can be detected by the use of adequate reading tests,[1] provided that their actual reading age is ascertained. It is essential, however, to differentiate between the younger ones—for instance, those aged 8–9 with a reading age below 7—who may be merely somewhat lagging in their grasp of the mechanics of reading; and the older ones, of 9 years and over, who have by then been 'stuck' for so long at a reading age below 7 that special efforts are required to help them.

Unfortunately the methods used in studying backwardness in reading have frequently not differentiated at all adequately between children who are merely slow and backward in reading, and those who, in spite of reasonable intelligence, appear incapable of mastering the mechanics of reading. It is of course difficult to draw a

[1] No detailed study of standardized reading tests is included in this book. An extensive list is given by Robinson (1953a). A large variety of these tests is in use in the U.S.A. But the author has had no opportunity of studying them or of assessing their validity. For British children, the tests of Burt (1921) and of Schonell and Schonell (1950) are probably the most widely used, and appear to be quite satisfactory. It would be unwise to apply the norms of American tests to assess the reading ages of British children. Although group tests of reading comprehension are valuable for making a rough assessment of the reading ability of large numbers of children, no child should be diagnosed as illiterate, or as suffering from specific reading disability, until he has been given individual tests, including an oral test of reading words.

hard-and-fast line; but nevertheless, if anything is to be done to understand real disability in reading, the merely backward must be differentiated from those who can do no more than recognize a few words at sight. But a great many of the studies of reading backwardness have been made on large, heterogeneous, and ill-defined groups of children. Sometimes all those with reading ages of a year, or even only half a year, below their mental ages are classed together, quite irrespective of whether or not they can read in any real sense of the word, and the frequency of certain characteristics in this group contrasted with their frequency among normal readers. Sometimes the frequency of such characteristics has been correlated with the reading performance or reading ages of a whole group of children of all levels of proficiency. It is clear that such studies can give only very imperfect evidence as to the characteristics of those with real reading disability. It is not surprising that an extreme diversity of factors has been suggested as having some connection with backwardness in reading; or even as being the cause of reading disability. There is not even much agreement as to the main features of these children's attempts to read.

It is clearly essential therefore to discuss first what the child does when he tries to learn to read; and what it is that he fails to do when he is unable to learn, his peculiar mistakes and difficulties. When the characteristics of those with real reading disability have been distinguished, it may be more possible to investigate the underlying causes of the disability. The only really satisfactory method of making this investigation is the intensive study of individual cases. Unfortunately the number of satisfactory case studies made in the past is all too small. Too often, superficial diagnoses have been made of 'narrow perceptual span' or 'poor auditory memory'—as if these characteristics could be in any sense regarded as inherent or basic. Or else the investigator has been content to point to the apparent multiple causation in each single case, and has failed to extract such factors as appear common to all, or to a large proportion, of cases. However, this failure is understandable. There is no doubt that these cases do present, at least superficially, a great and complex diversity of features. More-over, the cases are rarely recognized when their inability to learn to read is in its early stages. By the time that they are detected and studied, the original causes may have been overlaid and concealed by a whole tissue of confused cognitive processes, emotional resistances, and so on. Events which occurred early in the child's development may by now be altogether forgotten. Thus again and again we shall encounter the difficulty, if not impossibility, of distinguishing what is the cause from what is the effect of the reading disability. However, we hope that it may be worth while to make a thorough and detailed study of the experimental investi-gations that have been made; and to present and to weigh up the evidence as to the importance of the various factors which appear to be associated with the inability to learn to read.

CHAPTER II

VISUAL PERCEPTION IN READING

(1) THE DEVELOPMENT OF VISUAL PERCEPTION IN CHILDREN

Before we study in detail the characteristics of the illiterate individual's attempts to read, and the causes of his disability, we must first devote some attention to what appear to be the processes that occur as the child learns to read. Clearly, he must begin by perceiving some kind of shape or pattern which constitutes the printed letter or word. It is difficult to be certain exactly what the little child does perceive—though in all probability he does not see just what the adult sees.

Before the child can perceive printed shapes, he must be capable of perceiving small 'meaningless' shapes, containing a good deal of detail. It is therefore important to consider the evidence which has been obtained as to the development of this ability in children. Not many systematic investigations of the development of shape and pattern perception have been carried out; perhaps because the accurate perception of pattern is not very important to the child until he begins to try to read. The young child is concerned mainly with the perception of three-dimensional solid objects which can be touched and manipulated, as well as seen. He is eager to find out what they are like, what they do, and what he can do with them. His experience of two-dimensional form comes mainly through looking at pictures in books, and through drawing or scribbling. It does seem possible that he establishes a certain association between the shapes which he sees in pictures, and the movements, and images of movements, he makes in drawing them. It has been stated that children tend to draw from their ideas about objects, rather than by copying from pictures, or from their own imagery—though Gesell, Ilg and Bullis (1949) consider that the 5-year-old likes to trace and copy pictures. But we cannot assume that the child has much previous experience of a kind relevant to the establishment of an association between reading and writing the shapes of letters and words.

Even the *perception of pictures* may be partial and vague. Griffiths (1954), however, found that the average child began to look at pictures, though only momentarily, as early as his second year. The Terman–Merrill Intelligence Test (1937) expects an average child of $3\frac{1}{2}$ years to be able to name fifteen out of eighteen simple outline drawings of familiar objects; and to pick out and name three objects from a fairly complicated picture. Thus it may be supposed that by the time the child begins to learn to read, he can identify pictures of objects with which he is familiar, either as real objects or as pictures. Indeed, it has often been said that a child must be able to name pictures without difficulty before he can begin to learn to read (see Monroe, 1951). For in many reading books pictures are shown of objects and activities of various kinds, which the child has to understand in order to associate with them the printed description of the object or activity which accompanies the picture. Yet children are much slower to understand the meaning of a picture, and the nature of the activity it presents, than they are to name simple representations of objects. Binet and Simon (1908) drew attention to the inability of young children to 'understand' pictures. In the Terman–Merrill test, a child is not expected to give the meaning of the picture of the telegraph boy till he is 12 years old. This is perhaps rather a difficult picture to interpret. But the author (1940) observed that the average child could not fully interpret a picture till he was about 11 years old, though he could give a simple description of its more obvious activities by the age of about 7 years. This often included a considerable amount of irrelevant detail. Miller (1938) also found that children of 8 or 9 years could describe only about 20 % of the main items—those which gave the real meaning of the picture—in pictures taken from the books they were actually using in school. They tended to see these items as isolated details, with no relationship to the meaning of the picture as a whole; and often the most important items were altogether overlooked. Again, Poston and Patrick (1944) showed that, although, in general, children of 6–8 years could identify printed names of objects more readily when these were presented with pictures of the objects, in some cases the pictures had a misleading effect, because the children misinterpreted them. For instance, the word 'hen' was often read as 'chicken', presumably because the latter was a more familiar name for the picture given. Clearly then, if children are to be taught to read through the use of pictures, it is most important that the teacher should ascertain that they know what the picture represents and means.

But a more important problem lies in the *perception of two-dimensional shapes* without representational meaning, such as the shapes of letters and words. It is doubtful how soon the child is able to perceive such shapes. We know that very simple shapes such as a triangle, square and circle, can be differentiated from one another at 2 years (Gellerman, 1933); and that these shapes can be remembered and recognized in different settings, colours and spatial positions. In the Terman–Merrill test, the average child of 4 years is expected to match eight out of ten simple outlined geometrical shapes. Piaget and Inhelder (1948) found that in copying figures the 5-year-old could differentiate between a square and a rectangle, a circle and an ellipse, a horizontal-vertical and a diagonal cross. Gesell and Ames (1946) showed that children could copy a cross recognizably at 3 years, a square at 4½ years, and a triangle and diamond at rather greater ages. Copying a diamond appears in the Terman–Merrill test among the items for the 7-year group; that is to say, most normal children of 7 years should be able to do this.

More complex figures are not fully grasped till later. Thus Gesell and Ames found that the figure shown was reproduced at 4 years with a single central vertical line and numerous cross-lines. Between 4 and 5 years, the tendency was to draw the inner lines as spokes radiating from the centre, but unrelated to one another. At 6 years, there were a vertical-horizontal and a diagonal cross, but their centres did not necessarily coincide. Clearly the child analysed the complex shape into several constituents, without relating them to one another.

Piaget and Inhelder found much the same. In copying figures such as a circle within a triangle, each shape was correctly reproduced by the 5-year-old child, but their relationship to each other was not accurately reproduced. It appeared that the child's perceptions were fragmented, and that he could not combine them into a coherent whole. Line (1931) also noted that, when at 4 years the child began to differentiate detail within an outline, the details were at first seen as quite unrelated to the outline.

The most complete study of the ability of children at various ages to copy moderately complex figures is that of Bender (1938). She showed, as had Piaget and Inhelder, that younger children appeared to have some awareness of the details within a figure, but could not reproduce them accurately. Thus the directions of lines, other than the horizontal, were not copied correctly; vertical lines were approximately correct at 5–6 years, but oblique lines not till 9–10 years. When the figure consisted of two parts, these were not accurately related to one another by the younger children. They succeeded at 7 years with Fig. 1(a) and (i), but not till 11 years with (h). Fig. 1 also shows some of the typical reproductions made by the younger children.

Another study of the reproduction of these figures was made by Harriman and Harriman (1950). They found that there was a striking maturation in reproduction between the ages of 5 and 7 years.[1] At the later age, many of the reproductions resembled those of adults; whereas at the earlier age, they included many examples of figures reproduced as 'wholes' with little attention to detail. Townsend (1951), however, brought evidence to show that the ability to copy these figures correctly improved fairly steadily up to the mental age of $7\frac{1}{2}$–8 years; but after that, various individual factors seemed to determine the accuracy of copying. Even adult subjects did not always copy correctly the figures shown in

[1] Almost all the results of experiments on American school-children are expressed in terms of school 'grades'. These have been converted approximately into chronological ages by means of the table given by Gates (1935). This practice of assessing results in terms of grades is unfortunate, since, as McNemar (1942) has shown, there may be a spread of as much as 6 years of chronological age, and of over 4 years of mental age, in one of the lower grades, and even more in one of the higher grades.

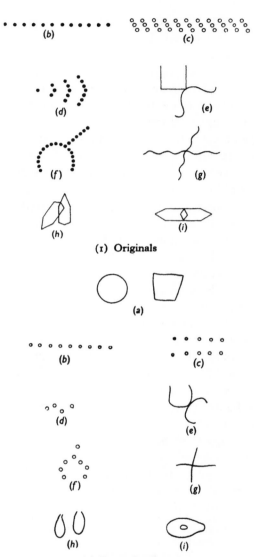

(1) Originals

(2) Reproductions

Fig. 1. The Bender Visual Motor Gestalt Test

Fig. 1(c), (d), (e), (g), (h) and (i); (h) and (i) were particularly hard to reproduce correctly. In Townsend's investigation, seven simpler forms (triangle, square, diamond, etc.) were given to the children to copy as well as the Bender figures. The errors were analysed and placed in three categories: (1) failure to reproduce the essential form correctly; (2) failure to include all the component parts; and (3) rotations. Their distribution according to mental age, in 287 children of chronological ages 6 years 1 month to 9 years 3 months, is shown in Table 1.

Table 1

Percentage errors in category	Mental age in years							
	4½–	6½–	7–	7½–	8–	8½–	9–	9½–10
(1)	67·2	56·8	41·0	29·5	35·8	30·1	29·5	26·6
(2)	49·1	37·9	24·0	20·0	16·1	14·5	15·4	13·8
(3)	20·6	19·9	10·5	8·3	5·7	5·8	6·4	6·4

Possibly Townsend's standards of correctness in copying were rather high. Some of the errors may have been due to inability to draw correctly, rather than to inability to perceive the shapes correctly. It is true that the correlation of the copying test scores with the scores for matching shapes (form perception) was 0·60 (0·42 with mental age partialled out[1]); and this was higher than the correlation with scores on motor tests, which was 0·52 (0·19 with mental ages partialled out). We may conclude, however, that form perception was highly inaccurate before a mental age of 7½–8 years.

These results cannot be explained entirely by the rather generally held opinion that young children tend to see shapes as wholes, and rarely see small details, a tendency sometimes called 'syncretism'. This view was possibly advanced originally by the Gestalt psychologists as part of their general theory of the primacy of 'wholes'. At about the same time Segers (1926), investigating children's perception of pictures, concluded that differences of form were poorly perceived by children under 7 years of age. There was apparently a

[1] The term 'partialled out' indicates that this correlation coefficient was independent of the relation of both the copying test scores and scores for matching shapes to mental age.

'syncretist' tendency to see things as a whole, but the number of details perceived increased with age. When children were shown pictures of animals having the head of one animal and the body of another, no child below 7 years perceived the discrepancy between head and body, and few did so under 9 years. But these results cannot properly be generalized to include all types of shape and pattern. It seems fairly clear, both from Bender's results and also from an investigation by Osterreith (1945), that the perception of shapes as wholes depends upon the 'goodness' of the shape, in the Gestalt sense; that is to say, whether the shape forms a coherent

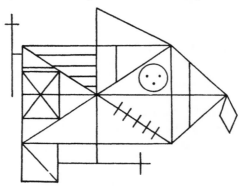

Fig. 2. Complex 'meaningless' figure

whole with a fairly obvious structure, or whether it consists of a complicated mass of unclear and unrelated detail. Osterreith required adults, and children from 4 years upwards, first to copy and then to reproduce from memory the complicated figure shown in Fig. 2. He found that the youngest children made very vague copies, with a few details dotted about irregularly. As their age increased, the children made increasingly exact copies of the details, juxtaposed together without any general scheme. Thus apparently they perceived the details separately, without inter-relating them. There was not much improvement in this procedure till 11 years of age, when the children began to produce a general structure based on an enclosing rectangle, into which the other details were fitted. Again, if parts of the figure were presented to the child, who was asked to recognize them within the whole, certain outstanding details were recognized at an early age, but the main outlines of the figure not till 9–10 years. These results agree with the argument put forward by Meili (1931), that syncretist perception occurs in children when they are shown simple forms of obvious and uncomplicated structure. These exert a strong determining influence on what is perceived; detail is neglected, and also the child ignores any modifications produced by the general setting. But if the total form is complicated or meaningless, its structure weak, or its details salient and obvious, then the latter tend to dominate the child's perceptions. Again, there is evidence that different children may vary in these respects. Petty (1939) found that some 6½-year-old children tended to copy drawings of real objects syncretically; but others selected details in an inconsistent manner, reproducing some very minute details but ignoring other more obvious ones.

The implications of these studies for reading are that children (or, at least, some children) are less likely to see words as wholes than as meaningless jumbles of details with no apparent relationship between these. On the other hand, letters may perhaps be seen as unanalysable wholes, and hence there is difficulty in differentiating their structure. Another point which was noted by Segers was that dissimilarity between shapes was more readily perceived than similarity. If this finding can also be applied to the perception of words, it suggests that it is difficult for the child to recognize a word he has learnt when it is shown in a different script or format or type size.

It seems from the study by Wood and Shulman (1940) that even if children can perceive shapes correctly, they may not be able to reproduce them accurately from memory. These psychologists found that children below the age of 8 years were unable to reproduce accurately from memory most of the forms shown in Fig. 3, when these had been presented for 5 sec. each. Even after this age, shapes other than 1 and 2 were often reproduced inaccurately; 9 and 10 were not reproduced correctly till about the age of 13. The percentage scores of correct reproductions are shown in

Table 2, for 908 boys and 738 girls. However, it is possible that greater accuracy was required in this test than would be necessary for the reproduction of letter shapes.

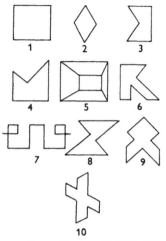

Fig. 3. Reproduction of simple shapes

Table 2

	Age								
	8½–	9½–	10½–	11½–	12½–	13½–	14½–	15½–	16½–17½
Boys	50	56	60	63	67	70	73	73	76
Girls	49	52	59	65	68	70	69	72	71

On one characteristic of the child's perception there seems to be general agreement: that he does not observe, or only observes and remembers with difficulty, the *orientations* of shapes and their *order* or direction in a sequence. That he overlooks the orientation of shapes is naturally to be expected, since one of the things which he has to learn in early childhood is that objects retain their identity when their spatial position and orientation are changed. Köhler (1939) quotes experiments by Mouchly as showing that little children could recognize outline drawings as easily when they were inverted as when they were upright. Frank (1935) found that children of 6–7 years frequently confused playing cards and their mirror images, but by the age of 9 years only 18% made this error. Davidson (1934) required children of 5 years and upwards to match silhouette shapes which were supposed to resemble the outlines of words (see Fig. 4).[1] The number of children who

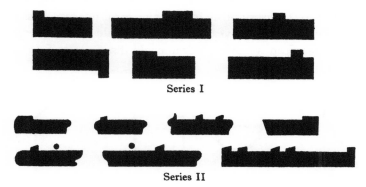

Series I

Series II

Fig. 4. Silhouettes resembling word outlines

Fig. 5. Reversible figures

matched these shapes with their mirror images decreased from 83% at 5 years to 50% at 8 years. These errors do not seem very surprising, for the shapes must have been hard to differentiate. What is much more surprising is the fact, commented on by Newson (1955), that 5-year-old children may be unable to see the difference between a shape and its mirror image even when it is pointed out. This indicates a real inability to attach any importance to orientation.

There is no doubt that certain shapes are particularly easy to reverse. Thus Krise (1952) found that even educated adults confused the shapes shown in Fig. 5, and had great difficulty in learn-

[1] In point of fact these figures are taken from an earlier paper by Davidson (1931). In the later paper (1934), Davidson stated that the figures used for matching were of the same kind as those employed in the earlier paper.

ing which was the correct one to associate with a given symbol. Hildreth (1934) showed that the shape ▨ was readily reversed by a group of children aged 7–8 years who were asked to reproduce it from memory; 15 % reproduced it in reversed form. Newson (1955) found that figures of the type shown in Fig. 6a were particularly hard to discriminate from their mirror images. Less than half of a group of 100 5-year-old children could do this correctly, whereas significantly more children could discriminate from their

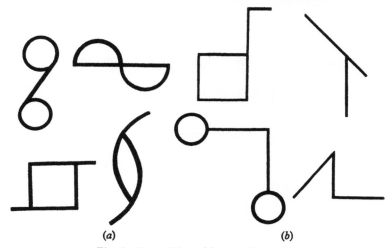

(a)   (b)

Fig. 6. Reversible and irreversible figures

mirror images the shapes shown in Fig. 6b. Now the shapes in Fig. 6a are characterized by the fact that if the top half is rotated, it becomes identical with the lower half, just as do the letters N, S and Z. Hence perhaps the frequency with which children continue to write these letters in reversed form long after other reversals have disappeared. However, it is doubtful if such reversals are of great importance in reading. But the reversal must be a perceptual one, since Newson used the matching method, and not the result of a tendency to draw clockwise which Gesell and Ames (1946) demonstrated between the ages of 3½ and 6 years.

Probably also of minor importance to reading is the tendency to rotate figures from the horizontal to the vertical position. Newson found that such rotations, and also complete inversions, were much more readily discriminated by 5-year-old children than were mirror reversals. As we shall see below, the same is true also in reading. The rotations of the Bender figures obtained by Fabian (1945) and by Townsend (1951) may have resulted from the well-known tendency to perceive symmetry, since the rotated figures were more symmetrical than the originals.

Closely related to the perception of orientation is the perception of *direction* and *order* in a sequence of shapes. The work of Piaget and Inhelder (1948) seemed to show that in the early stages children depend for their realization of order upon moving in such a way as to copy directly a perceived sequence. Thus they can reproduce the order of beads on a string only by taking up one bead after another and placing it exactly in the same position relative to the preceding one as it has in the original. They cannot until they have reached a certain age perceive visually the complete sequence of beads on the string as a whole with related parts. Teegarden (1933) found among fifty children aged 6–7 years, who were asked to name pictures of familiar objects arranged in five rows each of five columns, that eight did so quite irregularly—that is to say, they picked out pictures at random. Some moved up and down the columns; some from left to right and then back again; some consistently from left to right; and some consistently from right to left. Thus at this age, before they had begun learning to read, there were variable tendencies in direction of movement.

Recent work by Stambak (1951) showed that children had great difficulty in matching rhythmic tapping against visual reproductions of this (for instance, I II III II); and also the visual reproductions against a tapped rhythm. The first task was not carried out accurately till 12 years old, the second not until still later. Children under 10 could not always understand what they were supposed to do. This reproduction of rhythm appeared to have a certain relationship to the association of spatial and temporal order which occurs in reading (that is to say, order of printed letters and succession of letter sounds). This perception of correct order is vitally important in word recognition, writing and spelling; and inability to perceive in this way may be one of the factors making for difficulty in reading.

(2) THE VISUAL PERCEPTION OF PRINTED FORMS

We must now consider the part played by visual perception in the earliest stages of reading. Both the evidence already cited, and also that gathered in the study of reading itself, seem to indicate that the normal child of mental age 5–6 years can perceive simple forms without great difficulty. What is less certain is the extent to which he can remember accurately the small differences between a number of similar shapes, like those of the letters of the alphabet. And from the work of Bender particularly it appears likely that his memories of combinations of shapes, as in words, are most uncertain and unreliable.

Various experiments have indicated that there is little relationship between reading ability and the ability to perceive and discriminate shapes in children who have already begun to read. Thus Gates (1922) found that in children aged 8 years and upwards there was no significant correlation between the ability to detect small differences in shapes, and perceiving verbal material. Neither was there any correlation between the discrimination of small differences between numbers, and reading ability. When younger children, aged 6 years and upwards, were tested (Gates, 1926), a correlation of only about 0·3 was obtained between reading performance and the ability to note similarities and differences in geometrical figures, digits and words. A later investigation (Gates, 1940) showed a correlation of 0·42 between a picture directions test given to the children when they first entered school and their reading performance at the end of the term. Gates considered that a certain minimum perceptual ability might be required for reading, but that this minimum might be quite small. Kendall (1948) found a zero correlation between the reading achievement of children aged 6–8½ years, and their ability to reproduce from memory meaningless shapes of varying complexity which had been shown them tachistoscopically.[1]

[1] That is to say, the words were presented in a tachistoscope, a piece of apparatus for showing material for a very short period of time.

Davidson (1931), however, claimed that instruction in the perception of shapes such as those shown in Fig. 4 was of assistance in helping children of a mental age of 4 years in the beginning stage of learning to read. Unfortunately she could give no direct evidence of this, since she employed a number of different methods of instruction simultaneously. MacLatchy (1946) stated that training in the perception of visual form assisted 7-year-old children to learn to read; and Davis *et al.* (1949) claimed that training of kindergarten children in the rapid recognition of pictures improved subsequent reading progress. But these observations were not accurately controlled, and other factors may have been at work producing improvement.

It appears to be customary in testing children for '*reading readiness*' to include certain tests of visual perception. These tests are given frequently to children on entering the lowest grade of an American primary school at about the age of 6 years. From their results may be assessed the readiness of each child to be given formal teaching in reading. Moreover, the results may also demonstrate particular weaknesses, and indicate which aspects of teaching methods should be emphasized in particular cases (Gates, 1937). Three sets of 'reading readiness' tests, the Gates Reading Readiness Tests, the Metropolitan Reading Readiness Tests and the Monroe Reading Tests, include visual material. Much of this is pictorial. It has already been pointed out that if a child is to learn to read through the use of pictures—the commonest method of teaching—he must first be able to understand the meaning of pictures. But he must also be able to perceive and remember meaningless shapes. The Metropolitan and the Monroe tests include tests of the ability to copy, recognize or differentiate shapes and designs. But there appears to be little evidence of any close relationship between proficiency in this activity and ability to learn to read,[1] except that given by Petty (1939), who found a correlation of 0·48 between performance on a drawing test and the

[1] Among the very large numbers of 'Readers' and 'Pre-Readers' published in this country are books designed to teach 'reading readiness'. These include among other items the matching of printed letters and words. It is difficult to see the value of teaching children to match word shapes which they cannot read.

reading achievement of children aged 6–7 years. Possibly, as Gates pointed out, children must have reached a certain minimum proficiency in this respect before they can begin to read. However, these observations refer to the perception of relatively simple shapes; the perception of small details and of the relationship between these details may be another matter.

There has been much discussion as to what the child *actually perceives* when he learns to read a word. Children are no longer taught to read letters first of all, and then to build up the words letter by letter. Yet if they are to recognize whole words, there must be some characteristic of these words which they observe and memorize. Is this the total word form or outline of the word, or is it some grouping of particular letters within the word? Or are both aspects utilized?

Unfortunately a great deal of the earlier work on this problem was carried out on adults. This work was discussed by the author at some length in a previous book (Vernon, 1931, p. 118); and her conclusion may be quoted as follows:

The conclusion seems to be that some general form or contour is perceived, with certain dominating letters or parts arising out of it, as the 'figure' rises out of the 'ground'. The ascending letters seem to play an important part, and an alternation of vertical and curved letters may also help in structuralizing the form. It is improbable that any individual letters or parts of words are recognized as such. But they are the details, standing out from the rest of the field, which differentiate its flat clearness, and finally produce perception of the 'specific object'. The words are not necessarily recognized and named individually, but the structuralized visual percept of the whole phrase or sentence arouses the more or less subliminal auditory or kinaesthetic imagery of the sounds appropriate to that percept, or in some cases an incipient vocalization of these sounds. This total percept is then interpreted directly in accordance with the general meaning of the reading content.

But this is a description of visual perception in reading at the highest level. We cannot infer that anything of the kind takes place in the reading of beginners. Much of the work on recognition in children's reading is speculative and inconclusive. Sholty (1912) studied the reading of three children who had been taught to read for $1\frac{1}{2}$ years, by mixed methods, and found that one child tried to read words as wholes, whereas the other two analysed them into phonetic parts. Petty (1939), however, considered that children with syncretist tendencies, who saw words as wholes, learnt to read more easily than those who paid too much attention to detail, which was often irrelevant. This view agrees with that of Dearborn (1936), who stated that the better readers among the children he studied saw the total word form rather than the letters or parts of words. However, Petty also considered that the superiority of the syncretist type of reader was due to his greater facility in accepting the modern type of reading instruction, which is mainly syncretist in character. Payne (1930) found no tendency among children of 7–10 years to fall into any contrasting groups— those who saw total word forms and those who perceived only parts of words. She stated that both superior and inferior readers used both methods in word recognition, according to the type of word shown them. However, Sholty, Dearborn and Payne all used tachistoscopic devices for presenting words, which may produce methods of word recognition somewhat different from those used in ordinary reading.

Davidson (1931) found that 16 % of a group of thirteen children of mental age 4 years, who were learning to read, substituted for the words presented words of the same general shape. Bowden (1911) showed that similar length was the most common cause of confusion in the reading of five 6-year-old children, producing 24–42 % of the errors. When they were presented with words of similar general shape, they might not realize that these were different. But Davidson considered that younger children and poorer readers were liable to identify words by means of certain outstanding characteristics—certain particular letters; hence they confused words with similar letters. Gates and Boeker (1923) found no tendency to confuse words of similar general form. Words with similar endings were confused, but not those with similar beginnings, or middle sections. Some words were recognized by means of small and trivial details, such as the dot over the 'i' in 'pig'! In Davidson's study, 18 % of the words were confused with words of the same initial letter; 10% with words with the same final letter; and 7% with words containing the same 'oddly shaped' letter ('k', 'v', 'w'). Meek (1925) taught seventy-one children aged 4–6 years, of superior intelligence, to recognize the words 'ball', 'flag', 'doll', 'duck', 'lion' and 'rose', and to differentiate them from other similar words. She found that the children tended to confuse the first four of these words with other words containing similar or the same final letters, probably because the 'ascending' and 'descending' letters 'l', 'g' and 'k' stood out and caught their eyes. 'Lion' and 'rose' were most often confused with words having the same initial letters. Wilson and Flemming (1938) also found a tendency in children aged 6–7 years to substitute words of the same initial letter. But particular letters were sometimes recognized, for instance, the double 'o' in 'look'. Wiley (1928) showed that 19% of the errors in word recognition were caused by similar beginnings, 19% by similar endings. But confusion with words of similar configuration was also frequent. It seems therefore that letters which stand out in some particular way are noticed, and also that the initial and final letters of words are more often observed than those in the middle of the word. Bowden (1911) rather particularly stressed that even if words are perceived as wholes, the child is aware of the presence of absence of certain characteristic letters, but without any clear recognition of their position within the word. Whether a word will be confused with another word depends, as Payne noted, on the degree of similarity and the relative familiarity of the words. Thus she found that the word 'palace' was often confused with the more familiar word 'place'. However, the presence of ascending and descending letters which diversify the word structure does not necessarily lead to easy recognition. Rickard (1935) tested the recognition by children aged 6–9 years of 119 words taken from two lists of words used by children in their own vocabularies. He found that words containing no ascending or descending letters were among those most often recognized correctly. But these included some of the very short easy monosyllables. Shortness was certainly one of the factors making for easy recognition.

At first sight it is difficult to reconcile a tendency to notice particular letters with the categorical statement of Frank (1935) that backward readers, like young children, perceive the general structure of words and neglect details; and that words are solid wholes which defy analysis. But these findings are not perhaps altogether contradictory. The child may perceive the word as an unanalysable whole with its shape characterized by the shapes of certain particular letters. In the early stages of reading, he cannot analyse out these letters as separate entities which enter into different configurations in other words, yet retain their peculiar identity. Before reaching the later stages of reading, he must learn to make this analysis.

On another point there seems to be some agreement, namely, that children learn at a fairly early stage to recognize the shapes of certain isolated *letters*, and to give them their correct sounds. Gesell and Ilg (1946) stated that some identification of letters begins as early as 4 years of age; and these are fairly familiar by the age of $5\frac{1}{2}$ years. Smith (1928) obtained a high correlation between ability to match letters and to recognize words. Kopel (1942) also found that the reading achievement of children aged 6–7 years correlated more highly with the ability to perceive letters than with any other measure he used. Wilson and Flemming (1938) obtained a high correlation between the naming of letters and reading ability. In a further study (1940), they stated that a knowledge of the shapes, sounds and names of letters was one of the most important factors making for success in the early stages of learning to read. This conclusion was based upon the correlation of tests of letter recognition with reading progress. They gave the figures shown in Table 3 for the percentage of letters which could be named and sounded correctly at various ages (1939). Gates (1939) considered that letter sounding was important especially for children taught to read by methods which included a good deal of phonetic analysis.

Most advocates of teaching word or sentence 'wholes' recommend that the recognition of the shapes of single letters should not be taught before the child can recognize a certain number of simple

Table 3

	Age in years				
	4	5	6	7	8
Naming capital letters	36	54	74	91	97
Naming small letters	20	35	58	78	94
Sounding letters	—	13	23	51	64

words. This is partly because the letters by themselves are meaning-less to the child; and partly because their shapes are in some cases so much alike and so difficult to distinguish. Thus Smith (1928) found that shapes with *reversed orientation* ('b' and 'd', 'p' and 'q') were particularly liable to confusion; and there would be fairly general agreement on this point. Davidson (1934) showed that practically all children under the age of 6 years tended to confuse reversed and inverted letters; that is to say, 'p' with 'b' and 'q' with 'd', as well as 'p' and 'q', 'b' and 'd'. Errors of inversion tended to die out at a mental age of about 6 years, but reversal errors did not disappear until a mental age of 7½ years. The children began to see that 'b' and 'd' were different from each other before they could remember which was which. Wilson and Flemming (1938) showed that the tendency to confuse letters persisted up to the age of 8–9 years, but it was chiefly confined to confusions between 'b' and 'd', 'p', 'q' and 'j'. Frank (1935) found confusions between reversed letters, especially 'b' and 'd', to be very common in children of 6–7 years. But according to Ilg and Ames (1950) this becomes relatively infrequent after 7 years. Hildreth (1932) showed that even in the direct copying of letters, 70–80% of two groups of children aged 6–7 years made some reversal errors. It appeared that there was no consistent tendency towards the mirror writing of letters, but that it was almost a matter of chance which way they were copied. Ames and Ilg (1951) found that, in writing without a copy, children could print some letters at 3½ years, but they were placed at any angle. Reversals in writing letters and numbers occurred at 5 years, were frequent at 6 years, and began to die out at 7 years. This development seemed to be due to maturation rather than to learning to read, for Hildreth found that among the children she studied those who had begun to learn to read showed little superiority to those who had not. But Smith (1928) stated that even 6-year-old children were less likely to confuse the more similar letters when they were contained in nonsense syllables, than when they were given in isolation. Hill (1936), however, found that reversible letters caused more confusion to children aged 5–7 years when they were included in words than when they were shown in isolation. Reversals ('b' and 'd', 'p' and 'q') caused more difficulty than did inversions ('b' and 'p', 'd' and 'q', 'n' and 'u'). An experiment of the author's showed that reversals of 'b' and 'd', 'p' and 'q' still occurred in children aged 7–8 years, but were relatively infrequent; they occurred in 12% of possible cases. The only other confusion which occurred among isolated letters was between 'i' and 'l'. Hill (1936) also showed that in matching there was little tendency to confuse isolated letters other than the reversible ones. But Smith (1928) found considerable inaccuracy in matching the letters 'r', 'h', 'f', 'c', 'j', 'x', 'y' and 'v', when they were presented in isolation to 6-year-old children. Hers is, however, the only evidence of much difficulty in this respect. Most experimenters have found that if the child is given time to perceive the letters carefully, he can differentiate them with fair accuracy by the age of 6–7 years. The real difficulty lies in remembering which of the reversible letter shapes corresponds to which sound; and this difficulty persists up to 7–8 years, even in normal readers. It is probably due to an inability to remember orientations, a result of lack of maturation.

There is also fairly general agreement as to the inability of young children to recognize the importance of *order of letters* in words. Errors in word recognition are frequently due to confusion of words in which the same, or approximately the same, letters are placed in different positions, or even in *reversed order*. Bowden (1911) found that children could easily read words shown upside down. Nor did they notice the transposition of letters within the word, for instance 'nettims' for 'mittens'. Monroe (1928) gave the following percentages of all errors as reversals of the order of letters in words: 6 years, 12%; 7 years,

9%; 8 years, 8%; 9 years, 6%. Wiley (1928) tested the ability of five 6-year-old children to identify words when they were taught to recognize 60 words, over a period of 12 weeks. Only 11% of the 2518 errors made were due to reversals or partial reversals of words. But certain particular reversals were frequent, for instance, 'girl' for 'dog', and *vice versa*. Davidson (1931) found that 16% of the errors made in matching by children of mental age 4 years were reversals or inversions of words. In another study (1934) with slightly older children, 46% of the errors in word matching by 5-year-olds were reversals, and 40% of those made by 6-year-olds. But Hildreth (1932) found that when children aged 7–9 years were required to reproduce words from memory, other types of letter transposition were much more frequent than complete word reversals. Hill (1936) also showed that children of 5–7 years were very liable to confuse words containing the same letters in a different order. Ilg and Ames (1950) found that transposition of letters within words and complete word reversals persisted till 8–9 years, considerably later than did letter reversals. The same was true of writing (Ames and Ilg, 1951). The author noted occasional cases of matching reversed letters in words ('b' and 'd') in children aged 7–8 years; but matching with reversed words was much more common. Other forms of substitution were also fairly frequent, however, especially of the vowels within monosyllabic words.

It may be concluded that the order of letters in words is a matter of indifference to young children, and that they have great difficulty in remembering the correct order,[1] and hence in differentiating words containing the same, or almost the same, letters in a different order. Undoubtedly there is also a tendency to confuse words in which the order of the letters is completely reversed—words such as 'on' and 'no', 'was' and 'saw'. The total number of such words in the English language is not very great, but they may occur rather frequently in children's reading books. As we saw in the previous section, there does appear to be

[1] That this difficulty persists even in adults is shown by the common failure to remember when 'i' comes before 'e', and when 'e' before 'i'.

an inherent tendency in children to identify complete mirror images. However, in normal readers it does not persist, once the children begin to learn the correct order of the letters in words. It may appear to persist in backward readers, but again it may be no more than a part of the general confusion over order of letters.

It is fortunately true that errors in the order of letters in words are less likely to be of any importance in reading words connected in sentences than in recognizing or matching isolated words, since the child is helped to recognize the words correctly by the context. But a good deal of phonetic teaching necessitates the ability to match or identify isolated words correctly. Potter (1940) found that confusions due to reversals did not die out naturally, but that it was necessary to teach children the importance of the order or direction of letters in the word. Thus since teaching by word-whole methods does not impose any control upon direction, it must be supplemented by practice in writing words, which compels the child to observe each letter in turn, and thus forces their order upon his notice. Until he has learnt this, the whole process of reading is extremely unsystematic, consisting of a hit-or-miss recognition of a few words which the child has learnt to identify as wholes.

The general conclusion to be drawn from the studies of form and word perception in little children is that below a certain age they are too immature to perceive and remember small details of shape with great accuracy. In particular, they do not realize which details are significant and which comparatively irrelevant in defining the essential structure of a shape; nor do they understand the relationship of parts to the whole. They are also ignorant of the importance of orientation of shapes in space. Thus they may be capable of perceiving and recognizing rather unsystematically certain letters and certain words by means of their general shape or from some of their letters. But they have not acquired the ability to understand the importance of particular details in letter shapes, their spatial position, and their relationship to one another within the total word shape. Even if they can perceive these details, they do not remember their significance. However, in the normal child this ability seems to develop and mature rapidly at the age of 5–6 years, or at an earlier age in highly intelligent children, though recognition of the importance of correct order of letters in the word may come considerably later. The teaching of reading assists the development of these abilities, but cannot force it to proceed beyond a certain rate. Nor is it likely to take place in a very logical and systematic manner, since these children lack much ability to reason logically. But it can be concluded that in general the child is unlikely to be greatly handicapped in learning to read by any deficiency in the visual perception of word shapes. The auditory analysis of word sounds presents a more formidable difficulty; and this we shall now proceed to consider.

CHAPTER III

AUDITORY PERCEPTION IN READING

(1) THE DEVELOPMENT OF SPEECH AND THE HEARING OF SPEECH

It is, of course, obvious that the child cannot learn to read unless he has developed an adequate knowledge of words and of their meanings. For the normal child, this comes through hearing and understanding what is said to him, and through speaking words himself. It is generally agreed that the child 'understands' what is said to him before he can speak more than a few words. Thus, according to Seth and Guthrie (1935), he can understand simple sentences and commands by about the fourth quarter of the first year of age. This does not mean that he understands the full meaning of the words spoken to him, or even that necessarily he hears all the words correctly. But he can respond, by making appropriate actions, to patterns of sound in which the intonation of the voice is perhaps even more important than the sound patterns of the words themselves. The accurate discrimination and recognition of the latter is a later development.

But the child does not have to depend only upon hearing in the development of understanding word meanings. He also manipulates and experiments with the production of speech sounds in his own language. The production of speech sounds begins during the first year of life with babbling. This babbling apparently contains all the sounds necessary for speaking the English language, and indeed others besides, although the frequencies of sounds are different. It has been fairly generally postulated that the infant gradually adapts his own babbling sounds to the sounds of adult speech, partly by direct imitation, and partly by selecting those which adults can comprehend—since he finds sooner or later that only such sounds are successful in establishing communication with adults. Miller (1951), however, stated that the child does not use his own babbling sounds, but is obliged to re-learn speech

31

sounds from the language he hears spoken. In any case, children's speech sounds only gradually approximate to adult speech sounds. Thus McCarthy (1930) found that the following percentages of children's verbal responses were comprehensible to adults: 26% at 18 months; 67% at 2 years; 89% at 2½ years; 93% at 3 years; and 99% at 3½ years.

Sheridan (1955) has made an extensive study of the development of speech sounds in young children, based on records taken from 650 English children aged 4–5 years. She has described how, for some time after the child can himself understand adult speech, his own speech is so phonetically incorrect as to be incomprehensible to anyone outside his own family. Loudness is exaggerated and pitch distorted. The first words consist mainly of vowels (often differing considerably from adult vowels), with gaps where the consonants should be, and with intonations copying those of adult speech, for instance 'i–i' for 'dicky'. The consonants are acquired only gradually, and of these, 's', 'sh' and 'th' are the latest. In Sheridan's sample of children, only 20% of the girls and 10% of the boys could use 'th' correctly; it was usually replaced by 'f' or 'v'. Now Fletcher (1929, 1953) had shown that the audibility of consonants, and especially of 'v', 'f' and 'th', is relatively low. It appears likely therefore that the young child may be unable to voice these sounds because they are difficult to discriminate auditorily, and he is too inattentive to do so. The normal child of course grows out of this stage, and both hears and speaks accurately by about 6 years of age—though Sheridan showed that about 15% still possessed some defective consonants at 12 years. When these consonants were not correctly spoken at a later age than 6 years, it was not, according to Sheridan, a sign of impaired hearing, but of (a) mental defect, (b) some form of childish immaturity such as occurs in neglected or over-indulged children, or (c) lack of interest in or attention to speech—hence the greater incidence among boys than among girls (after 7 years of age, this defect was five times as common among boys as among girls). On the other hand, a defective 's', uttered as 't' or 'th' or omitted altogether, though sometimes due to malformation of the mouth or teeth, or to a particular local accent, may be an indication of impaired hearing if it persists after the age of 5 years. And defects of 'r'—pronounced as 'l', 'y' or 'w'—are often found in children with impaired hearing. Thus some degree of hearing loss should always be suspected when these defects appear in children of 6 years and older.

It is clear that any child who retains these or other speech defects after the age of entering school may have difficulty in learning to read. Furthermore, it is necessary not only that he should be able to enunciate correctly, but also that he should be able to speak grammatically and formulate sentences more or less correctly. In this again boys are usually more backward than girls. Children who have retained childish speech habits often outgrow them quickly when coming in contact with other children in school. But it is important that when the child goes to school, he should be taught to enunciate correctly. Again, he should be given practice in speaking grammatically. The understanding of the meaning of words in context is to a great extent a function of comprehending whole sentences, in their familiar grammatical structure. Children will only be confused if they say, like the child in *Punch*, 'Her b'ain't a-calling of we; u; don't belong to she'!

But even when the child can enunciate clearly and accurately, it does not follow that he can always perceive correctly the speech sounds of others, especially if these are given in isolation and not included in words. The threshold of hearing even for pure tones may be higher for children of apparently normal hearing than for adults, as Henry (1947) demonstrated. This may have been due to inattention, but inattention may also affect children's ability to hear speech sounds correctly. Kennedy (1942) also found that the auditory acuity of 6-year-old children was lower at almost every frequency than that of 8-year-old children. Pitch discrimination also seemed to be poorer in the younger children. Even children aged 14–15 years missed 31 % of all the consonant sounds presented in an articulation test.[1] Watson (1954) found that, at the age

[1] The score on an articulation test is the number of items (syllables or words) in a given list which the listener can repeat correctly.

of 9–10 years, there were considerable individual differences in the ability of children with normal hearing to hear words and sentences at near threshold intensity, though at higher intensities the differences were small. It seems likely that the failure to hear softly spoken words was due to lack of attention, but that these older children heard normally spoken words quite adequately. This might not necessarily be true of younger children.

Bennett (1951) found that 6-year-old children could hear on the average 79% of simple names to which they listened through headphones—in the sense that they could identify the pictures named. But Midgeley (1952), using the same technique, showed that 6-year-olds made frequent mistakes over the words 'house' (often confused with 'mouth'), 'rose', 'cage', 'hen', 'lid', 'mug' and 'frock'. The process of learning to read requires a more accurate discrimination of word sounds than does the naming of pictures. It necessitates hearing the consonant sounds correctly, which, according to Fletcher (1929, 1953), are in many cases very likely to be heard incorrectly—especially, as we have seen, the consonant sounds 'v', 'r' and 'th'. In normal adult speech, consonants are often slurred. In certain forms of English accent, they are almost completely dropped from the middle of the word— hence 'fa-er' for 'father', 'mo-er' for 'mother', etc. Sheridan indeed considered that this might be a prolongation of the childish habit of eliding these sounds. Even highly educated people are liable to under-emphasize or drop the final consonants of words, as in the well-known 'huntin', shootin' and fishin''. Hirsch (1952) stated that the intensity level of conversational speech must be 70 decibels[1] above threshold to be heard with 100% accuracy, and this is distinctly above the intensity of ordinary conversation. Moreover, continuous conversation is heard much more easily and accurately than are isolated words; and the latter are clearer than are nonsense syllables (Fletcher, 1929), the speech sounds which the child must hear accurately if he is to match them with the

---

[1] The decibel (db.) is the unit of intensity of sound. The intensity of a whisper is about 30 dbs., that of normal conversation 60–70 dbs. The cycle is the unit of pitch or frequency of sound vibration; the pitch of Middle C is 256 cycles per sec.

printed syllables. Thus Miller (1951) pointed out that the comprehension of continuous speech was much less affected by distortion than was that of nonsense syllables.

Again, it is clear that vowel sounds are greatly distorted in different English accents. Black (1937) found that the three characteristic frequency bands (ranges of pitch) of a vowel may vary by as much as 200 cycles in different speakers. The cockney child, for instance, may use vowel sounds which are almost completely different from those of standard English. Sheridan (1955) found the following words, which she spoke in standard English, to be incorrectly heard by Lancashire school-children: 'cart' was heard as 'cot', 'yard' as 'yacht', 'mud' as 'mad', and 'bush' as 'bash'. They pronounced 'cart' as 'ca-ert', and the 'u' in 'mud' as in 'should'. Though Bennett (1951) found no difference in the number of words heard correctly by 6-year-old children when the words were spoken in a Lancashire or a Fifeshire accent, in these cases the words may have been recognized mainly from their consonants. It is true that the vowel sounds, except for 'e' as in 'ten', are usually readily audible; and their intensity in ordinary speech is greater than that of consonants. But there are many monosyllabic words which are differentiated only by one vowel; and it seems inevitable that such sounds might be easily confused by children whose accent is very different from that of the teacher.

A good teacher of reading will of course articulate the individual speech sounds accurately and clearly, and will emphasize the consonants. But the child who has become accustomed to distorted vowels and elided consonants in the speech ordinarily spoken to him will now have to learn their correct sound patterns in the words which the teacher speaks. Furthermore, the teacher is often handicapped by the bad acoustics of the school class-rooms. In one of the schools where Midgeley tested, there was an average degree of noise of 11 decibels above threshold, and there was much reverberation of sound. The higher frequencies were the most affected, and these are especially important for the hearing of speech sounds. It seems quite probable that a child with a slight hearing loss would often find it difficult to hear accurately what the teacher said; and we shall give evidence in Chapter VI to show that such losses are not infrequent. Again, where there is a definite speech defect, such that the child cannot differentiate the vowel sounds, or confuses certain consonant sounds, such as 'f' and 'th', it seems very likely that he will be doubtful about the correct auditory patterns of words, and the sounds which constitute them. Williams (1937) is stated by Miller (1951) to have found that accuracy of articulation is correlated significantly with correct usage of words and sentence complexity. Thus it is likely that the child who does not himself speak fluently will have less familiarity with word sounds. Yedinack (1949) found little inferiority in language development in 8-year-old children with defective articulation; but they were inferior, on the average, to normal children in reading achievement. But the relation of reading disability to auditory defects will be fully discussed in Chapter VI.

(2) THE UNDERSTANDING OF WORD MEANINGS

The development of facility in language increases familiarity, not only with the sounds of words, but also with their meanings. It is generally agreed nowadays that children should be taught to read the words which they know best. 'Word' methods of teaching are based upon the connection of the shapes of printed words with their meanings as given by pictures, and it is therefore essential that the child should be familiar with these meanings. The majority of modern reading books claim to have vocabularies which are easily within the comprehension of children aged 6–7 years; though there are books in use in this country which contain lists of rhyming words some of which would be quite unknown to children of this age. But clearly a minimum vocabulary of words is essential before the child can begin to learn to read. Ilg and Ames (1950) and Durrell and Sullivan (1937) consider that 'reading readiness' depends upon the child's vocabulary and language facility. They found a close correlation between scores on reading achievement tests and tests of the understanding of words. However, it is often stated that the normal child of 6–7 has a vocabulary which is sufficiently large to cope with most reading instruction. There is considerable disagreement in the estimates which have been made of the size of children's vocabularies; and naturally the number of words a child can understand is greater than the number which he can use with facility. M. E. Smith (1926), testing the understanding of a sample of words, estimated that the 6-year-old child had a vocabulary of about 2000 words. But M. K. Smith (1941), using a different method of sampling words from the dictionary, and a more liberal judgement of understanding, obtained the very large figure of *c.* 17,000 basic words as the average vocabulary for children aged 6–7 years. Watts (1944) gave the more conservative estimate of 2000 words understood at 5 years, rising to 4000–5000 words by 7 years; but he did not state how he arrived at this estimate.

It must be remembered also that children may understand some meanings of a word from the context in which it is used without knowing all its possible meanings, irrespective of context. Young (1941) showed that children from poor-class homes had a narrower vocabulary than did children from better-class homes; and also they used different types of word. P. E. Vernon (1948) demonstrated similar differences in a study of the conversational vocabularies of Scottish children. Samples of the conversation of 200 of these children, aged $4\frac{1}{2}$–$5\frac{1}{2}$ years, included about 3000 different words. But there was a lack of overlap between the words spoken by different children. Over 1000 words were used by one child only, and only 12·7% of the words occurred among 10% or more of the children. A list was drawn up of the 1910 words used by two children or more; and another list of the 491 words used by fifteen or more children. It was pointed out that forty to fifty of these might not occur in the vocabularies of another sample of such children. Thus in selecting the vocabulary for use in a reading book, words should be chosen which are thoroughly familiar to a large proportion of children of the appropriate age.

It is usually advocated in modern methods of teaching reading that children should be given the opportunity of developing their vocabularies in various ways before they begin formal reading instruction. In a study of the words found in seven reading books in common use in Glasgow schools, Carrigan (1948) found that, except in one case, 70% and upwards of the words employed occurred in the word list of 491 words mentioned above. However, it was apparent that for these urban children there were too many words in the reading books connected with country life, with which they were relatively unfamiliar. From the words included in the reading books every fifteenth word was selected; and the list of ninety-six words thus obtained was given to 100 Glasgow school-children aged about 5 years. The children had to indicate whether or not they understood the meanings of these words by answering simple questions, matching with pictures, etc. It was found that on the average 76·5% of the words were known; but that the scores ranged down to 30% for some children. Such children would obviously have considerable difficulty in learning to read from these books. However, a recent study by Kelly (1954) showed that about 81% of the words found by Vernon (1948) to be known by 5-year-olds appear in at least one of a set of eight modern Scottish reading books. This is a fair proportion, particularly since some of the words listed in 1948 were war-time words which have now dropped out of use. It is probable that the criticism of unsuitable vocabulary is much less valid than it was even ten years ago.

The fact that a word is familiar to a child and is in common use in his vocabulary does not, however, guarantee that it will be easy to read. Rickard (1935), who tested the recognition of children aged 6–9 years of words commonly included in their vocabularies, found that on the whole the more familiar words were more often read correctly; but the factor of familiarity was by no means the predominant one in producing correct recognition.

(3) THE PHONETIC ANALYSIS OF WORDS

As we have already noted, the child may be familiar with sounds and meanings of words as they are generally used in conversation. But here they are integral parts of the total pattern of speech, the meaning of which is emphasized by the intonation of the voice, and often reinforced by gestures, and by the context. When the child speaks himself, his words are inherent parts of a total situation, from which he may not be able readily to isolate them. With less mature children, especially if they come from poorer-class homes, speech is seldom exact or grammatical. Thus Hartmann (1941), according to Anderson and Dearborn (1952), considered that before the child could learn to read, he must be able to understand and use simple propositional phrases—sentences with a subject and a verb, not the mere sequence of words which does, duty for a sentence with little children. Again, Werner (1954) showed that younger children tended to identify meanings of words with the sentence in which they were contained. The word was so deeply embedded in the sentence, and so impregnated with its meaning, that it could hardly be thought of in isolation. Furthermore, the child does not realize that a word may have a different meaning in a different context, yet still remains the same word, with the same sound and spelling. Thus the child has to learn to understand that: (a) each word and its sound pattern are separate entities, with their peculiar, invariable and universal characteristics; (b) each word's sound pattern can be analysed into a succession of sounds, with a characteristic and invariable sequence; (c) these unitary sounds can be generalized, in the sense that they occur, in approximately the same form, but in different sequences, in different words; (d) the sounds correspond to different letter shapes, visually perceived; but (e) unfortunately in the English language the relationships between sounds and visual percepts vary considerably from word to word. Thus Horn (1929) pointed out that the vowel 'a' has eighteen different sounds (including combinations with other vowels); indeed with minor variants as many as forty-seven different sounds can be detected. The combination 'ea' can be pronounced in eight different ways, from that of 'great' to that of 'idea' and 'ocean'. Thus even when the child has realized the importance of differentiating and attending to the phonetic sounds, he is set a formidable task in memorizing these differences. It is not surprising that many children cannot master these processes for a considerable period after they begin reading. Metraux (1944) found that the auditory memory span for speech sounds continued to increase up to 10 years with vowel sounds, and up to 12 years with consonant sounds.

We have seen that, in the early stages of reading, word shapes are visually perceived, remembered and recognized as separate wholes, each with its own identity. The child also learns that each of these shapes has its own different sound, and the sound is associated with the meaning he gives it in his own speech. This stage is covered in 'look-and-say' methods of learning to read. But sooner or later, if he is to be able to read properly, he must begin to analyse both the word shape and the word sound. Now the visual shape is extended spatially; in print the letters are separated from one another; and their spatial order for any one word is invariable. Thus the teacher can point to each letter in turn, and show the child the separate parts of the word shape, and their successive positions in that word. Incidentally, it is likely that as long as the 'look-and-say' method is being employed, this directional analysis is liable to be neglected. But when some phonetic teaching is introduced, the teacher will also sound the words, letter by letter and syllable by syllable; or, more commonly in modern teaching, as one phonetic unit after another. For the child, however, the sounded word is a meaningful whole, and the shorter words, at least, have no *natural* parts. It may be comparatively easy for him to hear the separate syllables in a polysyllabic word. But 'cat' does *not* sound to him like 'ke-a-te'. The simple monosyllables with which the teaching of reading begins are essentially unanalysable. The sounds of the phonetic units are something which the teacher appears to construct—from what, the child does not understand; and these sounds have no intrinsic meaning.

It is not surprising, therefore, that there are many reports of the difficulty encountered by little children at these stages of learning to read. It is clear why it is so important that the child should be able to discriminate word sounds correctly. Thus Gates (1940) found a correlation of 0·28 between the ability to rhyme words, in 'reading readiness' tests, and performance in reading achievement tests given one term later. Wilson and Flemming (1940) obtained high correlations between reading ability and the ability to pronounce phonetic units in children from 5 years upwards. Presumably they did begin to hear and copy these sound units at this early age, though hardly to read them. Schonell (1945) considered that a child who had reached the mental age of 6½–7½ years might begin to learn the connection between certain sounds and the corresponding printed syllables, provided that by then he was able to read 70–100 words at sight. Harris (1947) echoed this judgement, but did not think that the child need be able to recognize all the alphabet sounds and common phonetic units till he had reached the age of 9–10 years, which seems very late. Agnew (1939) considered that some actual teaching in phonetics could usefully begin at 6½–7 years, and that much improvement could be produced in reading by teaching them to 8-year-old children. An experiment by Bradford (1954) supported this conclusion. He gave to 336 children aged 6–8 years a test in which they had to pick out pictures, the names of which contained a phonetic unit which had previously been presented. The younger children could usually select correctly picture names containing the easier consonants, but were less accurate with vowel sounds and double consonants such as 'mp', 'dl', 'br', etc. The older children were fairly successful in this task, indicating that by the age of 7–8 years there is some ability to isolate letter sounds from the sounds of whole words. However, it must be noted that this ability depends on the children's intelligence. Thus Morphett and Washburne (1931) found that, among children with a mental age of less than 6 years when they began reading, only 8% had made such progress in 6 months as to be able to identify simple words. But 80% of those who had mental ages of 6½ years and upwards when they began to learn made satisfactory progress. Dolch and Bloomster (1937) showed that when children of 6–8 years were given tests of matching and differentiating words distinguished by their sounds rather than by their appearances, children of lower mental age were almost certain to fail. Those with mental ages under 7 years made only chance scores. Later, Dolch (1948) stated that children with mental ages under 7 years could never pick out correctly words and nonsense syllables sounded by the teacher.

It is doubtful if anything is gained by attempting to teach formal phonetic analysis until the child has had a certain experience of sight methods. Thus Sexton and Herron (1928), in a carefully balanced and controlled study of about 900 children, found that there was no advantage for 'phonic'[1] over 'non-phonic' methods during the first year of teaching reading. During the second year, however, those taught by phonic methods began to show some superiority over those taught by non-phonic methods. The results of Garrison and Heard (1931) also seemed to indicate that it was useless to begin teaching phonetic analysis to children below a certain age. Children aged 6–7 years, in their first year at school, tended to forget it in the summer holidays at the end of the year. Again, Dolch (1948) found that whereas some highly intelligent children, aged 6–8 years, were deficient in the ability to analyse words phonetically, almost all the less intelligent ones, with mental ages below 7 years, failed in this task. Whipple (1944), after an extensive study of eighty-three backward readers in the middle school grades, concluded that in 71 % of cases one of the causes of backwardness was learning to read too young. Many of these cases were of rather poor intelligence; about 70 % appear to have had I.Q.s below 90. Gates and Russell (1939) also showed that 'under-privileged' children, of rather poor intelligence (I.Q.'s 75–90), physique, emotional stability and socio-economic status, seemed to profit by the extension of 'reading readiness' activities and the postponement of formal instruction in reading until their second year in school.

On the other hand, the investigation by Taylor (1950) of the reading of Scottish children seemed to show that they profited by beginning to learn to read at an earlier age than that of American children. Taylor applied the Metropolitan Reading Readiness Test and the Metropolitan Achievement Test to 114 children of

[1] The term 'phonic method' seems to include any method which makes use of any form of phonetic analysis of words. 'Phonic drill', however, relates to the teaching of similarities and differences between isolated phonetic units not included in words.

average age 6 years 3 months in Glasgow schools. These children had already been in school a year, and had received teaching in reading which probably included some phonetic analysis. Their average score was 16·3 points above the norm for American children of the same age on the Readiness Test, and was approximately the same on the Achievement Test as the norm for American children of $7\frac{1}{2}$ years. Taylor concluded therefore that these children did learn a good deal from the year's teaching from 5–6. An enquiry by Macgregor (1934) suggested that this advantage was maintained. A group of 6000 11-year-old Scottish children, tested with Battery A of the Public School Achievement Test, had a median reading age of about 5 months above the American norm; and there were only about half the number of cases of severe retardation as in a comparable American group. In language usage and spelling, the Scottish children were 2–$2\frac{1}{2}$ years in advance of the American children. But a more recent investigation by Vernon, O'Gorman and McLellan (1955) showed a different result. They found that a group of 8-year-old Scottish children were significantly in advance of a comparable group of English children in word recognition and spelling (word recognition 5·0%, spelling 8·9%); but there was no significant difference in reading comprehension. At 11 and 14 years, the spelling of the Scottish children was still much superior to that of the English children. At 11 years there was no significant difference in reading comprehension. At 14 years, the Scottish girls were better than the English girls, but the Scottish boys were no better than the English. The authors concluded that the Scottish children were more thoroughly drilled than the English in the basic subjects; probably also the former began to learn to read earlier. The girls accepted this drilling and continued to profit by it; but the older boys rebelled against it and lost their initial advantage. It is true that the total sample, 881 children, was not as large as Macgregor's, and the results could not be applied to Scottish and English children in general. But whether a very early proficiency in the mechanics of reading is really of advantage in the long run must remain in some doubt.

Other evidence indicates that a suitable type of phonetic analysis may be used in teaching reading at quite an early age. Dolch (1948) considered that training in noticing the similarities and differences between word sounds can usefully begin before the child is able to analyse out and generalize about the phonetic units of word sounds. But a great deal of repeated instruction may be necessary before the child can be induced to associate clearly and definitely the sight and sound of words. Gray (1937) and Watts (1944) also recommended preceding any formal analysis by getting the child to recognize the similarities and differences between words. Bond and Wagner (1943) considered that some analysis of printed words could take place by vision alone, without any sounding, and that it should always precede phonetic analysis, the words being systematically inspected from left to right. Phonetic analysis is certainly more difficult than visual analysis, because of the variation in vowel sounds. However, the use of rhyming words is frequently recommended as valuable.[1]

It may then be concluded that the auditory perception of word sounds and their association with the printed shapes may present formidable difficulties to the young child. In his common use of words he may not hear or enunciate words clearly and accurately; he may be uncertain as to their precise meaning or range of meanings; and he may be incapable of using them grammatically—that is to say, in the way in which they are presented to him in his reading books. Thus he has first to learn to perceive and remember the word sounds accurately, as spoken in a 'standard English' accent, which may necessitate an accuracy of hearing and an effort of attention quite beyond his capacities. He must then realize that the whole sound of the word can be analysed into successive phonetic units, which are associated with the printed shapes of letters and letter groups, but in an unsystematic manner varying according to the particular word being analysed. All this necessi-

---

[1] A discussion of the general efficiency of the various methods of teaching reading will be given in Chapter VII.

tates understanding the meaning of the word in a particular context. Thus it is not surprising to observe, from the results quoted above, that the amount of detailed and systematic phonetic analysis of which children of mental ages under about 7 are capable is rather small. There is real danger, especially if they are drilled on isolated phonetic units, that they may fail to hear these correctly, or may find them so boring and incomprehensible as to develop a thorough distaste for studying them. Even if this does not occur, the children may fail to see any relevance of the phonetic units to reading. Thus it is better that the little child at any rate should begin by learning to recognize phonetic sounds within familiar words, for instance, by rhyming, before he attempts to analyse the word and to differentiate each separate sound that it contains. Moreover, when the analysis has begun, and the phonetic units are being matched to the corresponding visual units, it is advisable to give extensive practice in blending the sounds to form whole words, both auditorily and visually. Much evidence goes to show that difficulties frequently arise in remembering the exact order of sounds in the word, and in blending unitary sounds to form whole words. We shall return to this problem in section 5 of the next chapter.

CHAPTER IV

THE NATURE OF READING DISABILITY

(1) THE BEGINNING OF DISABILITY

The study of reading disability suffers from the great disadvantage that the disability seldom becomes apparent in the early stages. Indeed, we do not even know whether, if difficulty in learning to read were detected in its very early stages, it might not be over-

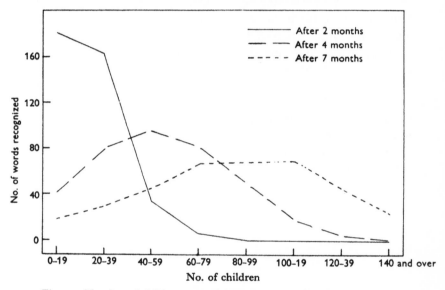

Fig. 7. Number of children recognizing a given number of words after 2, 4 and 7 months learning to read

come fairly readily by ordinary teaching of an appropriate kind. We do know that skill in reading varies very greatly from the beginning. Fig. 7 shows some results obtained by Donnelly (1935) as to the number of words which a group of 389 children aged 6–7 years could read 2, 4 and 7 months after they began to learn reading. Rickard (1935) found that the percentages of 119 familiar words which children of 6–7 years could read correctly varied from 8 to 92. And Dolch (1934) showed that, when children were tested at the end of their first year of school in the recognition of words which had been included in the books they read earlier in the year, some children could recognize hardly any of them. Again, Boney and Lynch (1942) tested children monthly during their first year in school, and found that the rate of learning varied greatly among different children. But whether the rate of progress was fast or slow, there was never any regression from a high to a low rate.

No doubt some of these differences were due to differences of intelligence. Table 4, obtained by Gates (1930), shows the number of repetitions needed by children of varying intelligence to learn words, when they began reading.

Table 4

I.Q.	No. of repetitions to learn word
120–129	20
110–119	30
90–109	35
80– 89	40
70– 79	45

But it seems probable that even some quite intelligent children begin to lag behind the others in reading progress almost from the beginning: this deficiency may be recognized when they leave the infant school and enter the junior school at the age of 7–8 years, or not till much later. They may be put into a backward class, and be given special teaching in reading. This often enables children who are only slightly backward to overcome their difficulties without more ado. But for the child with real reading disability, this teaching may be no more successful than was his earlier teaching. It appears that he may indeed have learnt that printed words have some relation to spoken words; and, with a few simple words, he has memorized the spoken word that corresponds to a particular printed shape. But he does not seem to understand why; it might be quite an arbitrary association. He appears hopelessly uncertain and confused as to why certain successions of printed letters should correspond to certain phonetic sounds in words. To make this association demands a particular type of reasoning process. Although, as we shall see below, there may be some failure to perceive all the details of printed shapes accurately, or to hear word sounds correctly, yet the fundamental trouble appears to be a failure in development of this reasoning process. But it is extraordinarily difficult for the teacher or the psychological investigator to analyse or to understand the nature of the failure. Most children seem to find no great difficulty in developing the necessary reasoning processes, provided that they go slowly and are given plenty of help and practice. These children alone seem to have become 'stuck', and to be incapable of further progress. Though we shall endeavour to discover something about the nature and cause of the failure, it cannot be said that anyone fully understands it.

(2) VISUAL PERCEPTION IN THE BACKWARD READER

It has already been indicated that, in general, children at the time at which they begin learning to read seem to be capable of discriminating shapes with sufficient accuracy to enable them to perceive the shapes of letters and words, provided that they make an adequate use of this ability. In other words, if they look attentively at words and letters, they can see their shapes and how they differ from one another. It is much more doubtful if they can analyse and memorize the differences logically and consistently and understand their full significance. But tests of the ability to perceive and discriminate shapes other than those of words have seldom shown that the backward reader is deficient in the perception of shape as such. Thus Fildes (1921) compared a group of non-readers, aged 9–16 years and mainly of poor intelligence, with a matched group of readers, in their ability to recognize twenty fairly simple irregular shapes, shown for 2 sec. each. The children had to judge which of the series they had already seen. The non-readers were inferior to the readers only in their ability to discriminate between the same shapes in different orientations. But the former were inferior to the latter in naming, learning and remembering lists of numbers. Gates (1922) found that backward readers, aged 8½ years and upwards, were not inferior to normal readers in perceiving small differences in drawings and numbers. Schilder (1944) showed that seven cases of children aged 8–14 years who could read little if at all could perceive even complex pictures accurately. But according to Eames (1933), speed of picture recognition was slower in backward than in normal readers. Stroud (1945) reported that Sister Mary Riley (1929) found negligible correlations between tests of discrimination of geometrical drawings and the reading performance of children aged 9–10 years. Wolfe (1939) showed that the difference between backward and normal readers, aged about 9 years, in reproducing geometrical shapes was not significant. Kendall (1948) found an approximately zero correlation between the reading quotients (reading scores/mental ages) of children of 6–8½ years, and their ability to reproduce fifteen straight-line designs from memory. Galifret-Granjon (1951) showed that backward readers[1] were not inferior to normal readers in differentiating shapes of slightly different structure. Only the younger backward readers made poorer performances than the normal readers in combining fragmentary pieces together to form whole figures.

The author also found that backward readers did not appear to be inferior to normal readers in the analysis of complex figures, as shown in a test in which they were given figures together with their constituent

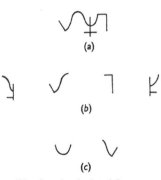

(a)

(b)

(c)

Fig. 8. Analysis of figures

parts, and required to arrange the parts in the same order of arrangement as in the complex figure (see Fig. 8).[2] The number

---

[1] Galifret-Granjon termed his group of 100 backward readers 'dyslexics'. Presumably they were clinic cases with severe reading disability, but the extent of the disability was not stated.

[2] The child was presented with a set of whole figures such as that shown in Fig. 8a, together with its correct parts (Fig. 8b) and some incorrect parts (Fig. 8c). He had to select the correct parts and arrange them in the right order to correspond to the whole figure.

of cases was few; but it seemed that the ability to perform this task depended upon age, and had no relation to reading ability.

It is probable therefore that after a certain age even backward readers can perceive most shapes quite adequately, and can even analyse them with fair efficiency. But younger children may be deficient in this ability to such an extent as to be impeded from learning to read. Some evidence in support of this conclusion was given by the results of Petty (1939), who obtained a correlation of 0·48 between the reading achievement of 6-year-old children and their ability to copy shapes of real objects by drawing them. It is true that some good readers made low scores, apparently because of a tendency to perceive the shapes syncretically. The poor readers who made low scores selected details inaccurately, including some very minute ones and omitting more obvious and important ones. This interesting observation seems to indicate the importance in reading of the difficulty mentioned above—the inability of children aged 6–7 years to analyse complex forms in a systematic and logical manner. Such a difficulty would make it hard for them to perceive the essential characteristics of word shapes. Frank (1935) also considered that backward readers were like young children in that they were incapable of analysing words, which appeared to them to be solid wholes defying analysis; or they perceived the general structure of words in a vague and inaccurate way without any real attention to detail.

The inability to perceive and reproduce detail correctly was also demonstrated in the investigation of Galifret-Granjon (1951). He compared the performance of 100 normal and 100 backward readers on part of the Bender test (Fig. 1, shapes (a), (c), (d), (e) and (h)). The performances were compared for accuracy in construction of angles, orientations of the axes of figures and relative positions of the elements, and were then grouped into good, medium and bad performances. Among the younger children, aged 7–10 years, 27% of the normal readers were good and 32% bad; 10% of the backward readers were good, and 70% bad. In the older group, aged 10–13 years, 89% of the normal readers were good and none bad; 52% of the backward readers were good and

16% bad. Thus although the backward readers did improve as they grew older in their ability to perceive and reproduce these particular details, they continued to be inferior to the normal readers.

This lack of attention to detail appears also in the tendency to ignore differences of *orientation* and of *order*, which was noted by Fildes (1921), Monroe (1928), Hildreth (1934) and Macmeeken (1939). Monroe found that 4·7% of a group of backward readers aged 6–10 years named rows of pictures in reversed order, as against 0·9% of normal control cases. In reproducing pictures from memory, backward readers showed disorientation in 35% of cases, normal readers in 27%. Hildreth's poorer readers, aged 8–10 years, also made more reversals in memory reproductions of shapes than did the better readers; but in addition they made far more errors of other kinds. Macmeeken found a considerable tendency among severely retarded readers, aged 7–10 years, to reverse the whole or a part of one of the Terman–Merrill figures ('Designs', Year IX, Item 3). Kendall (1948), on the other hand, obtained a zero correlation between reading performance and number of reversals made in reproducing designs from memory. But there is no evidence that any of these children was severely retarded in reading. Galifret-Granjon (1951) did find a tendency among backward readers to mirror reversal in reconstructing figures with match-sticks.

There is no doubt that backward readers, like beginners in reading, show a strong tendency to confuse words which contain the same letters in a different order, or even in reversed order; and to be unable to distinguish 'mirror image' letters such as 'p' and 'q', 'b' and 'd'. It should be realized that these two types of error are really different in nature, though they often appear to be associated and are often estimated together. The former is due to a reversal of *order*, the latter to a reversal of *orientation*. Reversal of orientation of whole words should not normally be a problem in reading; unless the child himself writes backwards, from right to left, he should never encounter words in that form. However, there do appear to be children who show a tendency to read lines of print from right to left, and possess unusual facility in this mirror reading (see Carmichael and Cashman, 1932). It is not at all clear how frequently they occur among backward readers. But the studies which have been made of the errors of backward readers suggest that transposition and reversal of letters within the word are the most commonly made errors. Monroe (1928) noted that a group of 120 backward readers, aged 6–10 years, were much more liable to reverse letters such as 'b', 'd', 'p', 'q', 'n' and 'u' than were a group of 175 normal readers. They showed greater facility in mirror reading and writing. But in addition they made many other errors, omitting, substituting and adding vowels and consonants to words. Table 5 shows the average number of reversals and of total errors made in a test of reading isolated words and words in sentence context.

Table 5

Age (years)	Reversed letters and words		Total errors	
	Retarded	Normal	Retarded	Normal
6–7	10·7	7·4	90·5	62·5
7–8	10·6	6·6	91·4	74·0
8–9	6·3	4·0	69·4	57·1
9–10	4·7	2·7	57·7	46·2

Teegarden (1933) stated that among 6-year-old children the tendency to reversal in copying letters, digits and nonsense characters was strong among reading failures. Hildreth (1934) found that the poorest readers among a group of children aged 7–9 years made slightly more reversals than the good readers in reproducing shapes, numbers and words from memory, but the former also made many more errors of other kinds. Some superior readers made reversals also. Frank (1935) showed that backward readers aged 7–11½ years were very liable to confuse the reversible letters, and also letters of similar shapes—for instance, 'm' and 'n', 'i' and 'l', 'n' and 'h', 't' and 'l'. Words of similar letter structure and reversible words were also mistaken for each other. Thus apparently shape, orientation and order of letters were all liable to confusion; and Frank considered that these errors were of exactly the same kind as those made by younger normal readers.

Blanchard (1936), on the other hand, observed a reversal tendency among only 34 % of a group of seventy-three clinic cases of backward readers aged 6–17 years. Only half of these confused reversed letters ('b' and 'd', etc.). Schilder (1944) stated that only two among seven cases of children aged 8–14 with extreme reading disability showed any mirror reversal in reading and writing, though confusions of similar letters within words were frequent ('p' and 'd', 'm' and 'n', 'b' and 'g', 'd' and 't'). Wolfe (1939) found more reversals of letters, words, and letters within words in the tachistoscopic reading of eighteen boys, aged about 9 years and retarded by about 2 years in reading, than among a matched group of normal readers. But the former also made more errors of other kinds. There was a tendency to reverse a less familiar to a more familiar word; for instance, 'nip' to 'pin', 'tub' to 'but'. The backward readers were able to read mirrored words better than could the control cases, and seemed less affected by whether the order of the letters was correct or reversed.

Bennett (1942) found that very backward readers, aged 8–10 years, made errors in the reading of 40 % of 594 basic words, mainly monosyllables, arranged in sentences. About 12 % were reversals; word reversals were more frequent and more difficult to eliminate than letter reversals. Schonell (1942) found the percentages of letter and word reversals shown in Table 6, in performance on a reading test. These figures indicate that although

Table 6

Age (years)	No. of cases	Confusion of letters 'b' and 'd', 'p' and 'q', 'w' and 'm'				Transposition of letters in words and word reversals			
		Backward		Normal		Backward		Normal	
		Boys	Girls	Boys	Girls	Boys	Girls	Boys	Girls
7–8	15	85	100	30	25	85	100	35	27
8–9	14	60	60	15	10	80	60	21	18
9–10	21	62	60	5	5	82	60	15	16
10–11	19	30	25	0	0	60	50	12	12
11–12	17	14	0	0	0	45	30	5	5
12–13	8	15	0	0	0	32	0	0	0
13–14	10	0	0	0	0	22	0	0	0

letter and word reversals and transpositions did persist for much longer in backward than in normal readers, nevertheless even in the former they greatly decreased with increasing age, and in the girls they disappeared altogether by the age of 12 years. This may account for the relative absence of such errors in some of the results quoted above which were obtained from older children. Schonell also found that some backward readers made no errors of this type. Johnson (1955), again, showed that 97% of a group of thirty-four clinic cases, aged $7\frac{1}{2}$–18 years, made reversal errors in reading, writing and shape discrimination; but she thought that these were symptoms rather than causes of reading difficulty.

It appears then that although most backward readers are un-certain about the order and arrangement of the letters in the word, and some of them also confuse letters of similar shape, there is not an invariable tendency towards mirror reversal either in reading or in writing. Certain cases seem to read and write backwards and forwards indiscriminately, but they are in the minority. It seems possible that the childish tendency to overlook the orientation and order of shapes and letters is prolonged in the backward reader, partly as the result of continued immaturity, but partly also because of his general cognitive confusion. Such a confusion also appears in an inability to *associate* shapes with names. Thus Hincks (1926) found that some of her cases, who were retarded in reading 2–4 years behind their mental age, showed a poor visual memory in associating shapes, colours and names. Fildes (1921) also found that her non-readers had difficulty in associating shapes and names together when either the shapes or the names were very similar to one another, though they could perform this task adequately when they were obviously dissimilar. In an experiment of the author's, the children were required to repeat from memory the names of a series of three or four simple geometrical shapes. The backward readers were inferior to normal readers in naming the shapes correctly, in the right order.

Thus we may conclude that in general there is not any real in-ability among backward readers to perceive at least the simpler type of shape, or to differentiate similar shapes. But memorization of shapes, or the names given to shapes, may be defective. And in the analysis and differentiation of small details of shape (including their orientation and order), the backward reader may be definitely inferior. But this is probably a cognitive rather than a purely perceptual disability. The child seems unable to distinguish what are the important features, or what are their characteristic relationships, or their essential orientation. This conclusion is supported by the results of Coleman (1953). He compared the mental ages of forty clinic cases of reading disability (aged 8–46 years), as measured by the Stanford–Binet and Wechsler Tests, with the mental ages calculated from the non-verbal section of the Otis Quick-Scoring Test. The latter consists of 100 items, each containing four pictures or diagrams, one of which has to be differentiated from the other three. The differences are sometimes differences of shape alone, and sometimes of meaning also (as, for instance, with a clock, a ruler, a thermometer and a pressing iron). The mental ages of the backward readers on the Otis test were on the average 2·24 years below their mental ages on the ordinary intelligence tests. Thirty-three of the cases were children, and twenty of these were lower by 10 months or more. Fifteen cases, aged 8–9½ years, were lower on the average by eleven months; and twelve cases aged 10–12 years were lower on the average by 32 months. But not all the cases made poorer performances on the Otis test; six of them made better ones.

Again, Ettlinger and Jackson (1955) found that five out of six cases of severe reading disability, aged 7–12 years, and retarded by 2½–5 years in reading, with normal or above normal intelligence, nevertheless gave very poor performances on the Kohs Blocks Test. The author has been informed that poor performances on the Coding test in the Wechsler Performance Scale are sometimes observed in cases of reading disability. These results again suggest an inability to relate and to reason about shapes; and the Kohs Blocks Test in particular requires abstract reasoning.

It appears, therefore, that some cases of severe reading retardation, but not all, do show a poor ability to relate shapes and details of shape, and to reason about them. We cannot assume, however, that the inability to read is due to this deficiency. It is possible, as Frank supposed, that it is a sign of lack of maturation. The normal reader may grow out of this immature type of behaviour. But backward readers may fail to do so because they have not developed habits of orderly and systematic analysis of shapes into their essential constituents. This deficiency then is the result rather than the cause of the reading disability; or both may be produced by some other defect. We shall discuss this possibility again later.

(3) AUDITORY PERCEPTION IN THE BACKWARD READER

If we can conclude that in general backward readers are not deficient in simple visual perception of shape as such, we can by no means be certain that they are not inferior in the auditory perception of speech sounds. Unfortunately the evidence is even less clear as to defects in auditory perception than as to failure in visual perception. There may be specific defects in the discrimination, analysis and remembering of words and speech sounds which are of major importance in cases of reading disability. But it is exceedingly difficult to analyse the exact nature of these defects; and too often in the past they have been labelled merely as defects in auditory perception and discrimination, without any study of their exact nature. Thus Monroe (1932) found that thirty-two non-readers, of average age 8 years 5 months, made 4·6 errors on a test of auditory differentiation of similar words, as compared with 1·5 errors made by thirty-two unselected children aged 6–7 years. Only 2 % of the former were defective in pure tone acuity. Monroe suggested that some of her group of 269 cases, aged 7–16 years, with reading deficiencies, had some form of specific innate defect in auditory perception of speech sounds, comparable to colour blindness. Wolfe (1941) also found that eighteen backward readers aged about 9 years, and retarded by about 2 years below their mental ages, were significantly worse than were normal readers on the Monroe tests of auditory discrimination and auditory memory for words, though not in auditory acuity. Schonell (1942) stated that weakness in the auditory discrimination of speech sounds was apparent in 38% of his backward readers, though he did not measure the extent of this weakness. Just as Frank (1935) attributed failure in visual discrimination to lack of maturation, so also Schonell attributed failure in auditory discrimination to innately delayed maturation in hearing speech; to inability to register correctly the sound values of the various parts of words, and their temporal distribution. Hester (1942) found that 58% of a group of 194 children of all ages referred to a clinic for reading difficulties showed an inadequate knowledge of letter names, sounds and blends. This group made on the average 7·5 mistakes in naming each letter of the alphabet; 29·0 mistakes in sounding each letter; and 43·5 mistakes in sounding combinations of two consonants. These difficulties in phonetic sounding reached a maximum at 10–12 years of age.

Wheeler and Wheeler (1954) gave tests of pitch discrimination and discrimination of word sounds and words to 629 children aged 10–12 years, with I.Q.'s of 76–139. The correlations of reading test scores and performance on the Seashore test of pitch discrimination were low, of the order of 0·2. The correlations between reading scores and tests of word sound discrimination were higher, 0·31–0·40. But the correlations between word sound test scores and intelligence were 0·38–0·40. Thus it cannot be concluded from these results that there was any specific effect on the reading of these children of inability to hear the word sounds correctly. Much the same results were obtained by Reynolds (1953) and Templin (1954). Reynolds found that when mental age was held constant, the performance of 191 children aged 9–10 years on tests of word and pitch discrimination and sound blending showed insignificant correlations with reading ability; though in one small group there was some relationship to word recognition. Templin compared the performance of the twenty-six best readers and the twenty-six worst readers in a group of seventy-eight children aged about 10 years, with comparable I.Q.'s, on tests of the identification of vowel and consonant sounds in isolation and when included in words and in nonsense syllables. Although the better readers did these tests slightly better, in general, than did the poorer readers, the differences were significant only for the identification of isolated sounds. However, there is no indication that the poorer readers in the groups studied by Wheeler and Wheeler, Reynolds and Templin were severely retarded in reading, as were the cases of Monroe, Wolfe and Hester.

A detailed study of auditory disability in younger backward readers was made by Bond (1935), with sixty-four children of mean age $8\frac{1}{2}$ years. The younger children were retarded by at least half a year, the older by at least 1 year. Their I.Q.'s were 85 and over. These children, and the sixty-four matched control cases, came from two types of school, in one of which reading was taught mainly by 'look-and-say' methods, and in the other mainly by phonic methods. Table 7 shows the mean scores obtained by these children on various tests. The differences between the poor and normal readers on the tests of auditory memory are insignificant or barely significant. But in tests involving a greater cognitive component, the differences are considerable. These include: ability to give words containing a given phonetic sound, to blend sounds into words, and to remember associations between visual symbols and sounds. The backward readers could apparently perceive the speech sounds, but could not understand or make use of them in an intelligent and systematic manner. It is interesting to note also that the children taught by phonetic methods did less well than did those taught by 'look-and-say' methods. This suggests that these children's deficiencies in auditory perception were at least in part functions of the particular teaching method. Thus they must have been to some extent acquired and not innate, as Schonell and Monroe postulated. However, many of these children were not greatly retarded in reading; and some innate defect might exist in cases of severe disability.

Monroe showed that her backward readers lacked the ability to blend sounds correctly to form words, as is shown in Table 8. The author also found that cases with considerable retardation in reading might be inferior in the blending of sounds to

Table 7

Word sound discrimination (pairs of like words)

	Experimental	Control
Phonetic teaching	12·9	14·6
Look-and-say teaching	15·1	16·3

Naming sounded letters

	Experimental	Control
Phonetic teaching	20·9	27·1
Look-and-say teaching	21·0	25·3

Giving words beginning with a given sound

	Experimental	Control
Phonetic teaching	5·6	8·6
Look-and-say teaching	6·6	8·0

Giving words ending with a given sound

	Experimental	Control
Phonetic teaching	5·6	7·5
Look-and-say teaching	5·4	7·1

Memory for

	Rhythms		Digits		Nonsense syllables	
	Experimental	Control	Experimental	Control	Experimental	Control
Phonetic teaching	12·9	14·6	5·7	6·1	4·1	3·8
Look-and-say teaching	15·1	16·3	5·5	6·2	3·5	4·0

Blending of

	Nonsense syllables		Phonetic sounds	
	Experimental	Control	Experimental	Control
Phonetic teaching	4·5	12·1	8·0	14·0
Look-and-say teaching	6·7	11·6	10·4	16·1

Association of phonetic sounds with arbitrary visual symbols

	Experimental	Control
Phonetic teaching	7·4	13·1
Look-and-say teaching	9·4	12·9

the hearing and enunciation of sounds. Thus nine children, aged 7–8 years, retarded in reading by an average of 1½ years, were able to recognize and match correctly 49% of a set of letter combinations ('la', 'zo', 'ed'). They could give the sounds of 51% of the single letters shown them. But when the letters were arranged in such a way as to make simple three- and four-letter words, they could blend these letters and enunciate the whole word in only 35% of cases. Thus although the sounding of letters and letter combinations was undoubtedly inadequate, the blending was even more defective. Indeed, it appeared often to be a matter of guesswork whether or not the letter sounds were correctly blended; the child might give the correct word, or he might produce a word which sounded something like the correct one but was quite differently spelt.

Table 8

Percentage of cases who blended sounds correctly

	0–1	2–3	4–5	6–7	8–9	10–11	12–13	14–15
269 backward readers	7	11	17	14	7	15	20	8
126 control cases	1	3	6	12	13	25	28	13

It has also been stated frequently that backward readers have an unusually poor *auditory memory*. Fildes (1921) found that her very backward readers had difficulty in remembering both numbers and words presented auditorily. Their performance was very variable, and those who were poorest were among the worst readers. Lord, Carmichael and Dearborn (1925) stated that 64% of a group of twenty-five cases of very backward readers of normal intelligence were deficient in auditory memory of both numbers and letters. Several of the cases of Hincks (1926) had poor auditory memory. Among the forty cases of Lichtenstein (1938), whose median age was 12–13 years, and who were retarded in reading by 3 or more years below their mental age, the auditory memory span averaged that for an age of about 8½ years. Rizzo (1939) found that the auditory memory span for the poorer readers in a group of 310 children was distinctly less than that of the better readers, especially among the younger children aged 8–11 years. A very narrow memory span appeared to be a contributory cause of severe reading disability in some of the children. Wolfe (1941) found that eighteen very backward readers, aged about 9 years, were significantly poorer in auditory memory for words than were the control cases. Johnson (1955) showed that 70% of a group of thirty-four very backward readers, aged 7½–18 years, referred to a clinic for their disability, had a deficient auditory memory span.

Table 9

	Backward children		Controls	
	Boys	Girls	Boys	Girls
Reading backwardness	6·6	3·8	2·0	0
Auditory perception defective	23·2	13·6	10·9	5·4
Scope of attention defective	12·4	10·1	3·6	4·0
Immediate memory defective	10·4	6·6	1·0	1·0

This defective auditory memory does not in most cases seem to depend upon poor auditory acuity. But it may possibly be due to inattention. Thus Burt (1937) found the percentage of defects shown in Table 9 among his generally backward readers. It may well be that many backward readers have not listened to and taken in what was told them, perhaps through day-dreaming or lack of interest. When they first began to learn reading, they may have failed to attend and to hear the words and word sounds spoken to them. The consequent failure to learn may then have made them still more uninterested and generally inattentive. It is clear that failure of attention would particularly affect auditory perception and memory, since auditory stimuli, once lost, are gone for ever. However, it seems impossible to prove whether or not inattention was the operative factor in these cases without a careful observation of their behaviour in class.

Some corroborative evidence as to the inability of certain children to hear the phonetic sounds of words correctly has been obtained in studies of children who were very poor at *spelling*. It is sometimes observed that children who have laboriously acquired the ability to read are still abnormally deficient in spelling.

Spache (1941) quotes McGovney (1930) as showing that poor spellers were deficient in the sounding of letters and syllables; and Russell (1937) as finding that they were inferior in the ability to distinguish between pairs of similar-sounding words and also in the systematic blending of letters to form syllables and words. Spache showed that when normally good spellers, aged 8–10 years, made spelling mistakes, these were usually phonetic errors—that is to say, words were spelt as they sounded. But poor spellers substituted letters which would give quite a different sound to the word. Thus bad spelling seems to demonstrate just the lack of phonetic appreciation which is so characteristic of many backward readers.

The inability to blend speech sounds correctly to form words may be due in part to poor perception of *temporal order* and *rhythm*. Though Bond (1935) found no significant difference between retarded and normal readers in this respect, yet Stambak (1951) showed that children with reading disability, aged 7–14 years, were much poorer than normal readers in copying temporal rhythms (groups of one, two or three taps with intervals between them) and repeating them over a period of time. Moreover, the former did not improve with increasing age as did the latter. The backward readers were less able to tap out the rhythm of a familiar song. When they were shown various rhythms drawn on a card, the older children could understand fairly well how to tap these out, but they could not do it accurately; whereas those normals who understood the task could also perform it.

The conclusions to be drawn from these data appear to be that in cases of reading backwardness there is frequently some inability to hear phonetic sounds of letters, letter combinations and words really clearly, and to remember them sufficiently accurately to be able to reproduce them in association with the corresponding printed letters and words. But we cannot be sure that, by the time the backward reader is tested (and the majority of those studied have been 8 years old or older), this deficiency has not resulted from his failure to learn to read. In other words, the normal reader acquires his skill in enunciating phonetic sounds correctly and systematically as he learns to read; but the backward reader remains in a state of confusion over the whole process. There is no evidence at present of any primary innate defect in the ability to hear phonetic sounds, such as that postulated by Monroe and Schonell, in cases where auditory acuity is normal. In any case, such a defect could not be of the same nature as colour blindness, as Monroe suggested, since colour blindness is a sensory defect. Moreover, it appears that the cognitive processes involved in phonetic analysis and re-synthesis (blending) in correct temporal order are usually more confused and ineffectual than is the initial hearing of the phonetic sounds.

(4) DEFECTS OF SPEECH AND LANGUAGE IN BACKWARD READERS

The relation between reading and the mechanisms of speech is also uncertain. It may be that defective speech affects only the ability to enunciate what is read; or that it also hinders the child from learning to read. Or it may be that some central disability of the nature of *aphasia* produces both defective speech and also reading disability. Ewing (1930) described cases of children aged 7–14 who were diagnosed as 'aphasic'. Their auditory acuity was normal, but their language development was extremely retarded. Indeed, two of them spoke an almost unintelligible jargon, and a third was very inaccurate in speech. A fourth could articulate familiar words, but had great difficulty with unfamiliar words, and could not repeat words and nonsense syllables accurately. None of these children was able to read. However, suitable treatment enabled them to speak fairly correctly, and to learn to read also.

These cases appear to resemble those described by Worster-Drought and Allen (1929, 1930), and by Barton Hall and Barton Hall (1931), as suffering from '*congenital auditory imperception*'—a term which they preferred to 'congenital word deafness', since the children were not deaf. Their auditory acuity was normal, and apparently their perception of auditory patterns was also fairly normal, for they could hear and imitate speech sounds, animal cries and usually musical notes and tunes. But they were incapable of understanding the meaning of words, and either they could not speak at all, or their speech was grossly distorted and incomprehensible. Their reading and writing were also defective. The term 'auditory imperception' was therefore incorrect also, and the defect should have been described as 'lack of ability to understand words'. The condition was said to be congenital, because it had existed either from birth or from a very early age; and in many cases there appeared also to be cases of speech defect in the family. These cases are extremely rare, and are unlikely to constitute more than a very small proportion of reading disability cases. But it is just possible that there may exist other less severe cases in which the understanding of words is defective though not completely lacking. It may be that some of Monroe's cases, described in the last section, suffered from such a defect rather than from 'poor auditory perception'. But the nature of this defect is obscure, and evidence as to its incidence and connection with reading disability is lacking.

In other cases there is evidence of the effect of *functional disorders of speech* upon reading. Travis and Rasmus (1931; see Travis, 1931) compared the discrimination of speech sounds of 382 normals and 186 individuals with mild functional disorders of articulation without motor disturbances of speech. At all ages, the latter made more errors in the discrimination of 300 consonants combined with the vowel 'a', and of 66 vowels paired in random order. Intensity, duration and pitch were held constant. The twenty most severely affected cases missed 63% of the vowels, which were the sounds they found hardest to articulate. Such defects of articulation might therefore be contributory to difficulty in reading.

Burt (1937) found the percentage distribution of speech defects shown in Table 10 among London school-children who were

Table 10

	Backward children		Normals	
	Boys	Girls	Boys	Girls
Marked defects	8·3	2·5	2·1	0·5
Slight defects	11·4	6·6	6·2	2·0

generally backward educationally. Lisping, lalling and mispronunciation of words decreased as age increased, and were less frequent among the more intelligent children, as is shown in Table 11, which gives the percentage frequency of such defects as found by Sheridan (1955).

Table 11

	Single defects *		Multiple defects *	
	Boys	Girls	Boys	Girls
Unselected primary and secondary school children:				
Aged 5 years	27	21	7	5
8 years	16	15	4	3
12 years	15	13	2	2
Grammar school children aged 11–13 years	9	8½	0	0
Mental defectives aged 11–13 years	42	25	24	18

* Single defects = defect of a single consonant; multiple defects = two or more phonetic abnormalities.

But though these defects become less frequent when the child goes to school, *stammering* may increase, especially among boys. Among Burt's cases, the numbers rose from 0·6% at the age of 5 years to nearly 2% at the age of 8 years. Despert (1946) also noted that stammering tended to appear most often when the child first went to school. It seems possible therefore that this increase was due to the difficulty experienced by many children in learning to read and write, rather than that stammering made reading difficult. But the effects of going to school may be less severe nowadays. Thus Cummings (1946) found that of twenty-five children aged 2–7 years with emotionally caused speech defects, who were followed up over a period of 18 months without being given any special treatment, six lost their defects and a further nine showed improvement.

As regards the incidence of speech defect among backward readers, Monroe (1932) found that 27% of 415 cases of reading disability had speech defects, as against 8% of 101 control cases. She considered that inaccurate articulation might confuse the child, who would hear the words spoken in one way by himself, and in another way by others, hence altering the phonetic sounds of words. Jackson (1944) found that 22·7% of a group of 300 readers aged 7–11 years in the lowest quartile on tests of reading achievement had speech defects, as contrasted with 10·2% of the 300 children in the top quartile. Robinson (1946) stated that 20% of thirty cases of severe reading backwardness, aged 6–16 years, suffered from dyslalia (lisping, lalling, etc.), as compared with only 2% of the normal school population. Schonell (1942) had five cases of gross speech defect among about 100 backward readers; and eight cases in a similar group of children backward in spelling. These spelling defects he attributed to a lowered power of auditory discrimination of speech sounds; thus the children could not discriminate between the sounds of 'sh' and 'ch', 'f' and 'th', 's' and 'sh'. But they could discriminate between words. However, it is exceedingly difficult to judge whether the children could not speak and read properly because they could not hear correctly, or whether their inability to read and spell was due to their lack of practice in hearing the correct speech sounds because they them-selves articulated them incorrectly. The latter difficulty probably occurred in the cases of faulty pronunciation associated with bad spelling.

It is quite possible that some cases of stammering are produced by *emotional disorders* which have a direct effect upon reading (see p. 132). Thus Despert (1946) found that many children begin to stammer between the ages of 2 and 4 years, during the period of considerable emotional resistance; and that 72% of the mothers of a group of fifty stammerers were domineering, over-anxious or over-protective. Hallgren (1950) also showed that there was a greater incidence of speech defects among his 122 cases of severe reading disability, aged 9 and upwards, than among the controls, especially among boys. But these defects were in the main slight, and he considered that they were associated with neurotic symptoms, which were also more frequent among the cases of reading disability, and not directly with the disability. Nelson (1953) also found that children with functional disorders of speech were less well behaved in school, and also generally retarded in school subjects, though their intelligence, health and school attendance were as good as those of normal children of their age.

It has been suggested that the *faulty breathing control* which characterizes stammering directly impedes language development and oral reading—and hence also silent reading. Murray (1932) found many of the disturbances of breathing characteristic of stammering also appeared during the silent reading of stammerers. These characteristics were: a much more variable amplitude and duration of inspiration and expiration than in normals; and also tonic spasms of the breathing muscles. The greater the difficulty of the reading material, the relatively greater the disintegration of breathing control. The reading achievement of eighteen stammerers correlated inversely with the amount of such disintegration. On the average, they were retarded by $1\frac{1}{2}$ years below the normal in reading comprehension, and $2\frac{1}{2}$ years in reading rate. Ketcham (1951) also considered that reading backwardness was related in some cases to inadequate breathing control. He gave special training in breathing control during oral reading to thirty-two boys, aged 7–10 years, who were seriously retarded in reading. They were also given training in the understanding of words as visual symbols. After training, they had gained the equivalent of 6·2 months in oral reading age, and 9·9 months in silent reading age. Control cases of backward readers who were not given this training gained little if anything during the same period. However, there is no evidence as to how much of the improvement in reading was due to improved breathing control, and how much to the training in understanding words.

Table 12

	Phonetic teaching		Look-and-say teaching	
	Experimental	Control	Experimental	Control
Stammering	8	12	2	0
Lisping, baby talk	21	21	14	22
Other speech defects	29	31	16	22

That speech defects are not always prevalent among backward readers is indicated by the results of Bond (1935) and Yedinack (1949). Bond found the percentages shown in Table 12 of speech defects among backward and normal readers. Thus there was no generally significant difference between backward and normal readers in the number of speech defects, but there were more of these among children taught by phonetic than by look-and-say methods. Children who were more backward in oral than in silent reading also had more speech defects than others. The effect of phonetic methods of teaching, then, may be to exaggerate natural difficulties in articulating words.

Yedinack (1949) quoted a study by Gibbons (1934) in which twenty cases of speech defect were found to be retarded on the average by one year in reading behind twenty control cases matched for age and intelligence. Fifteen of the twenty cases were sufficiently retarded in reading to need remedial treatment. It is not apparent whether or not the intelligence of these cases was subnormal; thus we cannot be certain if the speech defect alone was responsible for the reading retardation. In Yedinack's study, there were seventy-one cases selected by teachers on the basis of their poor articulation; their ages were 7–9 years, their mean I.Q. about 90 (none was below 76). These cases were defective in the pronunciation of at least one phonetic unit. In addition there were twenty-seven cases who were deficient in both speech and in reading. Children whose defective articulation was due to hearing loss were excluded. The cases of poor articulation were inferior to normal controls in oral reading by about half a year, and slightly inferior in silent reading, but were not significantly inferior on a non-oral vocabulary test. Nor were they inferior in the development of their written language, as measured by length and completeness of sentences and complexity of grammatical structure. Neither were these latter measures correlated with reading achievement, although this did show some correlation with vocabulary.

These studies appear to indicate that in some backward cases reading may be appreciably affected by severe speech defect and faulty articulation, but that these cases are not very numerous. However, it seems possible that even when there is no overt defect in the motor mechanisms of speech, there may be a distinct inability to understand words and to formulate them—just as there is a real difference between motor and sensory aphasia. Associated with this might be a lack of facility in the analysis of words into their constituent speech sounds. We know that sensory aphasia is produced by injury to a comparatively narrowly localized area of the cerebral cortex. It might be that in certain individuals this speech centre is inadequately developed and specialized; and that although it could function sufficiently well in ordinary speech, it could not supply the degree of sensitivity and refinement for the more highly developed language functions necessary in learning to read. There is also evidence, which we shall discuss in Chapter v, of an association between speech defects, reading difficulties, and left-handedness or ambidextrality.

It is generally agreed that a child requires a good *vocabulary* and a competent use of language before he can learn to read. Thus backwardness in *language development* may lead to backwardness in reading. Galifret-Granjon (1953) quoted Borel-Maisonny (1950) as finding that one of the important causes of reading disability was retarded development of language, both in expression and comprehension; and Linder (1951) as showing that 34% of a group of children aged 7–14 with reading disability were also retarded in speech. However, there is no evidence as to whether this retardation was due in part to poor intelligence. The same comment applies to the relationship established by Durrell and Sullivan (1937) between the reading achievement of young normal readers and their understanding of the meaning of words. Both of these may have been functions of intelligence. However, the author found that in six out of eight cases of severe reading retardation, aged 8–10 years, who could read only a few words at sight, the I.Q. on the Wechsler Verbal Scale was considerably below the I.Q. on the Performance Scale. Their scores on the Terman–Merrill Vocabulary Test were also low for their mental ages. Again it may be that these children through their inability to read had not been able to develop as good an understanding of words as a normal reader of the same mental age. But this inability to understand words would of course react back on their reading capacities. It might, for instance, make it necessary for them to continue using infant reading books, with contents quite out of tune with their natural interests at that age. Since lack of interest is a great deterrent in remedial reading, this defective vocabulary may be important.

(5) COGNITIVE DIFFICULTIES OF THE BACKWARD READER

We have indicated that backward readers can usually recognize a few words at sight which they have learnt to memorize. They can also guess a certain number of others, particularly if they are assisted by the context or by appropriate pictures. In the reading of isolated words, it is quite clear that the majority of the words they enunciate are little more than guesses. Often these guesses begin with the same letter as the printed words, and have about the same length; sometimes they contain other letters which appear in the printed words. Although as the children progress a little in reading they use more letters in the word as cues for guessing it, they do not perceive the whole structure of the word accurately. Often the errors they make seem to be quite illogical. Thus Davis (1939) studied cases of reading disability who remembered a word one day and forgot it the next; who substituted words with no apparent connection or resemblance; who could spell words but not read them. Lord, Carmichael and Dearborn (1925) described a case who could write words but could not read them when he saw them later. He attempted to sound them phonetically, but sounded the phonetic units in the wrong order and therefore could not blend them to form the word.

The author found that backward readers could often identify words which had been spoken to them from a group of similar words, when they could not read the same words. Also they could build up words when the letters were supplied to them, but not read them. Thus from a set of simple two-, three- and four-letter words, only 34% could be read at sight; but 68% could be identified by matching once they had been spoken to the child, and 58% could be built up from their letters. Quite a number of polysyllabic words could be built from their separate syllables, once the whole word had been spoken. Thus clearly the children were familiar with the general shapes of these words, and the letters they contained, but their knowledge was quite unsystematic. They knew something about the shapes of letters and letter groups and their associated sounds, and that the letters had to be blended together to form the words; but they were so confused that they had no certainty as to the correct manner of performing these processes, or of co-ordinating them together.

The commonest feature of reading disability is the incapacity to perform the cognitive processes of *analysing* accurately the visual and auditory structures of words. The backward reader guesses wrong letters, or the right letters in the wrong order. It might be thought that if he were told to spell the word, or to sound its consecutive phonetic units, this type of error would soon be remedied; and so, in many cases, it can. Such cases probably include the numerous children taught by look-and-say methods who have never learnt to study the letters and phonetic units consecutively in the right direction from left to right. But the severe cases of disability seem to have a deeply rooted incapacity to perform the process of analysis with facility, and to synthesize or blend phonetic units to form complete words. According to Schilder (1944), this failure in blending is the main characteristic of backward readers who can recognize a certain number of simple words as wholes. Perhaps for these children a word is an unanalysable whole. Or, as Durrell (1940) has pointed out, they may enunciate the phonetic units so slowly, focusing attention upon them as completely isolated units, that they defy integration into a total word sound.

Thus the fundamental and basic characteristic of reading disability appears to be cognitive confusion and lack of system. Why even quite an intelligent child should fail to realize that there is a complete and invariable correspondence between printed letter shapes and phonetic units remains a mystery which, as we shall see in succeeding chapters, has not yet been solved. It must be attributed to a failure in analysing, abstraction and generalization, but one which, typically, is confined to linguistics. Perhaps the obvious syncretism and familiarity of spoken words makes it particularly hard to apply cognitive reasoning to their analysis. Certain it is that in some cases only a drastic form of analysis proves efficacious, such as that utilized in the Fernald and Keller tracing method (1921).

But Fernald (1943) attributed the success of this method to quite another cause. She put forward the hypothesis that certain children are naturally defective in *visual* and *auditory imagery*, but rely greatly upon *tactile* and *kinaesthetic imagery*, which are not normally utilized in reading instruction. She stated that if beginners in reading were given the opportunity of learning words by first tracing and then writing them, certain children eagerly adopted this method and found it very helpful. Unfortunately, Fernald's evidence on this procedure was apparently obtained from the study of only one class of beginners of normal intelligence; and it does not appear to have been supported by corroborative evidence obtained by other investigators. But Fernald also stated that the majority of her clinic cases of extreme and total reading disability proved to be defective in visual and auditory imagery (though they were able to develop these when trained); but they were individuals who made great use of movement and gesture, their tactile-kinaesthetic imagery was excellent, and they learnt to read successfully when they were given the opportunity of using the tracing method. We shall discuss Fernald's remedial teaching methods more fully in Chapter VIII. But her hypothesis as to the functions of imagery in reading cannot be accepted as yet, for it has never been possible to prove satisfactorily that any lack of the appropriate imagery can completely prevent the development of any form of skilled activity. A tendency to rely on tactile-kinaesthetic rather than on visual and auditory imagery might, however, be a predisposing factor to reading difficulty.

But it may also be that the value of the tracing method lies to a great extent in directing the child's attention to the important features of the word, and in causing him to make an active attempt to incorporate these into his knowledge. It is well known that little children have great difficulty in concentrating for any length of time, especially upon rather recondite details such as the reading process necessitates. Even the continual repetition of procedure which takes place in the teaching of reading may fail to focus the child's attention upon some important feature of visual or phonetic structure; and once he has missed this, he may remain in an unresolved state of doubt and confusion. Ideally, the remedial teacher should seek to locate the source of the difficulty in each child, but this is usually extremely hard to do. However, practice in word analysis and the blending of phonetic sounds, while the printed word is being studied, are almost always valuable. Some modern reading books show the different phonetic units of the word in different colours; this should be of great assistance to the child in the process of analysis. But analysis should always be accompanied by immediate re-synthesis, and by frequent writing of the words.

To sum up the conclusions to be drawn from this chapter: There is no evidence of any general disorder of the visual perception of shapes in cases of reading disability. Children who cannot read at all may yet have normal visual perception. There may be some deficiency in the accurate discrimination of detail and of spatial orientation, related possibly to a general lack of maturation in analysis and visual memory, but resulting possibly from the reading disability itself. Apparent defects in auditory perception and memory may be due to lack of attention to details of phonetic structure which has also retarded reading; but again the latter may be the cause rather than the effect of the former. Speech defects and slow language development have often been found in backward readers, and may have been contributory to the retardation. But in the experimental study of these defects there has been little or no attempt to determine the frequency with which they appear in severe cases of disability, as distinct from their occurrence in the merely backward. Thus we do not know whether these defects are common among the former, except in the very rare cases diagnosed as exhibiting 'congenital auditory imperception'.[1]

[1] See also the cases of deafness described in Chapter VI and the congenital cases described in Chapter V.

The one universal characteristic of non-readers suffering from specific reading disability is their complete failure to analyse word shapes and sounds systematically and associate them together correctly. We have at present no evidence as to the cause of this cognitive deficiency, which appears to be confined solely to linguistic activity. We shall proceed to consider whether any more fundamental cause of the disability can be detected, studying first those causes which may be innate, and secondly those which are the result of the child's upbringing and environment.

CHAPTER V

INNATE FACTORS AS CAUSES OF DISABILITY IN READING

(I) INTELLIGENCE

It is of course obvious that a child of really low intelligence is enormously handicapped in learning to read. It is difficult for him to perform the complex cognitive processes described in Chapter IV. Also his vocabulary is smaller than that of the child of normal intelligence, and therefore he may not know the meaning of the words he is trying to read. However, as Wall (1945, 1946) and others have shown, children with I.Q.'s below 70 can learn to read. What is of greater importance is that there are considerable numbers of children of average intelligence who are nevertheless backward in reading. Few highly intelligent children suffer from specific reading disability; but there are many with I.Q.'s between 90 and 120. Schonell (1942) found that 1·3% of the backward children he tested had I.Q.'s below 70, as against 1·9% with reading quotients below 70. In the Middlesbrough enquiry (1953), about 3% were illiterate, but only 1·5% had I.Q.'s below 70. Schonell also stated that about 27% of all his cases of specific backwardness in reading had I.Q.'s below 80; and 11% had I.Q.'s below 70. In the special cases referred from schools, there were only 3% below 80. But 52% of those below 80 and 65% of those below 70 were retarded by 2·0 or more years below their mental age.

However, it must be noted that these children were tested with verbal intelligence tests. It seems probable that linguistic ability is particularly retarded in dull and backward children, and that this retardation affects both reading and verbal intelligence test performance. Moreover, group verbal intelligence tests require the child to be able to read; thus it is not surprising that a close correlation between verbal intelligence test performance and reading performance is often obtained. Mellone (1942) found that the verbal I.Q.'s of children of 8 years (tested on the Moray House

75

Test) were significantly lower than their I.Q.'s on the Sleight Non-Verbal Intelligence Test. The differences were not significant after 8 years of age. If cases at all ages with reading ages below about 9 years were considered, the difference between verbal and non-verbal I.Q.'s was significantly increased. Thus it might be supposed that in any really backward reader, the correlation between verbal I.Q. and reading age would appear spuriously high, because the inability to read fluently would affect performance on the verbal intelligence test.

Various American experimenters have found the correlations of reading performance to be lower with non-verbal than with verbal intelligence test performance. Thus Traxler (1939) obtained correlations of about 0·35 between the non-linguistic parts of the California Test of Mental Maturity and silent reading performance in seventy-four children of 14 years; whereas the correlations of the latter with the linguistic parts of the California test ranged from 0·68 to 0·73. Strang (1943) obtained similar results with younger children: the non-linguistic parts showed correlations of 0·36–0·56 with reading test performance, and the linguistic parts, correlations of 0·8 and over. Bond and Fay (1950) showed that among fifty children aged 9–12 years, those whose reading ages exceeded their mental ages excelled in the items of the Stanford–Binet test depending on the knowledge and use of words, whereas those whose mental ages exceeded their reading ages did better on the non-verbal items. Coleman (1953), however, found that in a non-verbal test consisting largely of items requiring perceptual discrimination, backward readers gave a poorer performance than on a verbal test such as the Stanford–Binet or Wechsler. But the author obtained a different result; she found that in cases of severe reading disability, especially among older children of 8–10 years, the score on the verbal section of the Wechsler test was often considerably below that on the non-verbal section (see p. 69).[1]

---

[1] It is true that Seashore (1951) has shown that discrepancies of 12–13 points occurred in a group of over 2000 children between the Wechsler Verbal and Performance scores; but the cases in which the Performance score was above the Verbal were approximately equal in number to those in which the Verbal score exceeded the Performance score.

It seems probable that at the beginning of reading, intelligence plays a major part with all children. However, as they grow older, and in most cases more skilled in reading, it becomes relatively less important. That is to say, the majority of children learn to read, though sometimes rather slowly, provided that they have a certain minimum I.Q., whereas those who do not learn are characterized by some specific defect. Thus Schonell (1942) found that the correlation between reading performance and intelligence decreased with increase in age, as shown in Table 13.

Table 13

Age in years	8	9	10	11
Correlation between reading and I.Q.	0·79	0·58	0·59	0·44

Woodrow (1945) found no correlation between I.Q. and gains over a measured period of reading scores in children aged 10–13 years. Further evidence to the same effect was obtained by Bliesmer (1954), who compared the reading performance of bright and dull children of the same mental age. Twenty-nine children with I.Q.'s of 116 and over were matched for mental age (which lay within the range of 10 years 7 months to 12 years 6 months) with an equal number of older children with I.Q.'s of 84 and below. There was little difference between the two groups as regards the mechanics of reading—that is to say, in reading rate, word recognition and understanding the meaning of words. The bright children, however, excelled in the comprehension of whole texts, and in reasoning about and drawing conclusions from what they read. Thus it appears that dull children, with I.Q.'s from 70 to 80, can learn to read with reasonable skill, though more slowly and at a later age, and with less adequate understanding of connected prose. Learning to read depends more on mental age, that is to say, level of maturation, than upon intelligence as such; and specific reading disability cannot be directly attributed to subnormality of intelligence.

(2) CONGENITAL WORD BLINDNESS

We have so far considered only the more obvious features of disability in reading. But the frequency of this disability, even among children of normal intelligence, and its resistance to treatment, suggest that at least in some cases it must have some more fundamental cause. We have seen that there is no evidence in backward readers of any general innate inability to perceive and discriminate shapes visually. There may be innate defects in the accurate hearing and understanding of speech sounds, but even this is doubtful except in deaf children, especially those suffering from high frequency deafness (see p. 124). We must now consider the evidence for the existence, and the causal importance, of other fundamental factors.

Perhaps the earliest to draw attention to the fundamental and possibly innate nature of reading disability was Hinshelwood (1917), who termed it 'congenital word blindness'. He supposed it to be a localized defect of visual memory for letters and words alone, which could not be remedied by ordinary school teaching. It might be congenital; and was caused by a localized defect in the development of that area of the cortex commonly associated with speech and with aphasia (angular and supramarginal gyri). It could be overcome by special treatment which set up a process of education of a centre in the opposite hemisphere to the affected one. Hinshelwood had no evidence for the existence of this cortical defect other than the extreme resistance of the condition to treatment. Wallin (1921) made some differentiation between mild cases of disability, which he called 'dyslexia', and severe cases, called 'visual aphasia'. But he classified them all as 'word blindness'; that is to say, they were defects in the perception of words, but not in other types of visual perception. He attributed them to lesions of the speech area in the angular or supramarginal gyri, originating congenitally or caused by birth injury; or to arrested development in these areas. Orton (1928) pointed out that the condition of 'word blindness' was assumed to exist merely from the similarity of the symptoms to those of 'alexia', the loss of ability to read as the result of injury or disease in the parietal lobe of the major hemisphere. Unfortunately the diagnosis of 'congenital word blindness' became popular among medical practitioners, though it has been repudiated again and again by psychologists; and many unhappy children have been diagnosed as cases of 'congenital word blindness', and all hope of teaching them to read has been abandoned. An article by Fogerty in the book *Abnormal Speech* by Boome, Baines and Harries (1939) shows that the term is still in use; though fortunately in this case the children were given remedial treatment in reading. Schilder (1944) also postulated the existence of an isolated cortical defect which prevented the backward reader from analysing and synthesizing letter sounds, but he differentiated this from the 'word blindness' of adult aphasics. He advanced no hypothesis as to the nature and basis of this defect.

In support of the theory of congenital reading disability, Dearborn (Lord, Carmichael and Dearborn, 1925) cited the findings of various earlier observers who collected family 'trees' of cases of reading disability. He himself obtained four instances where the disability was apparently congenital. In the first, the father was backward in reading and had three daughters, two of whom were non-readers. The second and third instances were of fathers and sons who had pronounced reading difficulties. In the fourth instance, the father had great difficulty in mastering linguistic subjects, and the daughter found it hard to learn to read. All these fathers were intelligent people, in professional occupations. Again, Eustis (1947a) described a family known to him through four generations which contained numerous examples of speech defects and unco-ordinated jerky movement. Many were restless, hyperactive and distractible individuals. There were six cases of reading disability, three boys and three girls; the boys were more severely affected than were the girls. Eustis attributed these defects to a congenital condition of slow myelination of the nerve tracts, a hypothesis also advanced by Karlin (1950) to account for the origin of stammering. This is of course a purely speculative hypothesis.

Hincks (1926) also found evidence of congenital disability. Nine out of eleven cases who were studied intensively had other cases of reading disability in their families. And again these families appeared to be emotionally unstable, with neurotic tendencies in some cases. Rather similar evidence was obtained by Burt (1937) as to the congenital nature of speech defects and emotional instability, among the backward children whom he studied. There were ninety-seven stammerers; in 62% of these there was some evidence of neuropathic inheritance, and in 23% a tendency among relatives to stammer. Bryngelson (1935) found that, among 700 cases of stammering in children aged 9–16 years, about 70% had some stammering relatives. It is of course possible that children might tend to copy such a defect from their relatives. Thus Despert (1946) pointed out that stammering often occurs among the children of over-anxious and over-protective mothers; and that if there is any tendency to stammering among members of the family, such mothers may be particularly anxious lest their children should develop the defect, and thus promote it by their anxiety and fussing. However, in 14% of Burt's cases there had been no contact with stammering relatives. Also these children had in many cases been backward in learning to talk, and there was a family history of backwardness in talking.

These cases of congenital speech defects are of course only indirectly relevant to the hypothesis of congenital reading disability. But more direct evidence was supplied by an extensive investigation carried out in Sweden by Hallgren (1950). He studied the test results, case histories and family histories of seventy-nine children registered at clinics as suffering from early and prolonged difficulties in learning to read and write, and forty-three children registered at school as 'word blind'. Some of these were unable to read after several years' schooling. He compared their performance with that of 212 normal controls in tests of reading, spelling, sound blending, memory for nonsense syllables; also on tests of hand, foot and eye dominance. The case histories of 160 sibs and parents of these children were also examined. The only characteristic difference between the normal children and the cases of reading disability was the greater incidence of speech defects and of neurotic symptoms among the latter. In some cases the neurotic symptoms had appeared before the reading disability, and might therefore have caused it, at least in part. But in many cases the neurotic symptoms did not appear till afterwards; thus Hallgren supposed that the neurosis could only have accentuated the disability, and in some cases might have been caused by it. The incidence of neurotic symptoms was higher among children who had undergone a medical examination, but was no greater among the parents and sibs of the reading disability cases than among those of the normal readers. But in all but thirteen cases there was some evidence of reading disability among the parents and/or sibs of the reading disability cases, and in some cases it could be traced back through three generations. Hallgren concluded that a primary disability was inherited as a unitary Mendelian dominant characteristic, independent of neurotic tendencies. Although it appeared more frequently in boys than in girls, the difference of frequency in the two sexes was not great enough to prove the inheritance to be sex-linked. But in addition to this primary disability Hallgren postulated the occurrence of secondary disabilities which were not congenital, but were caused by other factors such as poor intelligence, emotional disorders and environmental conditions. Eight of Hallgren's cases could be attributed to such factors.

It is difficult to accept Hallgren's conclusion that specific reading disability is in most cases a single congenital disability, unlinked to others, until further corroborative evidence has been obtained from other studies. What seems much more plausible is that there is a congenital disposition in certain cases towards the occurrence of certain related defects: reading disability, speech defects or infantile speech; motor inco-ordination; left-handedness or ambidextrality. We shall proceed to discuss these associated symptoms in the next section.

(3) CEREBRAL DOMINANCE

The most common suggestion as to the origin of these defects, and especially of reading disability, is that they are due to a failure to develop the dominance of the major over the minor cerebral hemisphere. The best-known exposition of this theory is that of Orton (1928, 1929, 1937). He attributed reading disability to what he called '*strephosymbolia*'. In learning to read, 'engrams' or 'traces' of the printed words were formed in both hemispheres, but those in the minor hemisphere were normally suppressed and elided through the dominance of the major hemisphere. This he considered was proved by the fact that the ability to read was destroyed by certain injuries to the major but not to the minor hemisphere. In certain cases, however, dominance was not completely established, or was established unusually late in development. There was then a confusion between the engrams of the major hemisphere and the unsuppressed engrams of the minor hemisphere which were mirror images of those of the major hemisphere. This confusion appeared in tendencies to mirror writing, to mirror reversal of words and letters in reading, in the ability to read mirror writing comparatively easily, and in difficulty in associating the reversed visual shapes with the straightforward phonetic equivalents. These characteristics appeared in backward readers, especially those who had been taught by 'look-and-say' methods, with their lack of emphasis on the order of letters in words. But they were not always associated with other signs of incomplete dominance, that is to say, cross-laterality of handedness and eyedness.[1]

This theory, then, rests upon two sets of experimental observations: (1) the frequency of reversals in the reading and writing of backward readers; (2) the greater frequency of left-handedness, ambidextrality and cross-laterality among backward than among normal readers. We have adduced evidence to show that *complete mirror reversal* in reading and writing occurs only in some cases of reading disability, whereas other types of error are much more frequent among backward readers than among normal readers, and especially transpositions of letters within the word. Now it might be expected that children suffering from 'strephosymbolia' would perceive the mirror images of letters and words relatively easily. But there is no reason why they should be prone to reverse the

[1] Left-handedness and right-eyedness, or right-handedness and left-eyedness.

order of letters in a word, while maintaining the correct spatial orientation of the letters. These reversals of order, and the other forms of transposition, should rather be attributed to the general confusion of the backward reader over order and direction which we discussed in the first chapter.

Before considering whether there is in fact any association between reading backwardness and cerebral dominance, we must first discuss the vast quantity of experimental evidence which has been adduced as to the relation of cerebral dominance to *laterality*, that is to say, the tendency to use one hand, one foot or one eye more readily or more skilfully than the other. In passing, it should be noted that in general when an individual is said to be right- or left-'eyed', this means that he tends to use one eye rather than the other in 'sighting', aiming or any other monocular task. This dominant eye is not necessarily the more efficient eye. Thus Gahagan (1933) found that in 27% of a group of 100 adults, the dominant eye in sighting had the lower visual acuity. Robinson and Huelsman (Robinson, 1953a) showed that there was no relationship between dominance and any other measure of visual efficiency. Nor does eyedness give any indication as to which is the dominant visual area in the cortex, since each retina is of course represented in both hemispheres (see Fig. 9, p. 90). However, some evidence as to the dominance of the visual cortical areas will be presented below.

Detailed discussions of the development and incidence of *right-* and *left-handedness* have been given by Burt (1937) and Hildreth (1949, 1950). It appears that the child begins to use one hand more frequently than the other at about 6–9 months, but he continues for some time to use either or both hands for many activities. However, Gesell and Ames (1947) were of opinion that laterality was related to the tendency of infants to turn the head predominantly to one side or the other when lying prone. This tendency disappears between the 16th and 20th weeks. The dominant hand is the one mainly used at about the second year, but a period of bilaterality in handling objects occurs from $2\frac{1}{2}$ to $3\frac{1}{2}$ years. After that the dominant hand is used mainly, but periods of bilaterality occur in some children at a later age. Differences in skill in the two hands are not pronounced until 3 years, and shifts of handedness may occur even later. Superiority of one hand over the other increases with age. Thus Burge (1952) showed that differences in the accuracy of aiming of the two hands increased up to the age of about 13 years. On the whole it appears that right dominance becomes fully established before left dominance; and that the proportion of right-handed individuals increases with age. This is due at least in part to the effects of training. Children are trained to use the right hand rather than the left, which training is intensified when they begin to learn to write. However, many children, and especially boys, retain the use of the left hand to a greater or less extent.

It has often been stated that left-handedness may be inherited. Thus Burt (1937) found that 14% of his left-handed cases had a left-handed parent, and in 31% of cases there were left-handed persons among other relatives. He quoted Chamberlain (1929) as having examined over 12,000 persons and found that in families with one or both parents left-handed, 17% of the children were left-handed, as against only 2% in families with both parents right-handed. Mills (1925), studying a group of about 1000 adults, found that over 20% were left-handed or had some tendency to left-handedness; and for 26% of these, there was some family history of left-handedness. There were left-handed or ambidextrous members in the families of five out of six of the cases studied by Ettlinger and Jackson (1955) of severe reading disability with tendencies to cross-laterality. Ojemann (1930) stated that handedness was bimodally distributed,[1] which pointed to a congenital basis, since environmental factors would be likely to give rise to unimodality of distribution. However, this demonstration of bimodality seems to have resulted from Ojemann's method of measuring handedness (see p. 88); and it cannot therefore be accepted unequivocally.

[1] That is to say, the numbers of ambidextrous, partially right-handed and partially left-handed people are less than the numbers of wholly right-handed and wholly left-handed people.

Whether because of congenital tendencies, or because of the social emphasis on right-handedness, left-handed individuals are much less frequent than right-handed, and their handedness is less well established. Thus there are in fact (contrary to Ojemann's findings) many in whom the skill of the two hands is about equal, and who use the right hand for some tasks and the left for others. According to Burt, the left-handed and partially left-handed are commonly more clumsy than the purely right-handed. Fitt and O'Halloran (1934) found that the speed of tapping of the two hands was more nearly equal in the left-handed than in the right-handed. Galifret-Granjon (1954) showed that children who were not strongly lateralized as regards handedness were slower at card sorting than those who were. Burt also showed that left-handedness was more common among the less intelligent than the more intelligent children. And Fitt and O'Halloran found that on the whole the left-handed were more backward educationally, which may be attributed to lower intelligence, greater clumsiness (especially in writing), or to the reading backwardness which we shall discuss below.

Burt drew a distinction, based apparently on general observation rather than upon exact diagnosis, between the congenitally left-sided and right cerebral-dominant cases, with left-handedness, -footedness and -eyedness; and cases with a considerable degree of temperamental instability and emotional resistance who were mainly left-handed in those activities which social convention allocates to the right hand, but were not left-footed or left-eyed. No evidence as to the correctness of this observation has been given in any other studies of the association between handedness and neurotic tendencies; though Cuff (1930) found that strongly left-handed and left-eyed children aged 7-9 years obtained rather poorer scores on the Woodworth–Cady Questionnaire[1] for neurotic tendencies than did strongly right-handed and right-eyed children. But there was no such difference among rather older children. And Wetmore and Estabrooks (1929) found that right-handed and

---

[1] Consisting of questions the answers to which are believed to indicate neurotic traits, emotional maladjustment, etc.

ambidextrous students and those with a tendency to left-handedness all obtained very similar scores for neurotic traits on the Laird Personal Inventory (see p. 85, footnote). Fitt and O'Halloran found a correlation of only 0·28 between degrees of left-handedness and neurotic tendencies, as measured by the Woodworth–Matthews Questionnaire (see p. 85, footnote), in sixty children of average age 12½ years. But these studies ignored Burt's distinction between the two types of left-handedness.

However, all these findings are somewhat vitiated by inadequate *testing for handedness*. In some enquiries it has been considered sufficient to ask the individual which hand he normally uses for various activities, for instance, writing, throwing, eating, playing various games. Answers to these queries are not always reliable, especially in children, though they may give the only available evidence as to the use of the left hand in early childhood, for instance, in beginning to write. Smith (1945) found a high degree of consistency in handedness (higher for right- than for left-handed individuals) in the answers to a questionnaire given to 120 students. But the agreement between handedness, footedness and eyedness was considerably lower. Moreover, consistency between answers to questions does not prove that the answers were always correct.

Thus it is much more satisfactory whenever possible to use a number of different tests, which assess speed and dexterity of movement of the two hands, as well as demonstrating the hand habitually preferred. Both practised and unpractised activities should be tested; unimanual and bimanual activities (such as eating with a knife and fork, digging with a spade); and activities requiring coarser and finer co-ordination. Hildreth (1949) has given an exhaustive survey of the most valuable tests. But when a number of tests are used, it is found that many children are not at all consistent in their use of the right or the left hand. For instance, Cuff (1931) found that children and adults who were predominantly right-handed in throwing, receiving and reaching, and right-footed in kicking, were often left-handed in sweeping. Johnson and Duke (1940) showed that children of 6–7 years were consistent in handedness only for a specific type of task, such as writing and drawing. However, many of the activities they tested, such as that of picking up objects, might not necessitate the use of the more skilled hand. Again, differences in performance between the two hands appear much more clearly in certain tasks than in others. Burge (1952) found no difference in speed of bouncing a ball for children aged 6–13 years, and comparatively little in strength of grip. Provins (1956) showed that there was more difference in adults between the two hands in a task such as tapping which required an organized series of graded muscular contractions than in a task in which a single pressure of the finger had to be reproduced.

Van Riper (1935) designed a test in which the two hands traced complicated patterns simultaneously, by touch alone, on two boards which were at first set in line, but which were then gradually rotated towards the parallel position. At first, with most people, the two hands traced similar patterns; but as the boards rotated, in time one hand, the less dominant, produced a mirror image of the tracing of the other. Ambidextrous individuals began to produce mirror images sooner than did normally right- or left-handed individuals; and they oscillated between mirroring the right by the left, and the left by the right. It must be noted that the reliability of this test has been questioned by Witty and Kopel (1935); and also by Jastak (1939), who produced a modification of the test called the 'ambigraph', which he claimed to be more satisfactory. This test was carried out with a vertical board placed parallel to the line of sight; observers had to trace a figure simultaneously with the two hands while drawing in the same direction, with one hand on one side of the board and the other on the other. They could not see what they were drawing. It was claimed that the dominant hand determined the direction in which a figure such

as ⌐ was drawn. The observers were also tested on a number

of other activities such as catching a ball, dealing cards, etc. Jastak found that the 820 observers varied considerably in consistency in using one hand or the other, and also in the consistency of dominance on the ambigraph. This agrees with the results quoted above. Thus many investigators have recommended that laterality should be measured by an index, such as $\dfrac{R}{R+L}$ or $\dfrac{R-L}{R+L}$, which indicates the tendency to right- or left-handedness. Johnson and Duke (1940) and Johnson and King (1942) found that when they calculated handedness in this way, the index showed a unimodal distribution, skewed towards the right-handed end, and not the bimodal distribution which would be expected if right- and left-handedness were all-or-none functions determined by cerebral dominance. It is true that Ojemann (1930) did obtain a bimodal distribution, but he used a different method of estimating handedness, combining test scores and parents' judgements. (The method of calculation was too elaborate for description here.)

Again, if the relative dominance of one cerebral hemisphere over the other determines whether an individual is right- or left-handed, then it might be expected that the right-handed individual would also tend to use the right *foot*, and the right eye in sighting—and vice versa. There appears to be some evidence to show that the right-handed person does tend to use his right foot, for instance, to kick a football. However, Provins (1956) found that there was no significant difference between the performances of the right and left foot in tapping by ten adults who showed marked differences between the right and left hand in tapping.

Although only about 10% of the population appears to be left-handed, something like 30% is left-eyed. But *eye-dominance* again varies greatly according to the way in which it is tested. Sometimes different eyes are used in different types of sighting, or on different occasions. Buxton and Crosland (1937) found an average correlation of only about 0·50 between four different tests of sighting and aiming. Moreover, the sighting eye does not always dominate in tests of lateral displacement. In these, the individual holds a pencil in front of his nose and focuses it with each eye in turn; the pencil should appear to move when the dominant eye is closed. Again, Crider (1944) found that sightedness varied with the number of times that the tests were repeated. After two sightings, 66% of approximately 1000 persons tested by him appeared to be right-eyed; but after forty-five sightings, only 38%.

We have already noted, however, that eyedness or sightedness cannot be connected with relative dominance of either of the visual areas of the cortex, though it might of course be associated with the dominance of one or other of the motor centres for eye movements. Some evidence has been obtained in other ways as to the relative dominance of the *visual areas*. That this does not correspond to dominance in the motor areas may perhaps be indicated by the observation of Jasper and Raney (1937) that the eye preferred in sighting does not necessarily dominate over the other in retinal rivalry. But Jasper and Raney did find some correspondence between handedness and dominance of the visual area as indicated in a test using the 'phi phenomenon'.[1] In this test, the observer was required to fixate a near point of light exposed in a dark box. Subsequently this light was extinguished, and another point of light exposed at a greater distance, which produced double images since it was not equidistant with the fixation point. Apparent movement was then perceived towards one or other of these images. The experiment was repeated with fixation of the far point and apparent movement towards one or other of the double images of the nearer point. It was necessary for the experimenter to make sure that the observer could see the double images clearly before he began to alternate the exposure of the two points; and 10–20 min. of observation might be necessary before the apparent movement was clearly seen. After that, the observer usually saw the movement consistently in one direction or the other.

The hypothesis was that movement which occurred predominantly to one side was determined by the dominance of a particular eye or hemisphere (see Fig. 9). Movement to the right with near fixation indicated the dominance of the right eye or the left hemisphere; and movement to the left, dominance of the left

[1] In the 'phi phenomenon', investigated extensively by the Gestalt psychologists, two points of light at some distance apart are exposed momentarily, the second shortly after the first. In general, a single point of light is perceived which appears to move from the position of the first point to that of the second.

eye or right hemisphere. Movement to the right with far fixation indicated dominance of the left eye or hemisphere; and movement to the left, dominance of the right eye or hemisphere. Thus if movement was perceived mainly to the right with both near and far fixation, it was determined by the dominance of the left hemisphere; and if to the left, by the dominance of the right hemisphere. But if movement was perceived to the right for near fixation and to the left with far fixation, it was determined by right eye dominance; and vice versa for left eye dominance. In a group of forty-four boys aged 9–12 years, 86% appeared to have left

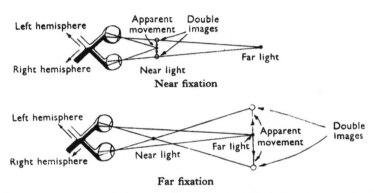

Fig. 9. Sensory stimulation occurring in perception of apparent movement with near and far fixation

hemispherical dominance, 12% right hemispherical dominance, and 2% were indeterminate. The consistency of these results on a re-test was 97%. But though there was considerable agreement between these results and cerebral dominance as indicated by laterality of handedness in manual preference, there was not much more than a chance association between the results and eye dominance in sighting.

McFie (1952) repeated the Jasper test with twelve normal readers aged 9–25 years, and found that they all reported consistent or predominant one-sided apparent movement in accordance with the dominance of one or other hemisphere; and that this dominance agreed with their prevailing handedness. His methods of assessing handedness were not, however, very adequate. Carter (1953) improved the Jasper technique by providing a separate fixation point, to ensure that the observer maintained his fixation of the near or the far point. He also employed an apparatus in which a central light alternated with two lights on each side of it. The observers, intelligent adults, tended to see a splitting movement at first, but in time this was replaced by a steady movement to one side or the other for observers with well-determined laterality. Of the nineteen observers, fourteen or fifteen were left-cerebral dominant, according to the test; of the seven left-handed observers, three showed right cerebral-dominance, and the remainder no clear dominance. Thus there does appear to be some correspondence between laterality in handedness, and a tendency to exhibit a particular function in the corresponding visual area of the cortex. The dominance of the latter does not seem to be very strong, however, since the percept in the opposite hemisphere is not immediately suppressed.

A study of reversed cerebral dominance as indicated in the Jasper test was carried out by Raney (1938) with *identical twins*. It had previously been noted that, in identical twins, one twin often showed reversed laterality, whereas the same tendency was not apparent in fraternal twins. Thus Jenkins *et al.* (1937) described two pairs of such twins, whom they had tested for laterality, though not very systematically. In the first pair, one twin was completely right-sided, the other mainly left-sided though she had been taught to write with the right hand. In the second pair, one twin was completely left-sided, the other right-handed and -footed though left-eyed. In Raney's study, there were seventeen pairs of twins aged 7–16 years. In addition to the Jasper test, they were given the Van Riper test, a test of sighting and a questionnaire on handedness. On the Jasper test, in 88% of cases one twin showed a dominance which was the reverse of the other's. In 70% of cases there was some indication of reversed handedness, and in only 12% of cases did both twins show clear right dominance. But there was little or no reversal of sightedness; it was in general similar in the two twins.

In a further study, Raney (1939) recorded the *electro-encephalograms*[1] of the twins, to find if there were any characteristic differences between the two cerebral hemispheres of the pairs. In general, the *alpha rhythms* of a pair of twins were similar to one another, in amount, frequency and amplitude—more similar than were those of unrelated children of the same ages. There was also a tendency for one twin (in 71 % of cases, the right-dominant twin) to have larger differences than the other between the amount of alpha rhythm in the two hemispheres. On the whole, there appeared to be a greater degree of alpha rhythm, and a greater amplitude of rhythm, in the hemisphere indicated by the Jasper test to be the non-dominant one. However, the differences were not always consistent; and they were not always the same in the occipital (visual) as in the motor area. Thus Raney concluded that lateral dominance was a localized specific function of a given area, rather than a completely unilateralized gradient of the whole hemisphere. But he suggested that in general the 'central excitatory state' and the peripheral nerve sensitivity of the dominant side of the cortex were greater than those of the non-dominant side, since the alpha rhythm was less. There was also less differentiation in the left-handed twin, indicating a lesser degree of lateral dominance than in the right-handed twin. Thus the difference in the central excitatory states of the two hemispheres was less in the former, which suggests that dominance might be more easily upset or reversed. Hence possibly the considerable frequency of left-handedness and mixed dominance in unstable personalities such as mental defectives, psychotics and neurotics. Furthermore, the changes of hand dominance which often occurred in the Van Riper test and in other bimanual tests could be explained by the amplitude of the alpha rhythm being greater first in one hemisphere and then in the other.

[1] In the electroencephalogram, the rhythmical electrical discharges from different areas of the cerebral cortex are recorded. When the eyes are shut, a rather marked slow rhythmical discharge called the 'alpha rhythm' may be obtained, predominantly from the visual area of the cortex, but also from other areas. The alpha rhythm is thus associated with lack of excitation from the external environment.

A study by Lindsley (1940) indicated that cross-laterals showed less synchronization of alpha rhythm between the two hemispheres than predominantly right- or left-sided individuals. He recorded the electroencephalograms of sixty-five normal children aged 5–16 years, of whom forty-eight were shown by tests to be right-handed, eight left-handed and nine ambidextrous. Thirty-seven were right-eyed and right-handed, and seven right-eyed and left-handed. The mean percentage of alpha waves out of phase between the two hemispheres was 8·6 for the right-handed and right-eyed, 16·9 for the left-handed and right-eyed, 22·3 for the ambidextrous. This indicates again a lack of cerebral dominance for the left-handed cross-laterals, though possibly of a less important kind, since the alpha rhythm functions in resting rather than in active states.

The evidence for consistent differences in the electroencephalograms corresponding to differences of laterality appears somewhat weak, however. Glanville and Antonitis (1955) quoted Cohn (1949) as noting a definite asymmetry of rhythm between the two hemispheres, but only on the basis of general observation. They themselves calculated the ratios of amount of alpha rhythm and mean amplitude of rhythm between the right and left occipital cortex. But they found no significant differences in these ratios between strongly right- and left-handed adults, as measured by the Jastak ambigraph test. It is possible that there are other differences in the electroencephalograms of the two hemispheres which relate to laterality. But at present the evidence is not at all clear or definite.

We must now consider other important symptoms which have often been related to lack of cerebral dominance—slow development of *speech*, and speech defects. Some interesting data as to the former association were adduced as long ago as 1918, by Nice. Four related children of educated parents (two siblings and two cousins), all girls, were ambidextrous or partially ambidextrous at 2–3 years. All were retarded in speech development at 2 years, though two appear to have developed normally by 3 years. Two unrelated cases with a similar association of ambidextrality and slow speech development were also described. These cases suggested that a slow development of cerebral dominance may in favourable circumstances be overcome long before the child goes to school. But it is reasonable to suppose that in other cases its effects are not so easily overcome, as for instance in the cases described by Castner (see p. 142).

Travis (1931) was particularly concerned to prove an association between lack of cerebral dominance and of control of the speech mechanisms. Indeed, he stated quite categorically that the latter is caused by the former. He described a case of a child who showed delayed speech development and stammering up to the age of 4 years, and was also ambidextrous. From 4 years he used his left hand to an increasing extent, and the stammering disappeared. Travis quoted results obtained by Bryngelson (1926), who found that 61 % of 200 cases of stammering, with ages ranging from 5 to 25 years, were also ambidextrous; 55 % had stammering relatives. Ballard (1912) found that 17 % of a group of 271 ambilateral adults still stammered, and 25·8 % had done so in the past; whereas none of a group of completely left-handed individuals stammered. In a group of 13,189 children aged 8–14, 4·3 % of the ambilaterals stammered, as against 1·2 % of the right-handed and 1·1 % of the left-handed. Scripture, Glogan and De Bra (1917) reported that, among 500 cases of speech defect, 25 % were left-handed or had left-handed relatives, 92 % of whom stammered. Wiseley (1930) found that among 18,560 school children, 5 % of the right-handed stammered and 12 % of the left-handed. Burt (1937) showed that among the children he studied, 6·5 % of the left-handed stammered, and 11·9 % had done so in the past; of the right-handed, only 1·7 % stammered, and 3·2 % had done so in the past. In another survey, 8·4 % of the left-handed and right-eyed stammered, as against 4 % of the left-handed and left-eyed. Among a group of ninety-seven stammerers, 14 % were left-handed, and an additional 18 % had left-handedness in the family. Downey (1927) found that in a group of 450 right-handed and partially right-handed adults and children, 11 % had some kind of speech defect, compared with 20·5 % of a group of 171 left- and partially left-handed individuals. But there appeared to be no greater incidence of speech defects among cross-laterals than among others. Again Oates (1929) showed that among a group of over 4000 schoolboys, aged 9–18 years, 7·5 % of the left-handed suffered from stammering or allied speech defects, as against 1·9 % of the right-handed. But many of these were not completely right- or left-handed; a considerable number were right-handed for unimanual tasks and left-handed for bimanual tasks, or vice versa. Of the completely right- and left-handed, 2·0 % had speech defects; of those with mixed handedness, 11·8 %.

A recent study carried out in France by Gille *et al.* (1954) on over 98,000 school-children aged 6–11 years showed that about 3·8 % of the right-handed suffered from speech disorders, and 10·2 % of the left-handed. The judgement of handedness was made by the teachers; and since in France left-handed children are strongly encouraged to write with the right hand, only the most obvious and recalcitrant cases would have been reported as such.

It is impossible to rely upon the accuracy of assessment of handedness in most of the above studies. We saw earlier that, if laterality was accurately tested and measured, it was seldom as complete as would be indicated by a rough estimate based on observation or questioning. When more accurate measurements are made, little association may appear between laterality and incidence of speech defects. Thus Johnson and King (1942) measured the laterality index on the Van Riper test and on answers to a questionnaire in ninety-eight adult stammerers and seventy-one non-stammerers. There was no significant difference in the index between the two groups. Thus although there may be some tendency for speech defects to be less common among completely right-handed individuals, especially children, than among others, such an association does not always hold. It may also be affected by pressure brought to bear on children to write with the right hand, a factor which we shall discuss below.

It must, however, be noted that some attempt has been made to link up *electroencephalographic* differences with speech defects. Lindsley (1940) found that in stammerers there was a tendency for the alpha rhythm to be out of phase between the two hemispheres. In two adult stammerers, 22·2 and 16·6 % respectively of the alpha rhythms recorded were out of phase. Furthermore, there was considerably more unilateral blockage (failure of alpha rhythm in one hemisphere but not in the other) while the stammerers were speaking than when they were silent. This difference did not appear in normals. The alpha rhythm tended to reverse in phase just before marked stammering began. Lindsley suggested that blockages and out-of-phase waves tended to interfere with the control of speech, and this was particularly likely to occur when there was lack of clear lateral dominance. Rheinberger, Karlin and Berman (1943), however, found the electroencephalograms of ten male adult stammerers and ten non-stammerers to be essentially similar, although the former appeared to be less completely lateralized. Douglass (1943) again could not demonstrate any difference between adult stammerers and non-stammerers in the overall amount of unilateral blockage of the alpha rhythm; but there was greater bilateral blockage of both alpha rhythms in the occipital (visual) cortex while the stammerers were speaking than when they were silent. Possibly this was because speech demands more attention from the stammerer than from the normal speaker. Moreover, the stammerers showed more blockage in the left hemisphere during silence, and non-stammerers more in the right hemisphere. This difference disappeared during speech. Knott and Tjossem (1943) repeated the observations with another group of stammerers, and obtained similar results, but found that there was a considerable overlap in the degree of blockage between stammerers and non-stammerers. No studies have been made more recently than these which clear up the evidence as to hemispherical differences in the electroencephalogram, and the whole question remains obscure. Nevertheless, it seems that if there exists any fundamental difference in function of the two hemispheres, it must ultimately be demonstrated in this way.

However, a further doubt is cast upon the existence of any interference between the functions of the two hemispheres by the observations of Smith (1945). He found that when right-handed epileptics were operated on by severing the commissural fibres linking the two hemispheres, there was little or no shift in laterality after the operation. But left-handed cases showed a decrease of laterality which persisted for two or three months. Footedness, which was less permanently established before operation, showed a greater change; eyedness, little or none. Smith concluded that the commissural fibres played little part in lateral dominance, and that one hemisphere does not dominate over or inhibit the other directly by means of impulses passing through the commissural fibres. In innate laterality, dominance and inequality of function are established at the sub-cortical level. But such lateral dominance as has been acquired by learning, for instance, in writing right-handed, may function at the cortical level and be interfered with by injury to the commissural fibres.

The association between left-handedness or cross-laterality, and the effect of *teaching left-handed children to write with the right hand* is also a matter of some importance. Travis (1931), for instance, supposed that the left-handed had their speech centres in the right cerebral hemispheres. Thus right-handed writing would necessitate an interaction between the opposite hemispheres, the effect of which was to inhibit the speech mechanisms. Burt (1937), in a lengthy discussion of this theory, maintained that there was little evidence to support it. Among children of normal intelligence he found 4·2 % of stammerers among the left-handed who wrote with their left hands, and 6·1 % among those who wrote with their right hands—only a small difference in frequency. In fact, stammering was much more frequent among those of mixed laterality. Again, he contrasted the incidence of stammering in schools where all children were rigidly forced to write with the right hand, and in those where the left-handed were permitted to use which hand they preferred. In the former schools, 8·0 % of the left-handed children writing with the right hand were stammerers; in the latter schools, only 4·3 %. Burt considered that the writing situation imposed a considerable strain on the left-handed child, since it was awkward and difficult for him to write even with the left hand. This is clear to anyone who has observed a child trying to write with the left hand. This emotional strain was then liable to interfere with the speech mechanisms; and hence the sudden increase in frequency of stammering at the school age (see p. 65). Wallin (1916) also found that about 85% of stammerers began to stammer at the time of learning to write in school. In support of Burt's view, results obtained by Schiedemann (1931) were quoted by Hildreth (1950), which showed that 250 cases of left-handedness among children of 4–5 years were reduced to 66 by suitable training, without producing any speech defects. Lauterbach (1933) found that among thirty-seven cases of adults with speech disorders who were left-handed, 50% had been forcibly compelled to change to right-hand writing by tying the left hand; or had been punished by scolding, ridicule, etc., for using the left hand. The majority were individuals with a high degree of left-handedness.

Other writers have maintained the view that stammering is more often associated with the compulsion of left-handed children to write with the right hand than with left-handedness or ambidextrality as such. Bryngelson (1926) found that 62% of 200 stammerers aged 5–25 years had been made to write with the right hand. In a later study (1935) of about 700 stammerers from a speech clinic, he found the percentage distribution of right- and left-handedness, ambilaterality and shifted handedness shown in Table 14. Though clearly the degree of stammering was very high among the children who had been induced to write with the right hand, we do not know what methods were adopted to bring about

Table 14

	Males (aged)			Females (aged)		
	4–8	9–16	16	4–8	9–16	16
Present handedness:						
Right	55	33	33	20	17	78
Left	0	1	2	0	0	1
Ambidextrous	45	66	65	80	83	21
Present eyedness:						
Right	4	28	31	69	69	11
Left	90	63	67	13	7	78
Amphi-eyed	6	9	2	18	24	11
Handedness shifted	67	67	61	85	83	95
Disabilities after shifting:						
Reading	20	35	60	27	20	3
Spelling	30	11	13	27	0	1
Writing	17	8	14	0	5	1

the change. Neither did Bryngelson give any figures for the percentage of reading disability among those who had not changed. But he did state that as part of their treatment about 74 % of all these cases were recommended to use the left hand as far as possible in all manual activities; and that satisfactory therapeutic effects were obtained by this treatment.

Further support for the view that compelling left-handed children to write with the right hand may lead to speech disorders was given by Kovarsky (1938), according to Gille *et al.* (1954). She studied 2500 children with speech and reading difficulties, and concluded that they were generally left-handed children who had been taught to write with the right hand. Ombredane is stated to have found that 45 % of a group of stammerers were obviously right-handed, 8 % obviously left-handed, 5 % ambidextrous, and 42 % had left-handed tendencies but had been made to write with the right hand. Hildreth (1950) was of opinion that stammerers behave very much like ambilaterals; and their difficulties in both speech and handwriting are very similar. If a child's habits of left-handedness are broken, tension will be set up which will interfere generally with motor habits, in speech as well as in writing. We shall discuss more fully in the next chapter the relationship between stammering and emotional maladjustment. It is clear, however, that, as Burt has stated, any forcible compulsion of the strongly left-handed to write right-handed is always in danger of setting up emotional disorders which may affect performance in school, and particularly in the activities of speech and reading which are closely connected with writing. Whether cerebral dominance is directly impaired in addition is difficult to establish. But it seems possible that in so far as dominance is variable and unreliable, or is impaired by too much emphasis on the language functions of the non-dominant hand, other language functions, namely speech and reading, may also be affected. We shall now proceed to discuss the association between laterality and *reading disability* when there is no evidence of disordered speech.

We have already mentioned Orton's theory of 'strephosymbolia', which would suggest that ambidextrous, partially left-handed and cross-lateral individuals would be particularly liable to reading difficulties. However, Orton himself, in a later study (1937) found that some of his backward readers were completely right-sided, and others completely left-sided. Monroe (1932) found the following distribution of cross-laterality: in 101 completely normal children, 27%; in 155 cases of specific backwardness in reading, 38%; in forty-five defective and border-line cases also backward in reading, 50%. Thus cross-laterality appeared to be linked more closely with poor intelligence than with specific reading disability. The children with cross-laterality showed no greater tendency to reversal errors than did the children with pure laterality, though they were somewhat better at mirror reading. Completely left-sided children were better at mirror reading than were completely right-sided children. Woody and Phillips (1934) also found no greater tendency among left-handed than among right-handed children to make reversals in reading, writing and drawing. Witty and Kopel (1936) obtained approximately the same frequency of left-handedness and cross-laterality among normal readers as among readers aged 8–14 years who were retarded by about one year; the percentages of cross-laterality were 43 and 40% respectively. Gates and Bond (1936) also found approximately the same number of cross-laterals among normal readers and readers retarded on the average by $1\frac{1}{2}$ years (mean age $8\frac{1}{2}$ years). Dearborn (1939) showed that there was no difference in handedness between a group of seventy-six backward readers and 124 normal readers, all of them cases referred to a clinic. But among the severely retarded readers there was 14% more left-handedness and 17% more cross-laterality than among the normal readers. Wolfe (1941), however, found the same proportion of right, left and mixed laterality among his normal and retarded readers. The latter group, of eighteen boys aged about 9 years, was retarded in reading about 2 years below mental age. Smith (1950) gave extensive tests of laterality (handedness, eyedness and footedness) to 100 boys aged 9–11 years with I.Q.'s of 90–131. Half of these were normal readers with reading quotients of 100–120; and half were retarded, with reading quotients of 69–88. There were no significant differences between the retarded and normal readers in most of the tests, though there was a slight difference in the Van Riper test. The retarded readers made significantly more reversals than the normals in reading lower-case letters, but clearly these could not be attributed to laterality differences. And the parents of these children, who were interviewed, reported no significant differences in their own hand preferences.

Table 15

| | Percentage of cases | |
	Backward readers	Normal readers
Right-handed and right-eyed	43	60
Left-handed and left-eyed	5	4
Right-handed and left-eyed, left-handed and right-eyed	48	28
Right-handed and either eye, left-handed and either eye	4	8

However, Schonell (1940, 1941) found that there was a greater proportion of cross-laterality among 104 readers, aged 7–13 years and retarded by 1½ years or more, than among seventy-five normal controls. The figures are given in Table 15.

In a study of French children, Galifret-Granjon and Ajuriaguerra (1951) tested 108 normal readers and ninety-seven children with specific reading disability, falling into two groups aged 7–10 and 11–13 years respectively. They used two tests of handedness (speed and sorting), two of eyedness (sighting and aiming) and two of footedness (kicking and hopping). The percentage distributions shown in Table 16 were obtained. Thus it appeared that the younger backward readers were much more often incompletely lateralized than the normal readers. Though lateralization in-

Table 16

| | Completely lateralized | | | |
	Right	Left	Cross-lateral	Ambilateral
Retarded, 7–10	28	16	42	23
Normal, 7–10	38	12	28	21
Retarded, 11–13	38	16	29	17
Normal, 11–13	52	8	29	10

creased as age increased, it was still less complete for backward than for normal readers. Indeed, the proportion of older backward readers with complete right lateralization was exactly the same as that of the younger normal readers. However, in all cases there was a fair number of backward readers who were completely lateralized, and of normal readers who were not.

Harris (1947) expressed the opinion that whereas large-scale school surveys tended to show no excess of cross-laterality among backward readers, intensive clinical studies of severely retarded cases did indicate a lack of clear cerebral dominance (weak laterality or cross-laterality). He found three times the normally expected number of cases of cross-laterality among severe cases. Bakwin and Bakwin (1948) quoted Eustis (1947 b) as finding eighteen out of twenty cases of reading backwardness to be ambidextrous; many of them sighted with either eye; and about half the cases had speech defects. But in Hallgren's study (1950), although reading deficiencies appeared to be severe and innate, there was no excess over normal readers of left-eyedness or cross-laterality, and only a slightly higher incidence of left-handedness.

Some investigators have attempted to stress the relationship of backwardness in reading to laterality specifically of the *visual functions*. Thus Macmeeken (1939, 1942) studied the association between backwardness in reading and spelling, and left-eyedness. In the first study, 12·2 % of the boys and 6·2 % of the girls in a group of 392 elementary school children aged $7\frac{1}{2}$–$10\frac{1}{2}$ years were found to have reading quotients of 85 or less (the reading quotient being the reading attainment expressed as a percentage of the norm for that mental age). Their mean I.Q. was 103·2. All these forty-nine children were left-eyed, though only four were left-handed. Two tests of eyedness were used, but handedness was assessed by observation only. In the second study, of a group of eighty-two intellectually retarded children, aged 7–12 years, with mean I.Q. 88, there was still greater retardation in reading and spelling, the reading quotient being only 88; 62 % of the boys and 45 % of the girls were left-eyed. Again only 7 % of these children were also left-handed, as measured by the Van Riper test. These children made frequent reversals in reading, and also showed a tendency to reverse shapes. It is difficult to see why these should be associated with left-eyedness as such—though clearly many of these children were also cross-lateral. But Macmeeken's figures are so unusual and disagree so greatly with the findings of other experimenters that it is difficult to explain them.

Spache (1944) designed a Binocular Reading Test, in which one half of a column of print was presented to one eye and the other half to the other, the two halves being combined stereoscopically. Certain readers with strong eye preferences tended to see one half more clearly than the other. Spache found that such readers were able to read ordinary print more rapidly with the preferred eye than with both eyes. However, he did not demonstrate that the ability to learn to read was affected in these cases (see, however, the results of Selzer, described on p. 118).

With respect to dominance in the *visual cortical areas*, McFie (1952) applied Jasper's apparent-movement test to twelve clinic cases, aged 10–34 years, whose reading ages were much below their mental ages. Only three perceived sufficient apparent movement to indicate dominance of either visual area. The remainder occasionally saw movement in both directions, or first in one direction and then in the other; but more commonly they saw no apparent movement. McFie suggested that this indicated that no clear dominance of either visual area had been established in these cases. But his controls, who were normal readers, matched for age though not for intelligence, in every case but one saw one-sided movement consistently or predominantly. There appeared to be a good deal of cross-laterality among the clinic cases, but it was not accurately measured.

One further suggestion has been put forward as to the effect of laterality on reading. Harris (1947) quoted Dearborn (1933) as stating that it is easier for a left-sided person to move the eyes from right to left than from left to right, thus reversing the normal direction of *eye movement* in reading. When there is mixed laterality, there is confusion in the direction of the eye movements; hence regressive eye movements, and reversals of letters in words and words in sentences. This suggestion was also made by Wile (1942), who found that in a group of fifty cases of reading disability, aged 5–12 years, brought to a clinic for some maladjustment of behaviour, 50 % were cross-laterals and 62 % left-eyed. But he did not in fact investigate whether his left-eyed cases showed any tendency to read from left to right, or to make more reversals than did his right-eyed cases.

A cognate piece of evidence was produced by Crosland (1938), who showed that thirty-four children of $11\frac{1}{2}$ years who were poor readers were left-eyed in 55 % of cases, and amphiocular in 6%. On the whole these children perceived letters in the *right half of the visual field* relatively better than in the left half. But thirty-one superior readers, 65 % of whom were right-eyed and 6 % amphiocular, perceived the letters better in the left and centre of the field. The letters were exposed tachistoscopically. LaGrone and Holland (1943) tested fifty-two children aged about 7 years by showing them pairs of letters tachistoscopically, one to the right and the other to the left of the fixation point. Those who were left-sided were mainly poorer readers than those who were right-sided, and were also on the whole less intelligent. The former showed a relatively greater accuracy of perception of letters on the right side of the fixation point, whereas the latter were more accurate with letters on the left side of the fixation point. Since these children had only just begun to learn reading, LaGrone and Holland argued that they could not have acquired the habit of emphasizing the left side of the field through reading, but must have had a natural tendency to do so. This tendency to see one side of the field more clearly than the other is corroborated by the experiments of Dallenbach (1923), Burke and Dallenbach (1924) and White and Dallenbach (1932). They found that when adult observers were required to assess the clearness or attentional value of circular patches of light to left and right of the fixation point, right-handed observers attributed greater clearness to the light patches on the left; but left-handed observers attributed greater clearness to patches on the right. These results did not seem to be affected by eyedness, since two of the left-handed observers were right-eyed.

But the effect of habitual reading direction seems to have been operative in the experiments of Anderson and Crosland, as reported by Anderson and Dearborn (1952), on Jewish children. In the first study, Jewish children were tested who were familiar with both English and Hebrew. They were presented tachistoscopically with sets of nonsense words printed in English and also in Hebrew, which is normally read from right to left. They saw more of the English letters on the left of the field, but more of the Hebrew letters on the right. The superiority of the right half of the field with the Hebrew letters was less than that of the left half of the field with the English ones, probably because these children were more familiar with English than with Hebrew. Mishkin and Forgays (1952), however, obtained quite opposite results when they exposed eight-letter words tachistoscopically to adult Jewish observers. English words were read more accurately on the right of the fixation point, and Hebrew words more accurately, though only slightly more, on the left. Orbach (1952), also working with adults, found that individuals who had learnt to read Hebrew before English perceived Hebrew words better to the left than to the right of the fixation point; but those who had learnt to read English before Hebrew perceived Hebrew words better on the right. In no case was there any relationship between eyedness and superiority of one part of the field to the other. Finally, Forgays (1953) tested groups of children at each year of age from 7 to 15 years with three- and four-letter words in English. The number perceived by the younger children was about equal to right and to left of the fixation point. But the number perceived on the right increased steadily with age; whereas the number perceived on the left increased slowly up to 10 years and then showed a very slight decrease. The general conclusion from these latter results seems to be that the effect of practice and familiarity in reading a language is to emphasize or strengthen fixation at the end of the printed line rather than at the beginning; whereas the earlier results of Crosland and of LaGrone and Holland indicated that it was the poorer readers who perceived the right side of the field better than the left. This disagreement makes it difficult to accept Dearborn's hypothesis. The effect of left-eyedness and cross-laterality on fixation direction and on eye movements in reading is therefore extremely doubtful. Moreover, there is ample evidence to show that irregular eye movements and frequent regressions are caused by inability to read and confusion in reading, rather than causing them (see Vernon, 1931; see also p. 122).

Clark (1935) has also obtained evidence to show that eye movements are not closely related to eyedness. He found that although there was a tendency for the dominant eye to 'lead' the non-dominant in the alternate convergent and divergent eye movements which accompany reading, nevertheless this did not happen invariably. There were numerous occasions when the dominant eye followed the lead of the non-dominant. Thus it seems unlikely that any inaccuracy in the convergent and divergent movements of the eyes necessary for fusion can be caused by cross-laterality.

What then is the upshot of all the experimental work on laterality and cerebral dominance, and of the theories to which it has given rise? It seems generally agreed that in the right-handed individual the speech centre is established in the left hemisphere. Brain (1945) considered that the dominance of one hemisphere over the other is due to the development of the speech centre in that hemisphere. If speech development is delayed or incomplete, then dominance will also be incomplete. However, Nielson (1940) stated that dominance of one or other visual area in the occipital region of the cortex developed before handedness or language determined the hemisphere in which the speech area is sited; and that laterality for language and non-language functions does not always correspond. But Gesell and Ames (1947) considered that laterality of handedness began to develop at a very early age, and was associated with the position of the head in the prone position during infancy. Thus there is no general agreement as to the functions in which laterality and dominance first appear, and whether laterality of one function determines laterality in others.

Evidence against there being any universal and permanent connection between speech and other forms of laterality was quoted by

Zangwill (1955), who pointed out that the speech centre for left-handed individuals may be situated in the right hemisphere, but is not always so placed. He noted that the number of cases in which aphasia was caused by a lesion in the left cerebral hemisphere was almost as great as the number in which it was caused by a lesion in the right hemisphere. Some right-handed aphasics have been found with right cerebral lesions; but there is often a history of left-handedness in the family, and some evidence that the patients were left-handed in early childhood. Some of these cases might show very severe disorders of writing, and even inability to write with the right hand, though they could re-learn to write with the left hand. Zangwill considered that, although handedness may be changed by learning, the speech centre does not change; it does not move from the right to the left hemisphere in the left-handed individual who uses his right hand to such an extent that it becomes dominant. On the other hand, according to Brain (1945), left cerebral lesions early in life may result in the re-establishment of the speech centre in the right hemisphere. In any case, it is clear that laterality in any function is likely to be modified by learning, particularly when that function undergoes some special training. Therefore it does not seem to be clear whether there is complete or persistent dominance of one or other hemisphere even in relation to language functions. But there is the possibility that those with disorders of language, including reading disability, may not have established as complete a dominance as exists in the individual whose language functions are normal.

But evidence as to the existence of complete or incomplete cerebral dominance is obviously very difficult to obtain; and it may be that completely lateralized individuals are less common than is generally supposed. Laterality of handedness is probably of more importance than is laterality of sightedness; and so far there is little well-established evidence as to laterality in the visual cortical areas. The relationship of all these to cerebral dominance, or lack of cerebral dominance, is extremely obscure. Certainly we are not justified in concluding that every one is either completely right-sided or left-sided; and that the former characteristic is an inherited Mendelian dominant characteristic, the latter a recessive (see Brain, 1945). Cobb (1943) also propounded this view, adding that heterozygous individuals showed apparent right-handedness with incomplete laterality or ambidextrality. Presumably the former class would include those with mixed laterality, of handedness, footedness, sightedness and retinal function. But we need to have much more evidence of congenital left-handedness and mixed laterality, investigated by careful experiment, before this theory can be established or disproved.

The explanation for the interest taken in innate cerebral dominance and its possible relationship to reading disability lies in the fact that some cases of reading disability appear to be so extremely resistant to remedial treatment. If it could be shown that they were suffering from a congenital, or even an innate, defect, it could then be concluded that such treatment was unlikely to remove the disability. But as we have seen, the evidence for such a conclusion is very conflicting. It seems possible that the reading difficulty is associated with difficulty in writing from left to right; and to the tendency to mirror writing in left-handed and ambidextrous children. Clearly it is not easy for left-handed individuals to write from left to right; and if their perception of the orientation of words is weak, they might at first see little difference between their own mirror writing and the printed words on the page. But sooner or later confusion over order of letters in words would be bound to occur. The evidence as to mirror writing tendencies in the left-handed and ambidextrous is not very extensive. Carmichael and Cashman (1932) examined seven cases of marked mirror writing, and found that one of them was completely right-sided. Moreover, the mirror writing was performed in different ways by different cases. Some could read mirror writing with ease, others not at all. Some could not even read their own mirror writing. Burt (1937) found that most mirror writers were to some extent left-handed; and considered that this was because their writing was uncontrolled by vision, and was guided entirely by kinaesthetic control. However, it is not certain if this tendency has any permanent and far-reaching effect on reading.

Woody and Phillips (1934) and Witty and Kopel (1935) found that reversals in reading were no more frequent in left-handed and cross-lateral children than in right-handed. But as we have seen, reversal of order of letters in words is not necessarily associated with mirror reversal. It seems to be merely one sign of the general confusion of the young or backward reader. Thus evidence for and against the existence of mirror reversal tendencies as a frequent causal factor in reading disability is lacking.

It is of course possible that incomplete lateralization is a sign of a general lack of maturation in the development of cortical functions, which also affects reading. As we saw in a previous chapter, the attempts at reading in cases of reading disability were similar to those of younger children beginning to read. But all theories which attribute reading disability to some general lack of maturation are unsatisfactory in that they give no explanation as to why reading alone should be affected, and not other cognitive activities.[1] We should expect some general retardation, or at least slow development of all language faculties, if the defect were due to lack of maturation. But it might be that lack of maturation is a predisposing factor, and that some other factor is necessary actually to precipitate the disability. Such possible factors will be discussed in the next chapter.

However, it does appear that there may be a class of individuals who are generally lacking in maturation. These are the cases described above who have no well-established laterality, and in addition exhibit speech and other motor disorders, temperamental instability and reading disability. This condition may be hereditary. Two such cases are described in Appendix I (Cases I and II); they were among those tested by the author. But clearly such cases form a small minority of all the cases of reading disability. Some of the latter exhibit poor lateralization, and hence possibly lack of cortical maturation. Others may have the writing difficulties

[1] The same criticism applies to the hypothesis advanced by Mateer (1935) that reading disability may be caused by pituitary dysfunction. She claimed that cases of pituitary dysfunction were more retarded in reading than in any other intellectual activity. But it is extremely hard to determine why this should be.

noted above. But many are completely lateralized; and for the cause of their disability we must seek elsewhere.

(4) SEX DIFFERENTIATION

One of the most curious facts relating to reading disability is its apparently greater incidence in boys than in girls. A typical finding is that of Durrell (1940), who showed that among 1130 children aged 12–13 years, 20% of the boys and 10% of the girls were backward in reading. In another study by Alden, Sullivan and Durrell (1941), of 6000 children aged 7–11 years, 18·6% of the boys were classified as backward in reading, as against 9·8% of the girls. Macmeeken (1939) found, among 392 Scottish children aged 7½–10½ years, that 12·2% of the boys and 6·2% of the girls were retarded in reading. In Schonell's group of 15,000 London school children (1942), about 5% of the boys were retarded by 1½ years or more, as against 2·5% of the girls. In the Ministry of Education report (1950), it was also stated that there were about twice as many boys as girls in the lowest, illiterate, grade. The same difference appeared in the Middlesbrough report (1953).

Even more striking differences have been demonstrated in cases referred to clinics. Monroe (1932) had approximately 86% of boys among her cases of reading disability, and Blanchard (1936) had the same proportion of boys among seventy-three clinic cases. Among Fernald's (1943) sixty-nine cases of severe disability, 97% were boys; and among Young's (1938) forty-one cases, 90% were boys. Park (1948) found boys outnumbering girls by 4 to 1 among 133 cases of reading disability of normal intelligence. Of Hallgren's (1950) 116 cases from schools and clinics, 77% were boys. However, among the parents and sibs of these cases, there was no significant difference between the number of male and female backward readers. Hallgren concluded that though specific reading disability appeared to be more frequent in the male sex, it was not a sex-linked characteristic.

Now various psychologists have found *left-handedness* to be more common among boys than among girls. Burt (1937) found the

Table 17

	Boys	Girls
Backward	9·6	6·0
Normal	5·8	3·7

Table 18

	Right-eyed	Left-eyed	Amphi-eyed
Males	50·8	21·5	27·8
Females	44·6	22·3	33·2

percentage distributions of left-handedness shown in Table 17 among 5000 normal and backward school-children. Brain (1945) stated that left-handedness was almost twice as common among men as among women. But Crider (1944) found that there was no significant excess of left-eyedness or amphi-eyedness among males, in the many hundreds of individuals he tested, as is shown in Table 18. However, as we have seen, eyedness has far less significance than has handedness as an index of incomplete laterality. It is just possible therefore that there might be a slower maturation of cortical function among boys than among girls. More evidence for and against this hypothesis is given below.

It has also been suggested that the greater amount of reading backwardness among boys than among girls is associated with greater backwardness in *language development*. The data shown in Table 19 were obtained by McCarthy (1930), and show the mean number of words, and the mean number of different words, used by boys and girls at various ages. Young (1941) also found

Table 19

Chronological age (months)	Mean no. of words		Mean no. of different words	
	Boys	Girls	Boys	Girls
18	8·7	28·9	5·4	13·6
24	36·8	87·1	16·6	37·3
30	149·8	139·6	52·8	49·8
36	164·4	176·2	60·1	66·0
42	200·8	208·0	76·7	90·6
48	213·4	218·5	91·1	93·8
54	225·4	236·5	95·8	104·0

that girls are superior to boys in the total number of words spoken in a given time; and also in maturity of speech. Thus boys used relatively more nouns, and girls more pronouns, verbs and adverbs. McCarthy (1946) quoted Davis (1937) as finding a greater maturity of language in girls than in boys up to the age of 9½ years. Speech defects also appear to be more common in boys than in girls. Lincoln (1927) found that twice as many boys as girls stammered; and Louttit (1935) stated that stammering was three times as common among boys as among girls. According to Missildine and Glasner (1947), some investigators have found the ratio to be as high as 8 to 1. Burt (1937) found only slightly more stammering among boys than among girls, but a great deal more immaturity of speech, as shown by lalling and lisping. The percentages of children showing these defects are given in Table 20.

Table 20

Age (years)	Lalling and lisping		Stammering	
	Boys	Girls	Boys	Girls
5–	19·9	9·8	0·6	0·6
6–	6·6	2·2	0·8	0·7
7–	9·1	3·8	1·0	0·8
8–	6·7	2·5	1·8	1·2
9–	4·6	1·2	1·8	1·1
10–	2·4	0·8	1·7	1·0
11–	3·4	0·8	1·6	1·0
12–	1·6	0·9	2·1	1·2
13–	1·7	0·7	2·3	1·5

However, Durrell (1940) stated that when their oral language achievement was equated, there were still twice as many cases of reading backwardness among boys as among girls. Another explanation advanced by Anderson and Dearborn (1952) was that girls mature physically at a more rapid rate than boys. Thus at any given age they have reached a state of relatively greater maturity. But though this might account for the greater backwardness of boys, it would hardly explain the larger number of cases of actual disability. Again, the variability of intelligence is greater in boys than in girls, and it might be that their reading ability was also more variable, giving rise to a larger number of very poor readers.

Table 21

Age (years)	Reversals		Other errors	
	Boys	Girls	Boys	Girls
5	3·77	3·17	4·68	3·17
6	0·77	0·87	1·38	1·08

Table 22

	Comprehension		Recognition	
	Mean	Standard deviation	Mean	Standard deviation
Boys	16·0	9·99	9·4	5·50
Girls	16·2	10·12	9·8	5·66

But some investigators have found that girls are not always superior to boys in reading ability. Thus Wilson, Burke and Flemming (1939) showed that there was little difference between boys and girls in general reading ability between the ages of 4 and 8 years, but that the boys made more mistakes in letter recognition, and were more prone to reverse both words and letters. Davidson (1934) found the same difference with 5-year-old kindergarten children; but the difference had largely disappeared by 6 years, as is shown in Table 21. Macgregor (1934) tested nearly 6000 Scottish children at the age of 11 years, and showed that the boys scored significantly higher than the girls on reading tests, though the girls did significantly better on tests of spelling and language usage. McClaren (1950) found that the average scores of Scottish children, aged 5–8 years, on tests of word comprehension and recognition were almost identical for boys and girls, as is shown in Table 22, and so also were the standard deviations of the scores. Vernon et al. (1955) found no superiority in reading or spelling among the younger girls they tested. The older girls were distinctly superior to the boys in spelling. These results seem to show that basically there is little difference even in variability in the capacity of boys and girls to learn to read. But possibly if the boys are less docile and assiduous and less interested in the task, they do after a time tend to fall behind the girls, especially in drilled tasks like spelling.

McCarthy (1953) also considered that there was no inherent difference between boys and girls in the ability to acquire language skills. As long as they were at the babbling stage, the girls showed no superiority; though they began to excel the boys as meaningful language developed. McCarthy suggested that in general girls may have a closer contact with the mother than do boys, and may feel more generally secure. Boys are more active, aggressive and independent, more out-of-doors and less in the house, and less close to the mother. McCarthy stated that girls with speech defects were usually found to have disturbed relationships with the mother, which supports her argument. Moreover, because the boy has a less close contact than the girl normally has with the mother, he has less opportunity for imitation and for the correction of incorrect speech. The difficulties of boys may be enhanced when they go to school. Because their language is less well developed than that of girls, they learn to read less easily, and they may come into conflict with the teachers, a conflict which is aggravated by their greater independence and resistance, and lack of docility and attentiveness. Furthermore, the actual physical limitations of the class-room bear more hardly on the more active boys, thus increasing their frustrations and resistance.

The great excess of boys among the more severe cases of reading disability referred to clinics may perhaps be explained along the same lines. Non-readers among boys create more trouble in school than do non-readers among girls; or at least they bring their disability more forcibly to the teacher's notice, whereas the girls suffer in silence! It is also possible that parents take a more serious view of the inability of a boy to read than of a girl. Perhaps the most likely explanation, to which we shall return in Chapter VI, is that the reading disability cases in boys often have emotional disorders in addition, and these are frequently aggressive disorders. Thus the boys are referred to clinics because these disorders, rather than the disability, have brought them to the notice of teachers and parents.

(5) CONCLUSIONS

The investigations which have been cited give no clear evidence as to the existence of any innate organic condition which causes reading disability, except perhaps in a minority of cases; though certain innate factors may predispose the child towards difficulty in learning to read. Poor intelligence will inevitably retard the progress of learning, and the unintelligent child may well have difficulty in reasoning out the systematic relationships between word shapes and sounds. However, even high-grade mental defectives can in time acquire the mechanics of reading, though it is unlikely that they will ever read fluently and with much understanding.

We may state categorically that no child exhibiting reading disability should be stigmatized as suffering from an irremediable defect labelled 'congenital word blindness' (except in cases of cerebral injury such as those discussed on pp. 129–30). Even the relationship to reading disability of incomplete lateralization and cerebral dominance is extremely obscure. It may perhaps be concluded that left-handedness need not in itself be a handicap to reading. But inevitably writing is harder for the left-handed child; and this may both make it more difficult for him to acquire an understanding of the correct order of letters in the word; and also set up a general dislike of linguistic pursuits, and anxiety over their performance. It is doubtful if sightedness is of great importance; and lack of dominance of one visual cortical area over the other is still of doubtful significance. But ambidextrality and mixed handedness may be associated with incomplete dominance of the major over the minor hemisphere, and this in turn produces general immaturity in motor and/or linguistic functions, or in certain of these functions in particular. Again, writing may be specially affected; and also there may be some direct influence on reading, which depends to such an extent on orientation and order. In some cases of reading disability incomplete lateralization may be an important factor, especially when it is congenital. But it is doubtful whether this in itself is sufficient to cause permanent inability to read, unless reinforced by some additional factor. Furthermore, there is undoubtedly a considerable number of non-readers who are completely lateralized; for their disability some other cause must be sought.

It may often appear that boys are slower than girls to learn to read, but not to the extent that they are innately incapacitated. The probable reason for the excess of male clinic cases of reading disability is secondary and indirect; namely, that they are more obvious and noticeable, and more resistant to school teaching and discipline.

CHAPTER VI

THE RELATION OF VARIOUS ACQUIRED DEFECTS TO READING DISABILITY

(1) VISUAL DEFECTS

It has often been postulated, especially by Eames and Betts (Betts, 1936), that backward readers show a higher incidence of ocular defects than do normal readers. Thus Eames (1932) measured the ocular defects of 114 cases of reading disability, referred to a clinic, and of 146 unselected school-children. He found that there was no significant difference in the visual acuity of the two groups; but that the backward readers showed significantly more *exophoria*[1] at the reading distance, and a significantly higher degree of hypermetropic astigmatism. In a later study (1935), he gave the percentages shown in Table 23 of defect among 100 cases of reading disability, and 143 unselected children. A more extensive study (1948a) of 1000 poor readers, of median age $9\frac{1}{2}$ years, showed that

Table 23

	Reading disability cases	Unselected cases
Exophoria	63·0	16·7
Hypermetropia	53·0	27·6
Low fusion	44·0	18·0

[1] *Heterophoria* is a visual defect such that, when a point is passively fixated, the two binocular images are not fused. Thus an active contraction of the eye muscles is necessary to produce and maintain fusion; and this may be relatively slow to occur, and may be maintained only with eye strain and fatigue. In *exophoria*, the eyes tend to turn outwards too much, and in *esophoria* to turn too far inwards. The amount of heterophoria is measured in degrees of angle through which the eyes are turned. The condition is usually due to some functional disorder of the external muscles of the eyes, known as imbalance, such that they do not rotate the eyeballs accurately into position. The ability of the eye muscles to rotate the eyes accurately is sometimes termed *duction*.

In *strabismus* or *squint*, the eyes cannot be converged accurately even by active muscular contraction, and one eye continues to deviate from the fixation position. It is therefore difficult to obtain and maintain fusion.

In *stereopsis*, stereoscopic binocular images are fused to produce perception of a single object exhibiting depth or relief.

43 % were hypermetropic, as against 12 % of 150 control cases, and that exophoria in near vision was also more frequent among the poor readers.

Park and Burri (1943 *a*) examined 225 children, aged 6–13 years, for ocular defects. They gave arbitrary scores for these defects, and correlated the scores with reading achievement expressed in terms of mental age expectancy. The correlation of reading achievement with total eye scores was 0·465; with total *duction* scores, 0·647; with scores for exophoria, −0·631. The correlations were slightly lower for the older than for the younger children. In another study (1943 *b*), of a group of eleven children aged 6–7 years who had not learnt to read, only four had good *fusion*, and one good stereopsis; duction was low and unstable, especially for the near point. Selzer (1933) went so far as to attribute all reading disability other than that caused by emotional and intellectual factors to *eye-muscle imbalance*, and lack of fusion. It is true that he found that 90 % of a small group of non-readers, aged 7–11 years, had 2–11° of esophoria or exophoria, as compared with only 9 % of 100 un-selected cases of the same ages. However, it is not very clear to what extent these cases of muscular imbalance actually showed the lack of fusion he attributed to them. He tested them with a test similar to that used by Spache (see p. 103), in which two columns of digits were presented, one to one eye and the other to the other, in a stereoscope. If the binocular images were fused, the digits were interspaced and both columns could be read; if not, they alternated, and first one set of digits was read and then the other. It appeared that this alternation did occur with some of the cases of ocular imbalance. But Selzer did not compare the frequency of alternation in his test cases with that in the controls. Moreover, he did not demonstrate that such an alternation of the visual fields occurred in normal reading, at least to any harmful extent. He claimed that the reading of some cases was improved by correcting their vision with prismatic lenses. But his study of the amount of improvement was quite unsystematic.

Wagner (1936) gave reading tests to 850 kindergarten children, and divided the group on the basis of their performances in the tests into an upper and a lower half. There were slight but non-significant advantages for the upper group in fusion, amplitude of fusion, absence of esophoria at near and far points; visual acuity; and stereopsis. The slightness of the differences may have been due to the lack of any considerable difference in their reading abilities. But Robinson (1946) found that duction was unsatisfactory in about two-thirds of thirty cases of severe reading disability, and over half exhibited phorias outside the normal range. Park (1948) showed that among 133 cases of reading disability, with average age about 12 years, 45 % were heterophoric; half of these were exophoric for near distances. Inadequate convergence and accommodation and lack of stereopsis were also frequent.

Both Macmeeken (1942) and Schonell (1942) reported cases of *squinting* among their backward readers. Schonell found that 4·0 % of his cases of backward readers suffered from squint, as against only 0·2 % in the control group; and he described certain cases who squinted so badly that they could hardly see what they were trying to read. It is to be hoped that the School Medical Service will nowadays remedy such severe defects.

Spache (1940) found a considerably greater degree than normal of muscle imbalance, particularly exophoria, and of *aniseikonia*,[1] among fifty cases of reading disability. Dearborn and Anderson (1938) also stressed the importance of aniseikonia in making fusion difficult and fatiguing to maintain. They tested 100 severe cases of reading disability, aged 9 years and upwards, with I.Q.'s of 80-170 (average 110), and reading retarded by 8 months to 5 years; and compared them with a control group of 100 cases with some degree of aniseikonia. But in this control group, only 23 % showed an appreciable degree of aniseikonia, as against 51 % of the reading disability cases. More of the latter showed a high degree of aniseikonia, and it was relatively more severe at reading distance than at far distances. Another defect, recently described by Miles (1953), which might have somewhat the same effect as aniseikonia is 'aniseidominance'. An individual who has better vision in one eye

---

[1] Marked size difference of the binocular images, due mainly to inequality of refraction in the two eyes.

than in the other may see the image in the former as brighter and nearer to him than that in the latter. This defect does produce some difficulty in fusion in reading.

As regards the frequency of defects from causes other than binocular inco-ordination: We noted above that Eames found a higher proportion of *hypermetropia* and of *astigmatism* among backward than among normal readers. Betts (1934) also considered that astigmatism might be a considerable handicap to some readers. Gates (1935) quoted a study by Fendrick (1935) which showed significantly greater percentages among backward than among normal readers (children aged 8½ years with normal intelligence) of failures in tests of binocular acuity (48 as against 23 %) and astigmatism (42 as against 23 %). As regards their efficiency of vision, they were classified as shown in Table 24.

Table 24

Vision	Percentage of backward readers	Percentage of normal readers
Normal	56	70
Slightly defective	22	18
Moderately defective	6	6
Seriously defective	16	6

Wolfe (1941) found more astigmatism among his group of eighteen backward readers than among his control group of normal readers. Robinson (1946) also observed numerous cases of hypermetropia among her group of backward readers. Schonell (1942) stated that 22 % of his backward readers showed mild or severe hypermetropia or astigmatism, as against 15·5 % of his control group. According to Park and Burri (1943b), many children of 6–7 years have immature visual mechanisms; over 50 % of one group had visual acuity below 20/20, and the eleven non-readers had particularly poor visual acuity. But the general correlation between reading scores and eye scores for those needing corrective lenses was only 0·24 (1943a).

As against this evidence for a high frequency of visual defects among backward readers, Witty and Kopel (1935) found that only in slow fusion were they inferior to normal readers, 29 % of the former and 1 % of the latter having slow fusion. However, their backward readers, 100 children of average age 10 years 4 months, were retarded by only about 1½ years. Again, Russell (1943 a) pointed out that children only gradually achieve complete co-ordination of accommodation and binocular focus. Robinson and Huelsman (Robinson, 1953 a) also found that these abilities improved between the ages of 9 and 12 years. Thus it is possible that poor reading may retard the attainment of this co-ordination, and that inco-ordination is the effect rather than the cause of poor reading. At the same time it is true that if the defects originated at an early age, when the child was just beginning to read, they may have made it difficult for him to see the details of the printed words sufficiently clearly. Or if they did not occur till after he had learnt the early stages of reading, they may have caused excessive fatigue which impeded practice and further progress. Thus Farris (1936) found that children aged 12–13 years suffering from hypermetropia and strabismus made less gain in reading achievement over a period of one year than did normal sighted children. But when their defects were corrected, by suitable lenses, their reading improvement was increased. Again Clark (1935, 1936) found that young adults with a high degree of exophoria clearly showed disordered convergent and divergent movements during reading. It appears that, even in those with normal eyesight, the eyes tend to 'over-converge' during the return movements from the end of one line to the beginning of the next, and to make compensatory divergent movements at the beginning of the new line. In readers with a high degree of exophoria, these divergent movements were appreciably greater than they were in those with normal binocular balance. Such excessive movement might be very fatiguing.

To sum up the findings as to the relationship of ocular defects to reading disability: It is impossible to say what proportion of reading disability is due primarily to such defects. It is obvious that severe defects make it difficult for the child to focus the print clearly, and this may become increasingly apparent as he gets older and is required to read small print. It is equally obvious that from every point of view it is desirable that such defects should be diagnosed and corrected immediately. Even mild degrees of muscular imbalance which do not prevent the child from learning to read may cause unnecessary fatigue and eyestrain. Hence he will find reading unpleasant, and may try to avoid it whenever possible. The study of Farris showed that correction did result in better reading among older children. It is doubtful if it would do so automatically among younger children, or among very backward readers, unless the defects had been so severe as to make it almost impossible for the child to see the print. It is true that Taylor (1937) found that orthoptic training, by reading with prismatic lenses, improved the reading efficiency of cases suffering from muscular imbalance. But again this improvement occurred in children who could already read, but who read rather slowly and with irregular eye movements.

It has often been suggested that because poor readers show irregular and confused *eye movements*, and constant regressions, therefore these movements should be regularized, which would then produce improvement in their reading. Indeed, Taylor (1937) designed an instrument, called the 'metron-o-scope', for this purpose. It exposed words and phrases consecutively, at a rate which could be suitably adjusted, thus compelling the reader to read the words exposed consecutively and at a regular speed. But it has been made abundantly clear that, except possibly in cases of ocular defect, it is failure to attend to and to comprehend what is read that causes irregular eye movements and regressions. Thus these children require to learn the mechanics of reading if they have not already done so; and if they have, they need training in understanding rather than in eye movement.

It has also been stated that backward readers have a narrower *perceptual span* than normal readers, or that they have limited *peripheral vision*. Hincks (1926) stated that this occurred in many of her group of fifteen children with severe reading disability. But this may have meant that they could read only a few words or a few letters at a glance. Rizzo (1939) found a low correlation between the reading achievement of, and the number of words perceived tachistoscopically by, 310 children aged 7–17. But some of the poorest readers were conspicuously bad in tachistoscopic perception, and Rizzo considered that this narrow span was to some extent contributory to their reading difficulty. However, Knehr (1941) argued that the size of the perceptual span was not a limiting factor in reading performance. He found that during a considerable proportion of the time taken in a fixation pause in reading, the reader did not really see the words at all. This was because during this time the eyes were performing convergent and divergent movements in focusing the word, and were therefore not accurately focused upon it. Thus he argued that the visual mechanism was inoperative during a considerable period of time while the assimilation of meaning was taking place. The rate of reading was therefore limited by the rate of comprehension of what was read; and the efficiency of the visual mechanisms, and the speed at which the eyes covered the print, were unimportant. Again, the evidence from numerous experiments is that although the span of perception can be increased by giving exercises in reading with short exposures —as with the metron-o-scope—this effect does not necessarily transfer to ordinary reading. An equally good effect can be produced by actual practice in rapid reading and in effective comprehension. It is true that all these results were obtained with adult observers who had already mastered the mechanics of reading. But it is only at this stage of reading that perceptual span really becomes important. Narrowness of perceptual span cannot be supposed to limit the reading capacity of a child who stumbles through print, one word at a time.

(2) AUDITORY DEFECTS

It will be convenient to discuss in this section the relationship between reading disability and all defects of the hearing mechanism, whether innate or acquired at an early age, since their effect on reading is similar. It is quite clear that learning to read must be exceptionally difficult for the deaf child, whatever the cause of his deafness, and that the greater the degree of deafness, the greater the difficulty. Thus Gates and Chase (1926) pointed out that the reading ability of a group of deaf children was greatly below that of normal children of the same age. However, they compensated to some extent for their difficulty in apprehending words auditorily by an unusual ability to perceive them visually. LaGrone (1936) gave the reading ages of groups of deaf children which are shown in Table 25. Sheridan (1955) showed that, as might be expected, reading in general became poorer as the degree of hearing loss increased. Unfortunately, although Burt's word-reading test was used, no actual reading ages were quoted. The reading performance was graded from 0—no reading, through 3—average, to 5— very good. The grades were then averaged, and are shown in Table 26.

Table 25

Chronological age	10	11	12	13	14	15	16
Reading age	2·9–3·0	3·8–4·7	3·6–5·1	3·9–5·4	4·0–5·7	4·7–6·6	5·1–7·4

Table 26

Hearing loss (%)	Under 10	10–19	20–29	30–39	Over 40
Reading: average grade	3·0	2·43	2·34	1·85	2·06

But special teaching can enable even severely deaf children, who cannot speak without special training, to learn to read adequately. Thus Ewing and Ewing (1954) tested twelve such children, aged about 11 years, with normal or above normal I.Q.'s. In three cases the retardation in reading was about 3 years; but in one case it was only 4 months, and in one the reading age was above the chronological age. In another group of deaf children aged 6½–7½ years, all but one had learnt to read sufficiently well to understand 50–90% of what they read. However, a correspondent in the *Times Educational Supplement* (21 January 1955) stated that it was estimated that deaf children of 15 years were retarded in reading ability by 5 years on the average below normal children of the same age.

In some cases in which there is only a slight hearing loss at low frequencies, *high frequency deafness* may make it exceedingly difficult for the child to hear speech sounds, and hence to learn to read. Ewing (1930) described five cases, aged 4–14 years, where the hearing loss above 256 cycles was so great that they were unable to speak, or, apparently, to hear speech sounds. However, they possessed sufficient residual hearing capacity at high frequencies to be able to learn to hear speech when they were taught to attend to it closely, and after a time to speak, though not very accurately.[1]

What so frequently happens, as we pointed out in Chapter IV, is that *slight hearing loss*, and even quite high degrees of high frequency impairment, go unnoticed. The children are given no special teaching, nor even any special consideration in class, and they are obliged to try and read on the basis of a more or less sketchy idea of what the teacher says, and what speech sounds are like. Recent audiometric examinations have shown that a considerable number of children have slight losses of hearing which would not be detected except by audiometric testing. Thus Kennedy (1942) demonstrated that some degree of high frequency loss was fairly frequent among 6-year-old children. Henry (1947) quoted Crowe *et al.* (1942) as finding that approximately 40% of the school-children they tested had some high frequency impairment. Henry herself found that, in a group of 288 children aged 5–17 years, about one-quarter showed losses, at high frequencies, of 17–65 decibels. Bennett (1951) showed the following incidence of defects among the 500 Lancashire children she tested: Grade I (hearing loss up to 35 decibels), 7·5%; Grade II (hearing loss 35–60 decibels), 3·6%. Sheridan (1955) gave the following estimates of frequency made by the Ministry of Education: Grade I, 5·0–8·0%; Grade II A, 0·05–0·20%; Grade II B, 0·05%; Grade III (totally deaf), 0·07–0·10%. She quoted Dr Burn, the Medical Officer of Health for Salford, as finding that about 2% of the school population showed an impairment of hearing sufficient to cause them inconvenience or difficulty in following the normal school curriculum. In a group of 100 of these children, fifty-seven

---

[1] Froeschels (1944) has described cases of apparent 'psychic deafness' who do not respond to audiometric tests. But that they possess some hearing capacity can be demonstrated by their reflex responses (blinking, starting, etc.) to the sound of a whistle conveyed by an air current into the ear. Such cases, which are however very rare, can often be taught to hear fairly normally.

also had speech defects. When their pure tone loss was examined, it was found to be slight in many cases; in forty-three it was under 10%, in thirty-six 10–20%, and in twenty-one over 20%.

Now Bennett stated that slight losses, such as those of children in Grade I, do not constitute a problem, since the children can be educated in ordinary schools. It does seem possible, however, that they may be handicapped in *learning* to read, especially in a noisy class-room. Thus Utley (1944) found a correlation of 0·80 between the amount of hearing defect of fifty-one slightly deaf children, and their ability to discriminate monosyllables differing by only a single vowel or consonant. But the Grade IIA children are perhaps more important. Although they can be educated in ordinary schools, nevertheless they cannot learn properly unless they are given a suitable position in the class-room, and probably also a hearing aid, and some tuition in lip-reading. Unfortunately it is often not realized that these children are deaf. They may be classified as of subnormal intelligence, as backward, or as lazy and inattentive. Often their parents will refuse to believe that they are deaf, or allow them to have special teaching.

Even more serious is the case of the child with a high frequency loss, at 512 cycles and upwards, since this defect makes speech more or less unintelligible, consonants becoming very indistinct and vowels hard to discriminate from each other. With an extensive loss, of 45 decibels and upwards, a child cannot discriminate speech sounds at all without special training, and therefore cannot speak. But children with less extensive high frequency losses can go undetected, without special examination, although their speech is usually flattened and monotonous and sometimes defective. Sheridan (1955) described four such cases, all apparently of normal intelligence or over, though regarded as being mentally defective. Their ages and reading ages were: (1) C.A. 13 years 8 months; R.A. 8 years 5 months; (2) C.A. 12 years 5 months; R.A. 15 years; (3) C.A. 9 years 4 months; R.A. 5 years 4 months; (4) C.A. 8 years 1 month; R.A. 0. Thus only the second case, a child of very high intelligence, had learnt to read fluently; he could not write from dictation. Therefore there is always the possibility that extreme reading disability may be due to high tone loss; and that milder degrees of disability might be due to small amounts of loss. Or again, disability might be due to an undetected Grade II A loss at all frequencies. Burt (1937), on examining fifty of his cases of general backwardness, found that 20% were suffering from some form of hearing loss, as compared with 6% of a group of fifty children with normal school attainments.

Unfortunately, though many experiments have been performed to demonstrate the connection between hearing loss and reading disability, only too often the method has been adopted of calculating the average hearing acuity of backward readers, rather than the frequency of backward readers with appreciable hearing loss. Therefore we have little evidence as to how numerous these cases may be, since in calculating average hearing acuity they are swamped by the children with normal hearing. Thus Bond (1935) found that the medium hearing loss of sixty-four poor readers, of mean age 8½ years, was 10·7%, as compared with that of 7·1% for sixty-four matched controls. Kennedy (1942) correlated reading performance and summed scores for pure tone acuity at various frequencies, and obtained a correlation which was positive but too small to be significant. Among the younger children he tested, aged 6–8 years, no child of relatively poor acuity was in the top quartile for reading. Among the older children, those with poor acuity at low frequencies were sometimes good readers; but those with high frequency losses were in general poor readers. The poorer readers also tended to do worse on the Seashore test of pitch discrimination. Hincks (1926), again, found that three-quarters of her cases of severe reading disability were below average on the Seashore test, but she gave no evidence as to whether this was due to hearing loss. Henry (1947) quoted Conway (1937) as testing 1000 children aged 10–13 years; sixty-seven had a loss of 10 decibels or more. The reading retardation was 2·3 months for those with a 10% loss, and 12·2 months for those with a 20% loss. Henry herself made a thorough study of this problem, testing the acuity of 288 children aged 5–17 years. The sixty-two subnormal readers, with reading quotients of 52–82, had a greater average hearing loss than the normal readers at all frequencies; and this loss was greatest at high frequencies. At the 'worst spot' of hearing, the loss was 25·1 decibels, compared with 16·9 decibels for those with reading quotients of 110–145. Also the variability of hearing was considerably higher for the poor readers. The mean reading quotient for children with 17–65 decibels loss at high frequencies was 97·7, as against 108·3 for those with no hearing loss; this difference, though small, was statistically significant. On the other hand, though 35% of this group had reading quotients below 90, 18% had reading quotients above 110. The former were particularly poor at reading phonetic sounds. These results indicate, therefore, that not all children with poor auditory acuity are bad readers, and not all bad readers have poor acuity. But in a number of cases, poor acuity may have been an important contributory factor to reading disability.

The importance of other factors is shown in the results of Rossignol (1948). She tested 229 children, aged 6–8 years, and found a significant relationship between hearing acuity and the accuracy of repetition of nonsense syllables; and also between hearing acuity and reading performance. This correlation was considerably reduced, however, when mental age was held constant, which indicates that the ability to do well in hearing acuity tests was directly influenced by intelligence. Again, Reynolds (1953) found that, when the effects of intelligence were eliminated, there was no significant correlation between the auditory acuity and reading ability and word recognition of children aged 9–10 years.

It may be concluded that not all poor readers have deficient hearing, and that many children with mild auditory defects can nevertheless learn to read normally. But it is desirable that all severe cases of reading disability should be examined for a possible hearing loss, and particularly for high frequency loss. It is true that these tests are difficult to administer to little children, and every possible precaution should be taken to see that they understand what they have to do. These difficulties were fully discussed by Midgeley (1952). It is possible that many of the cases who have been diagnosed as having poor auditory discrimination have in fact been suffering from hearing loss, and particularly high tone loss. Such children should be provided with adequate hearing aids, if the hearing loss is considerable. If it is slight, they should always sit close to the teacher; and should whenever possible be taught individually, or in small groups.

(3) INJURIES AND DISEASE

Since the ability to read can be destroyed in adults by injuries to the speech area of the cortex, it is not surprising that there have been attempts to diagnose brain injury in children with severe reading disability. Indeed, Jensen (1943) advocated confining the term 'reading disability' to cases in which inability to read could be attributed to organic defect resulting from *birth injury*; and differentiating these cases from those of mere backwardness in reading. But in the cases which he described there was little direct evidence of birth injury, other than difficult delivery. His twenty-two cases were characterized by other defects—motor inco-ordination, clumsy gait and speech defects; poor visual and auditory discrimination and memory; and, in nine cases, neurotic symptoms. These cases clearly resemble the cases of congenital disability described, for instance, by Dearborn and Eustis (see p. 79), and may in fact have resulted from hereditary factors rather than from birth injury.

Harris (1947) quoted Gesell and Amatruda (1941) as stating that birth injuries are not uncommon, though often unrecognized when they are slight. But they may result in poor muscular co-ordination, speech difficulties, poorly defined laterality and delayed integration which leads to reading difficulty. Though they form only a small proportion of all cases of reading difficulty, they may be more frequent among the severer cases referred to clinics. They can be diagnosed with certainty only by a neurologist; but they may be suspected in cases showing the above defects who have histories of prolonged, difficult or instrumental deliveries, and where congenital tendencies are contra-indicated.

A neurological examination was made by Anderson and Kelley

of 100 of Monroe's cases of reading disability (Monroe, 1932); and also of 100 normal readers. Possible neurological injury, due to birth injury, head injury or neurological illness, was found in 27 % of the backward readers, and in 20 % of the controls. Six of the cases with severe reading disability were diagnosed as having brain injuries. Johnson (1955) found that 21 % of a group of thirty-four clinic cases of reading disability had suffered from serious accidents involving brain injuries. Preston and Schneyer (1956) referred for neurological examination nine children, aged 8–18 years with I.Q.'s of 71–129, of whom five were non-readers, and four had very small sight vocabularies. It was found that three of them definitely had brain damage, and the remainder may have been affected. Thus four had abnormally difficult deliveries, three had head injuries during childhood, and two had had high fever accompanying childhood illness. Monroe (1951) described a similar case whose electroencephalogram indicated serious impairment, as the result of serious illness during childhood, possibly encephalitis. When given training by the tracing method, he learnt to read, but only very slowly. Ettlinger and Jackson (1955) reported studies by Spiel (1953) and McFie (1952). In the former, two boys with reading difficulties, in themselves and in their families, showed poor development of the parieto-occipital rhythm in their electro-encephalograms. In the latter, unusual or border-line features were reported in the electroencephalograms in four out of six cases of reading disability.

Eames (1945) found that 15 % of 100 cases of reading failure were *prematurely born*, a considerably higher incidence than is found among unselected cases. The prematurely born had 31 % more cases of neurological lesion, and 17 % more of defective vision. Quite apart from injury, it is possible that the cerebral cortex in the prematurely born might not develop normally as regards the linguistic and visual functions. However, the significance of prematurity is not at all clear; and the findings of Eames do not seem to have been confirmed by other investigators.

The results of Anderson and Kelley showed that *other diseases* were no more common among the reading disability cases than among normal controls. Burt (1937) estimated that poor health and illness were major causes of general backwardness in only about 4–5 % of cases; but were minor or predisposing factors in over 50 %. Jackson (1944), comparing 300 children, aged 7–11 years, in the top quartile of scores on reading achievement, with 300 in the bottom quartile, found that 27·3 % of the latter had histories of personal illness, as against 12·3 % of the former. Johnson (1955) also found that 65 % of her clinic cases had suffered from serious or recurring illness. Eames (1948b) compared the incidence of various diseases among 875 reading failures, of average age 9 years 7 months and I.Q. 102, with that among 486 normal readers, of average age 11 years 7 months and I.Q. 103. Among the former, 36·1 % had suffered from serious diseases of some kind, as against 15 % of the latter. However, these figures included, for the former, 6·2 % with speech defects and 2·6 % with urogenital diseases including enuresis; as against 1·2 and 0·4 % respectively. These can hardly be included as cases of physical disease. But certain other complaints showed a considerable difference of incidence in the two groups: ear, nose and throat diseases, 7·8 and 3·2 %; diseases of the circulatory system, 2·5 and 0·4 %, endocrine disorders, 2·6 and 1·6 %. Thus it seems possible that some of the reading failures had been handicapped by illness.

It is possible that disease, other than neurological injury, may have no direct effect on reading ability, apart from decreasing the child's energy and persistence in mastering a difficult task. But it has an indirect effect in causing him to be absent from school, and hence possibly to miss some essential stage in teaching. We shall give further evidence on this point in Chapter VII. The school work of such children might be improved by suitable medical treatment, special diet, etc. And some attempt should be made to discover what part of the reading instruction they have missed, and to provide special teaching to make good their loss. There is the further possibility that if illness has been severe and frequent or prolonged, especially if it necessitated much hospitalization, a condition of insecurity and emotional maladjustment may have resulted, or a failure to mature normally. This in turn may have affected progress in learning to read, as we shall discuss in the next section; and as appears with Case I, described in Appendix I.

As to whether there is any possibility of remedying the reading disability of neurological cases, there seems to be little evidence. Clearly they would require special individual teaching, and possibly the Fernald method would be the most helpful.

(4) DEFECTS OF PERSONALITY

It seems advisable to consider in this section all forms of defect in the personality including those due to innate temperamental instability, as well as those due to acquired neurotic tendencies, behaviour maladjustment, etc. It is seldom possible in practice to differentiate between innate and acquired defects of this kind. However, it is pertinent to recall the cases of families, described in Chapter v, in which there seemed to be a history of reading disability, combined with emotional instability, speech defects, left-handedness and motor inco-ordination. In these cases, the emotional instability and motor defects seemed to be innate, or acquired at a very early age, and therefore to have constituted a predisposition to reading disability. Indeed, there appears to be a fairly general association between *speech defects* and *emotional disorders*, and certain writers have held that the former were directly caused by the latter. Despert (1943) attributed stammering to emotional tensions arising, between the ages of 2–4 years, between the child and his mother, just at the period of maximum language development. She also found (1946) that stammering was associated with poor social adjustment, often originating before the stammering began, especially in children with overbearing and over-protective mothers. The stammering increased considerably when they went to school. On the other hand, Kopp (1943) believed that it was stammering which set up the emotional disorders. Diatkine (see Gille *et al.* 1954), McCarthy (1946) and Robin (1952) all considered that emotional disorders enhanced difficulties in speech and language development, and indeed caused them in some cases, but not in all. Madison (1956) stated that in a small number of cases stammering is due to auditory deficiencies or to physical factors affecting articulation; but in the great majority of cases it is caused by some deeply-rooted emotional conflict, or it appears as a neurotic defensive symptom. Even in some apparently congenital cases of stammering in father and son, he attributed the son's stammering to some form of identification with the father. However, it is probable that there are genuine cases of inherited defect, such as we described on p. 79.

But the evidence as to the relationship between personality defects, innate or acquired, and reading disability (apart from any linkage with speech defect) is very far from clear. There appear to be numerous cases of reading disability in whom such defects exist. But some of them may not have caused the reading disability, but may have resulted from it, and from the consequent frustration, anxiety and feelings of inferiority experienced by the child who is educated in a society in which the ability at least to stumble through a page of print is regarded as so important. Thus Blanchard (1928) pointed out that reading disability extending over a number of years was likely to lead to failure in school; and that unless there were adequate and socially acceptable compensations for the feelings of inferiority aroused, behaviour deviations might result. These might be of the avoidance type: inattention, day-dreaming, lack of interest. But in many cases, they might be more aggressive in nature, and there might be resistance against parents and teachers. Fernald (1943) stated that out of seventy-eight cases of extreme reading disability referred to her clinic, only four had any history of emotional instability before entering school. Several of the cases of Hincks (1926) showed aggressiveness and also anxiety because their parents were distressed by their backwardness. Indeed, if the parents react to the child's backwardness by blaming or reproaching him, or even merely by undue pressure, urging him to work harder, a severe emotional conflict may result. Thus Young (1938) described the case of a child who was excessively distressed by his disgrace. In two-thirds of Young's forty-one cases, unnecessary pressure on the part of parents and teachers had contributed to the appearance of emotional disturbance in the children. Even more devastating were the results obtained by Preston (1939), who interviewed the parents of 100 children of normal and above normal intelligence, aged 7-17 years, who had failed to learn to read normally. She found that 66% of the mothers and 28% of the fathers were worried, anxious or upset by their children's reading failure. Many of them were shocked, angry or resentful. About three-quarters of the parents taunted their children with their failure, and made cutting comparisons with other children who were more successful. (Incidentally, 61% of these children had siblings who could read normally; only 12% had siblings who were retarded in reading.) Of the parents, 52% thought it was entirely the fault of the children that they could not read. About one-third of the children were punished by deprivation of privileges and one-third by physical punishment. There may have been some improvement in parental treatment since this study was made. But Johnson (1955) found that 62% of a group of thirty-four cases referred to a reading clinic were hampered in their remedial treatment by the parents' attitudes. In 38% of cases there was too much pressure on the children's achievement.

There was some evidence in Preston's studies (1940) to show that, quite apart from the effects of reading failure, the home atmosphere and the degree of security it afforded was poorer among the backward readers than among the sixty-seven matched control cases. Thus security was estimated to be satisfactory for 57% of the control cases, as compared with only 37% of the backward readers. It is interesting to note that 18% of the backward readers, as against 11% of the controls, were 'over-secure'; that is to say, in their early years the children were spoilt, indulged, overprotected or treated as perfect, until they failed to learn to read. Their fall from grace was then all the greater. But even those parents who treated their children excellently before their failure was obvious often seemed to reproach or even punish them after prolonged failure. There was no doubt whatever that any emotional weakness was greatly aggravated by the effects of failure, partly through the parents' reactions, and partly because of the inferiority and hopelessness experienced by the children in the school situation.

Thus it is probable that any innate temperamental defects of fearfulness or aggressiveness would be exaggerated by the undesirable treatment of parents and teachers, whether as a reaction to the child's disability, or merely as a general occurrence. Gates (1941) reported cases in which there was evidence of indifference, hostility or anxiety in parents and/or teachers; of conflict between the parents; or of over-protectiveness towards the child. The associated defects of mirror reading and writing might, however, according to Park (1953), be symptoms of emotional dissatisfaction shown by children to express resistance to adult authority. If such children are emotionally reassured, the reversals and the reading disability may disappear. But Park gave no evidence as to the frequency of such cases among backward readers. In contrast, Anderson and Dearborn (1952) quoted Missildine (1946) as finding that, in the majority of thirty cases of emotionally disordered backward readers, these disorders existed before the children entered school. These children were already insecure, restless and emotionally unstable, and were therefore predisposed to difficulties in school life. However, we have no evidence again as to whether such cases are frequent among backward readers in general. Nor can we be certain if the frequency of symptoms of emotional disorder was really much greater among backward readers than it is among children generally at the time of entering school. Cummings (1944) showed that minor symptoms of this kind were common at this age. In particular, about 37% of a group of 239 children, aged 6–8 years, showed lack of concentration, restlessness, laziness and tendencies to day-dreaming, a considerable increase over the incidence in younger age groups. She attributed the increase to the transition from the free play of the nursery school to the formal teaching of the junior school. Among a small sample of forty-five cases who were followed up over a period of 18 months (1946), 65% showed little improvement. If this behaviour is fairly general, it is not surprising that reading is often difficult.

There must also be numerous cases, at least in this country, in which reading disability is not detected until the child reaches the secondary school stage at the age of 11 years, and perhaps not even then—especially in rural all-age schools. Such children are unlikely to have suffered from contempt, ridicule or condemnation by parents or teachers, though they might be conscious of their own inferiority. It would be interesting to know whether such children show a smaller degree of maladjustment than those who were detected earlier. This view would accord with the opinion expressed by Hallgren (1950), that cases of reading disability who had undergone medical examination showed more frequent emotional disorders than those who had not. It is also true that cases in which there is some type of emotional or behaviour disorder in addition to reading disability are more likely to be referred to clinics, and to undergo psychiatric examination, than are cases of reading disability alone. Gates (1941) considered that something like 75% of the more severe cases of reading disability, referred to clinics, showed some degree of maladjustment; but that these severe cases constituted only about 10% of all cases of reading retardation in schools. In only about one-quarter of the severe cases did the maladjustment appear to have caused the reading disability; in the remainder, the maladjustment was the accompaniment or the result of the reading disability. But Johnson (1955), all of whose thirty-four clinic cases showed signs of emotional maladjustment, stated that the more extensive observation which was possible while these children were receiving remedial instruction demonstrated that maladjustment was more severe than it had appeared to be at their original diagnosis. Of these, 85% showed extreme need for attention and affection; but there were also many symptoms directly related to the reading situation, such as fear of failure (68%), avoidance of work (65%) and inattention (44%).

Studies of maladjustment in large school groups tend to show a much lower frequency than do studies of clinic cases. It is true that Burt (1937) found a larger percentage of temperamental instability and neurotic defect among children who were generally backward in school than among normal children, as is shown in

Table 27

	Backward children		Normal children	
	Boys	Girls	Boys	Girls
Temperamentally unstable:				
Excitable	21·2	18·7	11·9	7·6
Repressed	7·8	10·1	4·7	5·6
Neurotic symptoms	24·9	29·3	16·6	21·2

Table 27. And Peck and McGlothlin (1940) obtained a correlation of 0·617 between the reading achievement of 100 children aged 6–8 years, and their personality adjustment as measured by behaviour ratings. But Wilson and Flemming (1938) found very small correlations, of the order of 0·1, among twenty-five children aged 6–7 years, with various measures of maladjustment based upon parents' reports. Possibly in the study of Peck and McGlothlin the ratings were partially influenced by the children's behaviour vis-à-vis the reading situation. Jackson again (1944) found that in a group of 300 children, aged 7–11 years, who were in the lowest quartile in reading achievement, 18·8% were classified as subnormal in personality, on the basis of information given by the teachers, as against 8·8% of the 300 in the top quartile. On the other hand, Wolfe (1941) showed that his group of eighteen backward readers were only slightly inferior to the matched controls in emotional adjustment. The maladjustment showed itself largely in greater lethargy, inattentiveness and lack of persistence, all of which may have been caused by total lack of interest in reading. Bennett (1938) and Ladd (1933) obtained very small differences between good and poor readers in personality adjustment, as measured by personality questionnaires and tests. But there seems to be some doubt as to the adequacy of these measures (see Wilking, 1941). However, both Bennett and Ladd found that poorer readers were lacking in persistence and concentrated attention, and indeed were unable to persist for long even at a task in which they were interested. Thus it is possible that they had never properly developed the power to concentrate by attending to reading instruction.

We have noted above that the clinic cases of Blanchard and

Hincks showed considerable emotional disorder. Robinson (1946) also found that there was some emotional disturbance in about 60% of her thirty cases of severe reading disability; that this might have been the cause of the disability in 43% of cases; and that 32% seemed to be in need of psychiatric treatment. Here the disorders were obviously more severe than among most of the school cases, and it is very possible that they were directly responsible for the reading disability. But Ellis (1949) found that 48% of a group of 100 clinic cases of reading disability, mainly mild in nature, had no apparent emotional problems, as against 24% with severe emotional problems.

In two other studies in which an association was demonstrated between reading disability and emotional maladjustment, environmental factors were probably also important. The first study, by Lantz and Liebes (1943), was of thirty-three boys living in a cottage orphanage, who were referred for treatment of reading difficulties. They were of varying age and intelligence, but the majority had I.Q.'s of 90–109. Among them, nine lacked self-confidence and showed fears of failure; six were uninterested in learning; seventeen showed poor attention and concentration; twenty-eight had emotional problems of some kind. (These figures presumably overlap, and are not mutually exclusive.) Their reading disability showed great resistance to treatment, and they also required considerable remedial instruction in other subjects than reading. It seems fairly certain that these children were suffering from their general circumstances, and especially from lack of parental care and affection, which produced both their disability and their emotional difficulties.

The second study, by Fendrick and Bond (1936), showed that the average reading age of 187 delinquent boys in institutions, of average age 18 and average I.Q. 92, was retarded by about 5½ years. For the boys with I.Q. 90–110, the average retardation was 5 years. However, the majority of these boys seem to have learnt to read after a fashion, but had not advanced beyond the elementary stage. Again, the general circumstances of their case may well have been responsible for their backwardness.

There is no very conclusive evidence that reading backwardness is associated with any particular *type of defect* or emotional disorder. Thus Monroe (1932), comparing clinic cases with reading defects with those without, found that the former could not be distinguished from the latter by the excess frequency of any particular form of emotional disorder. Gates (1936), according to Anderson and Dearborn (1952), noted the following disorders among 100 cases of reading disability: aggressiveness and defensiveness, avoidance and recessiveness (day-dreaming), nervousness and restlessness, indifference and inattentiveness, self-consciousness, and feelings of inferiority. In a later paper (1941), Gates stated that reading disability might appear in all types of personality pattern. He quoted Challman (1939) as finding nervousness, withdrawal, aggression, defeatism and anxiety in reading disability cases. There were many different types of emotional disorder among the cases of Lantz and Liebes (1943). But the aggressive cases appeared to require a longer period of remedial treatment than did the day-dreamers and the hyperactive cases. Among the cases studied by Preston (1940), some were submissive in character, and these became increasingly moody, apathetic, isolated and shut-in as the result of prolonged reading failure. Others were more aggressive in character; they began by showing off and behaving aggressively to other children, and then became increasingly anti-social in behaviour, particularly towards the school. Almost all the children in time lost interest in school work, and tried to stop away from school whenever they could.

Four studies of backward readers have been made using the Rorschach Ink-Blot Test and certain other projection tests; these have been discussed by Solomon (see Robinson, 1953 a). The first, by Gann, indicated that backward readers were more anxious and less socially adjusted than were normal readers. The second, by Stewart, showed that the backward readers were insecure, but aggressive rather than fearful. In the third, by Vorhaus, it was found that the backward readers possessed concealed aggressiveness, though they were outwardly restricted, inhibited and withdrawn. A separate study by Spache (1954), using the Rosenzweig Picture Frustration Test[1] with fifty retarded readers aged 6–10 years, also showed these children to be more 'cocky' and aggressive than Rosenzweig's norms; less insightful and less ready to admit fault and accept blame. Their aggressiveness appeared most clearly in the pictures of situations dealing with children. In situations in which there was frustration from adults, it seemed that the children had learnt to avoid open conflict by passive resistance.

In the fourth of the Rorschach studies, by Solomon herself, there was apparently little difference in personality characteristics of good and poor readers of about 8 years of age, though the latter were somewhat more rigid and controlled, and were inclined to niggle over unimportant details. This study was interesting, however, in that the children had been given the Rorschach Test two years earlier, on entering school. Solomon concluded that there was nothing which at this earlier age would have predicted failure in reading, except this concern with unimportant details—rather a surprising defect for backward readers. Thus such essential difficulties as they showed at a later age must have been the result rather than the cause of their reading difficulties. But Redmount (1948) obtained evidence by means of the Rorschach Test of marked personality disturbances in two-thirds of a group of twenty-four children, aged 8–18 years, who were referred to a clinic for difficulty in school achievement primarily related to reading. As well as stereotyping, rigidity and lack of spontaneity of behaviour, they also showed insecurity, anxiety and hostility towards their environment. However, the oldest children were the most maladjusted, and the two youngest were quite well adjusted. Thus much of this maladjustment was probably produced by the reading difficulties.

Further light was thrown upon both type and source of reading difficulties in maladjusted children by Stewart (1950) in a study of

[1] In this test, the child is shown a series of pictures depicting situations in which a child is deprived, disappointed or accused by an adult or another child, and has to give the first words that come into his head as a response to the situation.

thirty children, aged 8½–12½ years, suffering from a considerable degree of maladjustment. Half of them were superior readers and half inferior—that is to say, they were above or below their age norms by one or more years. Both sets of children were basically insecure. But the superior readers had parents who were of the rejecting type, and the children struggled to excel in reading apparently in order to win their parents' approval. They also found that reading afforded them a refuge in the world of phantasy, and a compensation for their other difficulties. The inferior readers, on the other hand, did not strive for success in reading, and had no fear of the consequences of failure, either because their parents placed no value on reading; or as an act of hostility towards their parents (the children were often of an aggressive type); or as a means of gaining the support of indulgent, over-protective or capricious parents. These findings suggest that fundamentally maladjusted children may exhibit reading backwardness as one symptom of the disorder in appropriate circumstances, possibly without any essential cognitive difficulty in learning to read.

Davis and Kent (1955) carried out a study of the intelligence and reading achievement of 118 children aged 8 years, who were divided into four groups according to the nature of their parental treatment and upbringing. Those with 'over-anxious' parents had reading ages which were similar to the reading ages of children who had normal parental treatment. Some of the children with 'demanding' parents were greatly retarded in reading, but the disability does not seem to have been caused by the parental treatment, although it was aggravated by the excessive demands of the parents. But the children with 'unconcerned' parents, who were indifferent to their children's progress in school and whose discipline was lax or inconsistent, were retarded on the average by two years in reading age.

These results to some extent corroborate those of Stewart, but do not agree with results obtained by Hattwick and Stowell (1936). They studied the records of work habits and of social adjustment made throughout their school careers from the kindergarten to the age of 11–12 years by fifty-one children who were 'babied' by their parents—over-protected, spoilt or indulged; twenty-two children to whom was applied too much pressure to excel; and seventy-three children whose home life was well adjusted. It was found that a high proportion of the children who were babied and pushed showed poor habits of work; they needed constant pressure and encouragement from the teacher (90%); were not working to their full capacity (89%); were easily distracted and showed little power of concentration (26%); and were careless in their work (60%). Only a very small proportion of the children from well-adjusted homes showed similar characteristics. The frequency of poor work habits and of poor social adjustment among the three groups of children at the beginning and end of the period recorded is shown in Table 28. Unfortunately, no records were obtained of actual performance in school work, nor of the children's intelligence. But these results do indicate that both over-protectiveness and excessive pressure exerted by the parents may make it harder for the children to settle down to normal school work, and hence to learn to read easily. This might certainly be a contributory factor in reading backwardness.

Table 28

| | Percentage with work habits | | | | Percentage with social adjustment | | | |
| | Beginning | | End | | Beginning | | End | |
	Good	Poor	Good	Poor	Good	Poor	Good	Poor
Children babied	27	73	20	80	24	76	16	84
Children pushed	18	82	18	82	18	82	23	77
Children well adjusted	75	25	77	23	70	30	73	27

A study by Castner (1935) indicates that maladjustment from causes other than parental treatment may exist from an early age as a factor contributory to reading backwardness. This is a particularly interesting study, to which we shall devote detailed consideration, since it suggests the possibility of predicting a tendency to reading backwardness on the basis of a combination of factors. Unfortunately, the diagnosis of these factors was a clinical one, and it does not appear to have been subject to rigid experimental analysis and control. In particular, there was no comparison with children who had learnt to read normally. Hence, possibly, the reason why Castner's conclusions have not been directly confirmed by others—though a number of other studies which we have described give indirect confirmation. Among a group of pre-school children referred to a clinic, who were subsequently found to be deficient in reading, the following factors, appearing at the pre-school age, were diagnosed by Castner to be prognostic:

(1) Specific weakness in drawing tests, such as the copying of a square, cross, triangle and prism. (But the average child of pre-school age cannot draw all these forms correctly, and it is doubtful if he can copy them.)

(2) Some tendency to total or partial left-handedness or cross-laterality.

(3) Delayed language development in infancy, defective articulation or stammering.

(4) Emotional instability; and particularly over-activity, rest-lessness and distractibility. Castner pointed out that if such children, on entering school, find their lessons easy and interesting, their energies may be employed by their school work. But if not, their instability may be aggravated, and their school progress retarded.

Table 29

	Case												
	1	2	3	4	5	6	7	8	9	10	11	12	13
I.Q.	112	100	102	102	91	100	116	100	105	104	114	99	103
Years in school	2·3	1·7	2·2	1·0	2·2	1·2	1·3	1·4	2·5	2·5	2·5	1·6	1·6
Years progress in reading	0·9	0·4	0	0	1·9	0·4	0·8	0·7	0·4	0	1·1	0·4	0
Weakness in drawing	+	−	+	Slight	+	+	+	+	+	+	+	Slight	Slight
Reading disability in family			+	+			+	+		+			
Left-handedness, ambidextrality	+	−	−	+	+	−	+	+	−	−	+	+	+
Speech defect*	+	+	?	−−	?	+	+	?	?	?	?	+	−
Emotional instability	−	+	−	+	+	+	+	+	++	++	+	+	+

* Where a question mark is shown, no early history of speech development could be obtained.

Castner gave the data shown in Table 29 which relate to thirteen cases who subsequently showed slow progress in reading. This table does indicate that although no one symptom was universally present, there was a tendency for many cases to show a number of symptoms in common. It is not possible to decide whether these symptoms were interrelated, or originated in some general underlying factor; or whether the reading disability resulted from their reinforcement and enhancement of one another. It is interesting to note that only five out of the thirteen cases showed any congenital influences.

Table 30

	Case							
	1	2	3	4	5	6	7	8
Bad home background	+	+	+	+	−	+	−	−
Unintelligent or backward relations	−	−	−	−	+	−	+	+
Left-handed, cross-lateral	+	−	+	−	−	+	+	−
Visual defect	−	−	−	+	−	−	−	−
Auditory defect	−	−	+	−	−	−	−	−
Other defects or illnesses	+	+	+	+	+	−	+	
Nervousness, emotional maladjustment	+	−	+	+	+	−	−	−

Rather similar evidence of possible *multiple causation* was obtained in a study of a small number of children made by the author. There were eight cases of children aged 8–10 years who could scarcely read at all. Since these children were much older than Castner's cases, their symptoms of nervousness and emotional maladjustment might have been caused at least in part by their failure to learn to read. However, the conditions included under the heading 'bad home background' were, except possibly in one case, entirely independent of the child's reading failure; they were: bad (possibly delinquent) home, father deserted, mother committed suicide, child adopted, father an invalid who exerted too much pressure on the child, child very spoilt by mother. Thus it appears possible that a general insecurity was at least a contributory factor in many of these cases. Table 30 shows that multiple factors were involved in all but one case.

It might be supposed that if the emotional disorder were acquired, and were the fundamental cause of the reading disability, then *therapeutic treatment* would be essential; and that if it were successful, the reading disability would also disappear. Thus Stevenson (1949) showed that in a group of thirty-five children given remedial teaching for a period of a year, twenty-one improved satisfactorily and fourteen did not. Only 9 % of the former showed emotional maladjustment, as against 79 % of the latter. Blanchard (1935, 1936) found that emotionally disturbed children who could not be taught to read merely by remedial teaching were nevertheless able to learn when they had received suitable though prolonged psychotherapeutic treatment. Sylvester and Kunst (1943) found the same with two of their cases. The third case learnt to read after his teacher of remedial reading had shown a thorough understanding of his emotional difficulties and had enabled him to overcome them. Axline (1947), according to Anderson and Dearborn (1952), showed that thirty-seven backward readers, aged 7–8 years, many of whom were emotionally disturbed, improved in reading when they were given a form of play therapy in school, rather than specific remedial teaching. Spache (Robinson, 1953 *b*) claimed that if backward readers with symptoms of negativism and resistance were encouraged at the clinic to verbalize and dramatize their feelings in secure surroundings, these feelings of resistance and of inferiority and guilt were relieved, and this made it much easier for them to learn to read.

Bills (1950) studied the effect on eight backward readers, aged $7\frac{1}{2}$–9 years, who were lacking in emotional adjustment, of the Rogers type of non-directive play therapy. These children had each about six individual sessions and three group sessions of therapy during a period of 6 weeks. They showed gains of 0·45 to 2·05 years of reading age, and further gains during a subsequent follow-up period. But a group of well-adjusted retarded readers, comparable in age, I.Q. and reading retardation, made no significant gains as the result of play therapy. This study, then, demonstrates quite clearly that some cases of retarded reading result from emotional disorders which can be remedied by psychotherapeutic treatment; but that others are emotionally stable, and are quite unaffected by it.

The results of Preston (1940), however, give a different picture. We have already mentioned that she found that cases of prolonged reading failure became extremely maladjusted and maladapted to school life. In one group of twenty such cases, six eventually learnt to read normally. Before long these children recovered their social and emotional adjustment, and became quite normal and happy children. Fernald (1943) stated that the majority of her cases of reading disability who showed symptoms of maladjustment had developed these as the result of failure to learn to read. She described several cases of children who had excellent school reports when first at school, but who by the time they were referred to the reading clinic were sullen and unmanageable, negative and aggressive, or solitary and unadjusted socially. Conscious efforts to improve and parents' exhortations had no effect. But the children became normally adjusted when effective remedial teaching enabled them to read successfully. Johnson (1955) also found that remedial teaching of reading over a period of three years not only assisted the reading of her clinic cases, but also immensely improved their attitudes to their work generally.

It seems fairly clear that in some cases the emotional difficulties are the primary and fundamental factor in causing reading disability; whereas in others, the emotional difficulty is largely caused by the reading disability. The efficacy of therapeutic treatment and of remedial instruction is different in the two types of case. Thus Mehus (1953) described different types of clinic treatment in which there was relatively more play therapy and less remedial reading instruction when emotional disorders, produced, for instance, by home circumstances and difficulties in upbringing, had prevented the child from accepting the reading situation; and relatively less play therapy and more remedial teaching when the technical difficulties of reading had upset the child to such an extent as to create emotional trouble. Mehus emphasized, however, that even the latter profited by individual remedial teaching in the clinic, where they were helped, encouraged, re-assured and freed from the pressure of the school situation.

If, as with the cases of Lantz and Liebes (1943), the children are old enough to have established bad reading habits and extensive emotional conflicts connected with the reading situation, they may require prolonged specific remedial teaching in reading before they are able to surmount these difficulties. On the other hand, that the progress of remedial reading is often so slow may be due to the fact that the children do also require some therapeutic treatment of their emotional difficulties, whether these preceded or resulted from the reading disability. Thus Blanchard (1936) showed that children who responded less well to remedial teaching often had emotional conflicts. And Ellis (1949) found a correlation of -0.33 between the severity of psychiatric diagnosis of 100 clinic cases, and their improvement under remedial teaching. Even if the defects are temperamental in origin, it is likely that, as we have suggested above, they have become aggravated by the reading difficulties. Naturally aggressive children will have become more aggressive and resentful; timid children more anxious and fearful; apathetic children more inert; and restless and flighty children more inattentive and lacking in concentration and persistence. The milder cases may be remedied by a revival of interest produced by skilful teaching, especially if this can be given individually. The more severe cases, especially those with marked signs of emotional and behaviour disorder, would profit from psychotherapeutic treatment.

In conclusion, the studies we have described in this section do not finally answer the query whether there is some temperamental defect or some acquired emotional maladjustment in every case of reading disability. One difficulty in reaching any conclusive answer is that, as we have noted so frequently, mild cases of retardation which often show little sign of maladjustment have often not been differentiated from severe cases of real failure to learn to read. Even among the latter, however, it has not always been possible to detect any obvious signs of emotional maladjustment (see, for instance, Cases III and V, described in Appendix I). Undoubtedly many of these cases have not been investigated very thoroughly, and it is possible that more deeply seated types of disorder have passed unnoticed. Rorschach Test results might demonstrate the existence of such disorders; but unfortunately those described on pp. 139–40 were not obtained from severely retarded cases. Perhaps we might conclude, however, that a thorough investigation of possible temperamental or neurotic defect should be made in every case of severe reading disability; and that psychotherapeutic treatment of such defects should be administered whenever it seemed likely that they were remediable.

CHAPTER VII

THE EFFECT OF ENVIRONMENTAL FACTORS ON READING ABILITY AND DISABILITY

(1) HOME CIRCUMSTANCES

We may consider first whether the general circumstances of the home, its situation and socio-economic status, have any effect upon children's reading performance; and whether any of these circumstances are in themselves likely to lead to reading disability. It would probably be accepted immediately that in this country at least the reading achievement of children of lower *socio-economic status* is generally inferior to that of children of higher socio-economic status. In the first place, the intelligence of the former is on the average inferior to that of the latter. Apart from the effect of his intelligence, the child from the better type of home has great cultural advantages over the child from the poorer home. The parents of the former provide him with intelligent conversation, with books and with stimulation and encouragement to learn to read;[1] whereas the poorer parents may be unable to do any of these things. They may have a narrower vocabulary, and in general less time for talking to their children. On the other hand, it is possible that the child of well-to-do parents may have fewer opportunities than the poorer child of talking to other children.

It is, however, understandable that Burt in 1937 found the distribution of general backwardness in school work shown in Table 31 among children from different types of London home. Burt also calculated the correlation between the percentages of backward children in the different London boroughs, and various indices of poverty. The correlation with percentage below the poverty line was 0·727; with percentage on poor relief, 0·568; with

---

[1] Perhaps this is less true today than it was twenty years ago. Nowadays parents in the upper socio-economic classes may provide too many amusements and distractions. But we have no evidence that the children's reading has been affected by this, or by the possible tendency to over-anxiety in mothers in these classes.

percentage unemployed, 0·676; with percentage of overcrowding, 0·890; with infant mortality, 0·934. Into these figures enter all the different effects of poverty—sickness, malnutrition, overcrowding and lack of proper sleep in overcrowded homes—as well as the cultural effects described above. However, Burt considered that poverty was a major factor in backwardness in only 8·4% of his cases, though a minor predisposing factor in over 50%. In a later book (1952) he remarked that, although poverty had greatly decreased since the time of his earlier investigations, educational backwardness had not. Thus so far as low socio-economic status is connected with backwardness, it may be that the cultural factors are of relatively greater importance than is sheer poverty.

Table 31

Home	Backward children		Controls	
	Boys	Girls	Boys	Girls
Very poor	16·1 ⎱ 53·4	24·7 ⎱ 64·6	14·0 ⎱ 47·1	16·2 ⎱ 51·0
Poor	37·3 ⎰	39·9 ⎰	33·1 ⎰	34·8 ⎰
Comfortable	35·2 ⎱ 46·6	31·2 ⎱ 40·9	39·4 ⎱ 52·9	35·2 ⎱ 46·8
Well-to-do	11·4 ⎰	9·7 ⎰	13·5 ⎰	11·6 ⎰

Table 32

School in	Percentage cases of reading backwardness	
	Boys	Girls
Good neighbourhood	4·0	2·4
Average neighbourhood	5·7	2·5
Poor neighbourhood	6·2	3·1

Schonell's figures for reading backwardness in London school-children, though published in 1942, were probably also collected before the war. They relate to the percentage of backward readers among 15,000 children from schools in different types of neighbourhood, and are shown in Table 32. It may be thought surprising that the differences are not greater. But London neighbourhoods are not completely homogeneous, nor are school populations; and there may have been children from poor homes in all schools.

However, it was stated by Child (1955) that in London there were still 'pockets' in certain boroughs of large numbers of backward readers in primary schools. Three-quarters of the schools with a high incidence of backwardness were situated in one-seventh of the area. Moreover, these particular areas maintained their relatively high incidence throughout a 2-year period of observation. But even in the worst areas, there were some schools that showed only a small proportion of backwardness. Possibly the teaching in these schools was particularly good; and the parents who were anxious to have their children well taught selected them rather than others. Again, the areas with a high incidence of backwardness were by no means always those with the worst housing and economic conditions. This evidence suggests that the parents in these areas, whose children attend the schools with the highest incidence of backwardness, are not necessarily poor, but are indifferent or perhaps even antipathetic to their children's progress in school. There was definite evidence in some of the cases studied by the author of parents who were quite unworried by their children's reading backwardness, saying that there were several other members of the family who were no good at reading (see Appendix I, Case III).

On the other hand, there may be instances where good teaching is as important as good cultural tradition and socio-economic status. This is indicated by the data for 11-year-old children shown in Fig. 10, which are taken from the Ministry of Education pamphlet (1950). Though the urban primary schools do possess fewer superior readers and more backward readers than do the private schools, which would mostly contain children of higher socio-economic status, the former actually have slightly fewer illiterates and semi-literates at the age of 11 years than the latter. And both are much superior to the rural primary schools. This seems to suggest that type of education may be more important than socio-economic status in preventing or causing illiteracy, since many of the rural schools were probably all-age schools, sometimes with only one class-teacher. The difference persisted in the 15-year-old children; illiterates and semi-literates were more than three times as numerous in the rural schools as in the urban schools, and there were half as many again of backward cases.

A study of the reading ability of Glasgow school-children by McClaren (1950) appeared to show the inferiority of children coming from poor homes. A group of 1000 children, aged 5–8 years, were given tests of reading comprehension and word recognition. The forty-five schools tested were graded into eight

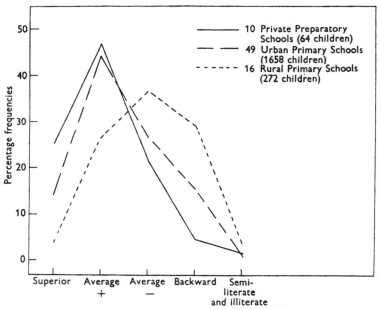

Fig. 10. Distribution of good and poor readers among 11-year-old children in various types of school

categories, according to the percentage of children in them receiving some form of public assistance, such as free milk; this percentage varied from 0·4 to 60·2 in different schools. The scores shown in Table 33 were obtained on the two tests. Here there is a definite advantage for the better class schools, though there was of course considerable overlap between the children in schools in the different grades. The differences in scores were much the same at all ages from 5 to 8 years; and they affected both the mechanics of reading and also the understanding of what was read.

Table 33

	Average percentage scores in schools in grade							
	1	2	3	4	5	6	7	8
	Boys							
Comprehension	77·8	66·0	60·3	53·8	49·1	46·2	44·1	41·0
Word recognition	67·5	64·6	55·7	43·6	41·0	39·7	37·5	36·1
	Girls							
Comprehension	68·0	64·3	59·8	54·6	50·7	49·0	47·0	44·2
Word recognition	70·8	65·9	56·9	46·1	43·3	41·7	40·0	37·5

But these data do not make any allowance for the effects on reading performance of varying intelligence in the different socio-economic classes. It may well be that the differences in intelligence were as great as, or greater than, those of reading ability. An earlier enquiry by Fleming (1943), also on Glasgow school-children, showed that the percentages of children, aged 8–12 years, with superior reading ability were very similar to those of children with superior intelligence. The schools from which the children came were placed in one of five grades, according to the percentage of necessitous children in the school (children receiving some form of poor relief, for food or clothing). Table 34 shows the percentage of children from these various grades of school who were above the 75th percentile in intelligence and in reading performance. The same type of result was obtained when the percentages of children with intelligence and reading performance above the 75th percentile were calculated for children coming from different types of home, namely, houses with various numbers of rooms; these are

Table 34

Percentage above 75th percentile in	Grade of school				
	1	2	3	4	5
Intelligence	51·8	28·5	23·2	12·6	7·0
Reading	39·6	27·3	27·2	17·3	6·5

shown in Table 35. These figures do not of course indicate directly the number of children retarded in reading in the various groups; but one is perhaps justified in inferring that they were inversely proportional. Fleming also calculated the correlations between socio-economic status at various ages, and I.Q. and reading performance, and found both to be of the order of 0·30. Thus clearly there is no evidence from these data that differences in reading ability are directly produced by differences of socio-economic status.

Table 35

Percentage above 75th percentile in	No. of rooms in house			
	1	2	3	4+
Intelligence	8·7	17·6	33·8	68·2
Reading	7·2	18·6	36·0	50·0

Some slight evidence as to the effect of bad housing and bad living conditions was obtained by Dawson (1936). He measured the I.Q.'s, reading and arithmetic quotients of 289 children whose parents were moved from a slum area in Glasgow to a slum clearance estate. Tests were given at the time of the move and 12–18 months later. It appears from the figures shown in Table 36 that the reading scores improved more than did the arithmetic scores and I.Q.'s; but all the differences except one were significant. A control group of children who remained living in the slum showed increases in some scores and decreases in others, but no overall improvement.

Table 36

	Boys		Girls	
	1st test	2nd test	1st test	2nd test
I.Q.	91·7	93·8	89·5	90·6
Arithmetic quotient	89·1	90·0	84·6	85·2
Reading quotient	91·7	98·0	91·5	98·0

Further evidence as to the relation between socio-economic environment and reading backwardness was given in the Middlesbrough study (1953). The evidence here related to children who were retarded by 1½ years or more below their mental age, and thus there was some allowance for the differing intelligence of different socio-economic classes. The percentages of retarded children found in the schools of three zones in the town are shown in Table 37; these zones, *A*, *B* and *C*, contained decreasing densities of population. Clearly there was a very wide range of incidence of reading backwardness in different schools in the same zone, and a considerable overlap of schools in different zones—a point to which we shall return in section 3 of this chapter. A questionnaire relating to 246 of the retarded children indicated that an adverse home background was a contributory factor to backwardness in 30·5 % of the children in Zone *A*, 27·2 % of those in Zone *B* and 23·6 % of those in Zone *C*. But the adverse home circumstances included many factors besides the poverty of the home.

Table 37

Zone	Average reading age	Average per- centage retarded	Range of percentages in different schools
A	10 years 4 months	17	8·3–45·9
B	11 years 4 months	12	4·0–31·4
C	12 years	7	1·0–16·6

As regards the data obtained from American school-children: It appears again that such differences as existed between children of different socio-economic status may have been due mainly to differences of intelligence. Thus Gesell and Lord (1927) studied two groups each of eleven children, aged 31–52 months, one from a good-class and the other from a poor-class nursery school. They graded the children's performance and behaviour in a number of tests and situations, including their language behaviour. The children from the good-class nursery school were superior to those from the poor-class school in everything except ability to dress and look after themselves. Teegarden (1932), according to Anderson and Dearborn (1952), found that satisfactory progress in reading was made during the first year in school by the percentages of children from different types of home which are shown in Table 38. Thus the best homes seemed to compensate for the lack of training in a kindergarten. Peck and McGlothlin (1940) obtained a correlation of 0·332 between the reading achievement of 100 children, aged 6–8 years, and their socio-economic status. This seems to have been partly a function of the amount of knowledge and information which

Table 38

	Kindergarten children	Non-kindergarten children
Superior homes	90	90
Middle-class homes	70	56
Homes in industrial districts	40	34

the children possessed, since this correlated 0·617 with reading achievement. And it was partly a function of intelligence, which correlated 0·773 with reading achievement. Again, Hilliard and Troxell (1937) found that kindergarten children with a narrower social background, with less in the way of picture books and of good speech and interesting ideas in the home, were inferior in reading readiness to children with a richer home background, although the children were of approximately the same intelligence. Furthermore, when the children were followed up for a period of two years, it was found that the children with the richer home background were 6 months ahead in reading achievement of the children with the poorer home background. The superiority was greater in sentence and in paragraph comprehension than in word recognition. Therefore the former superiority may have resulted from a better comprehension of what was read, produced by more adequate experience of play, picture books, etc., rather than from superiority in the mechanics of reading.

Some corroborative data were supplied by Sheldon and Carrillo (1952), although the children they studied do not appear to have been greatly retarded in reading. Questionnaires were sent to the parents of 868 children, of whom 290 were advanced by 1 year at least in reading, and ninety-five were retarded by at least one year. The retarded readers: (1) came from families of lower socio-economic status than the advanced; (2) came from larger families; (3) had a relatively later position among their brothers and sisters; (4) came from homes containing fewer books; (5) had parents who had reached lower school grades before leaving school. Again of course it is difficult to isolate the direct effects of these different factors from those of the parents' and the children's intelligence.

Ladd (1933) and Gates (1941), on the other hand, concluded that reading disability is not more frequent among children of lower socio-economic status than among children of higher socio-economic status. In reaching this conclusion, they were probably referring to children of equal intelligence. We may infer, therefore, that poverty and its attendant conditions do not necessarily lead to inability to learn to read. But it is likely that the more advanced stages of interest and facility in reading suffer from a lack of cultural influences in the poorer homes.

We have already described the unfortunate effects which can be produced in the home background by parents who show hostile and unsympathetic reactions to their children's failure to learn to read. However, Preston (1939) found that there were unsympathetic parents in all socio-economic classes. She was of opinion that there was no relation between the fitness of parents to bring up children and either their intelligence or their socio-economic status. It seems quite possible that in this country parents of higher socio-economic status would feel more anxiety over their children's reading failure than would parents of lower socio-economic status. But whether they reproach their children with their failure, or encourage them to surmount their difficulties, is probably an individual matter.

(2) SCHOOL ATTENDANCE

We have already mentioned that learning to read may be affected by illnesses which reduce the child's vitality and readiness to learn, and which also cause irregular attendance at school. Thus Whipple (1944) estimated that about half the number of a group of eighty-three backward readers in the middle grades at school were in generally poor health, or suffered from malnutrition or from physical defects of some kind. She also estimated that about half habitually came to school tired out because they were allowed to stay up too late at night.

Burt (1937) considered that *irregularity of school attendance*, whatever the cause, was a major factor causing general backwardness in 6·7% of the London and 8·2% of the Birmingham schoolchildren he studied; and that it was a minor predisposing factor in 4·9% of the London and 23·0% of the Birmingham schoolchildren. He obtained the percentage numbers shown in Table 39 of children who were irregular in attendance. Many more of the backward children seem to have missed school during the early stages of reading, and thus quite possibly have failed to grasp important steps necessary for learning to read. Schonell (1942) estimated that irregular attendance was three times as frequent among backward readers as among normal readers.

Table 39

	Backward children			Normal children		
	London		Birming-ham	London		Birming-ham
	Boys	Girls	Both	Boys	Girls	Both
Below 80% attendance in current year	3·6	4·6	21·4	1·0	2·0	2·6
Poor attendance in past years	12·4	10·6	31·1	1·6	2·5	5·1

It is of course true that the health of school-children in this country has greatly improved since the war. Nevertheless there is always a certain number of children who have frequent absences, or who have missed a rather long period of essential teaching through an operation or a serious illness. It is clearly difficult for such children to catch up lost time, and indeed they may never do so. Thus Harris (1947) cited among his cases of reading disability a child who had frequently missed school through illness; and two similar cases are described in Appendix I (Cases I and V).

Another possible cause of reading backwardness may be *frequent change of school*. Harris (1947) described a case who had been to five different schools and had a dozen different teachers in three years. Among the Middlesbrough children (1953), information about 246 backward readers showed the percentage incidence of

Table 40

Zone	Frequent change of school	Frequent or long absence
A	8·5	30·5
B	2·0	21·2
C	0	25·5

change of school and frequent long absence which is given in Table 40. Change of school is deleterious in that different schools and different teachers may adopt different methods of teaching reading. It is often stated that a rigid adherence to one single method of teaching is not advisable. Thus the 'look-and-say' and phonic methods, for instance, should be alternated and intermingled, in accordance with the needs of the children at the time. But clearly the changes must be systematic, and the methods must be integrated together. The child who changes schools may be exposed to the different methods in a purely random fashion, without in the least understanding how the processes taught by one method should be integrated with those taught by another. But although it seems likely that irregular attendance and frequent change of school may cause retardation in reading, we have no evidence other than that given by Harris that the retardation is permanent. The majority of cases may eventually acquire the mechanics of reading, although later than other children. We need further evidence to prove that any lasting disability results from these causes.

(3) EFFICIENCY OF TEACHING

The extent to which different schools can vary in the efficiency with which reading is taught is indicated by the wide range in the incidence of backwardness in the different Middlesbrough schools which was shown in Table 37 on p. 155. Some of this difference may have been due to differences in the sizes of the schools. A very small school may have a very wide age range of children in each class, and so small a staff that it is impossible to give any special teaching to the more backward readers; as, for instance, with Case II described in Appendix I. The same factor probably operated in the rural schools which were shown in the Ministry of Education pamphlet (1950) to have such a high percentage of illiterates. It is also possible that the teachers in such schools are less efficient. But it is exceedingly difficult to gauge the *efficiency of teaching*, and hence to measure its relationship to the incidence of reading disability, although it may well be responsible for much backwardness at least of a minor and temporary nature. A study was made by Brucker (1954) in which the teachers of 234 classes of beginners in reading were rated for the appropriateness of the materials used in teaching, the way in which they administered instruction and their efficiency in doing so. A reading test was given to the children, and the teachers of the twenty-five classes in the top quartile of reading scores were compared with the teachers of the twenty-five classes in the lowest quartile. It was found that although class-room equipment was very similar in the two groups, yet 64% of the teachers of the former classes were above average in teaching efficiency, as against 32% of the teachers of the latter. These results indicate that teaching efficiency was an important factor in promoting good reading, but obviously not the only factor.

It is also difficult to assess the relative efficiency of the various *methods of teaching reading*, since the skill of the teachers in applying them is always involved. Sexton and Herron (1928) tried to obviate this difficulty by requiring the same teachers to alternate between two different methods. But even then some of them may have been more skilful in employing one method than the other.

Another impediment to the assessment of efficiency of different teaching methods is that uniformity of name by no means guarantees uniformity of method. Thus there are many different types of 'phonic' method, each containing different amounts and different types of phonetic analysis. It is not surprising therefore that different investigators have obtained different results when comparing the relative efficiency of various methods.

But only too often the superiority of one method or another has been determined by fashion. Probably no one nowadays would advocate beginning by teaching the alphabet, or at least by teaching the names of the letters, though some methods introduce the sounds of isolated letters at an early stage. The 'phonic' method, which replaced the alphabet method, is not very popular nowadays; its use in isolation as a beginning method is not often advocated, though one very popular set of 'readers', the Beacon Readers, introduces it in conjunction with 'look-and-say' methods at an early stage, and most teachers employ some phonics sooner or later. At one time, 'look-and-say' consisted mainly of the recognition of words—names of objects, activities, etc. But later, in the 'sentence' method, short phrases and sentences were largely used, to provide the child with more familiar and meaningful units of thought. This practice was in line with modern 'activity' methods of education, since the sentences could easily be applied to the activities of the children themselves, and to those of people pictured in books. Recently there has been somewhat of a swing back from 'look-and-say' methods. The much publicized methods of Daniels and Diack (1954) and of Flesch (1955) advocated the phonetic analysis of words from the earliest stage of formal teaching of reading (see Appendix III).

The tendency to reject the freer methods of teaching reading was to some extent due to the considerable amount of illiteracy which was found to exist in this country in entrants to the Forces; and to the apparently lower level of reading skill in children in post-war years as compared with the level of pre-war years. This decline in reading ability has been greatly exaggerated. In the Ministry of Education pamphlet (1950) it was stated that the lag in reading ability after the war behind the ability in 1938 was equivalent on the average to 1 year 10 months for 15-year-old children and about 1 year for 11-year-old children. Undoubtedly this lag was due in the main to war conditions, and particularly to interrupted schooling.

There is no evidence that reading ability is poorer among children taught by the more progressive *'activity'* or *'free expression'* methods. Thus Gardner (1942) compared the reading ability of infant school children taught by 'progressive' methods with that of children taught by 'formal' methods; and found that only in one of the four types of school she studied, that attended by children from the poorest socio-economic class, were those taught by formal methods superior in reading performance to those taught by progressive methods. In a follow-up study (1950) of the progress in the junior schools of children taught by one or other of these methods, she found no significant difference in reading at 9 years, and a significant superiority for the children taught by progressive methods at 10 years. The only non-readers were among those taught by formal methods. Gardner's methods of investigation and calculation of results do not seem to have been entirely reliable; thus they give no absolutely definite evidence of the superiority or inferiority of progressively taught children. But Bergman and Vreeland. (1932) also found a slight superiority in word recognition in beginners who had been taught by a method encouraging individual activity over those taught by more formal group methods.

Among older children, aged 11–13 years, Evans (1953) found no significant differences in the gains in word recognition and reading comprehension test scores obtained by three groups taught by: (1) formal methods, including grammar; (2) activity and project methods; or (3) oral methods (including speech training and discussion). Kemp (1955) also obtained no significant differences in any kind of school achievement in children of 11 years taught by orthodox or progressive methods. Hunnicutt (1943) conducted an enquiry into the reading activities of about 4000 children aged 11–12 years, half of whom were taught by activity methods and half by formal methods. The children were matched for ability and for home background. The former had read on the average 3·78 books in the preceding ten weeks, and the latter, 3·42. The former also read on the whole a better type of book; and also read more 'for fun'.

However, Dice (1942) found that beginners in reading showed more spontaneous interest in reading when they were taught by a *direct* approach than by a *preparatory* approach. In the former, they began to read a book immediately, and went right through it, reading principally for comprehension, and not receiving any special drill in word recognition. In the latter, they were given activities designed to produce 'reading readiness' for their first half year in school, followed by formal teaching and drill in word recognition. Word recognition was also slightly superior in the children taught by the first method, especially among the poorer readers; and so also was the ability to attack new material. However, we do not know if these children maintained their advantage over those taught by the preparatory method at a later period, or whether they developed the ability to analyse and synthesize words systematically.

It is probably true that the newest and most progressive methods of teaching often give good results because they are adopted by teachers with more initiative and enthusiasm than those who are content to abide by the more conventional methods. It may be claimed as a recommendation for such methods that they do appeal to the more original and active teachers. But there is no guarantee that some still newer method (which perhaps is really a return to an old method) will not be adopted by yet another set of enthusiasts. In any case, it is difficult to assess the relative efficiency of the methods as methods.

There have been numerous investigations of the relative efficiency of *phonic* and *look-and-say* methods of teaching reading. One of the earliest investigations was made by Winch (1925). A whole class of 5-year-old children with rather poor mental ability from a school in a poor district in London was divided into two groups, each of thirty-two children, equated on the basis of pre-liminary tests of ability to learn associations between shapes and sounds. They were then given twenty-five reading lessons, the first group by the phonic method, the second by a look-and-say method, in both cases starting with whole words. In the look-and-say method, the words were recognized as wholes; in the phonic method, they were analysed phonetically. At the end of the lessons, the children were tested individually for their ability to read material consisting of words they had already learnt, and material containing a certain number of new words. The phonic group obtained a total score of 79·1, with averages of 21·9 and 13·5 on the familiar and unfamiliar material. The look-and-say group scored a total of 62·8, with averages of 17·5 and 10·1 on the familiar and unfamiliar material. A similar comparison was made between the phonic and the alphabet methods of teaching, and the total scores were 87·4 and 75·6 respectively (here the tests were somewhat different). Now it might be said that twenty-five lessons, spread over a two-month period, were too few to give a reliable comparison between the methods. The phonic method might have had an initial advantage which was not maintained because the children would have lost interest—for the phonic method has often been criticized because it makes reading so uninteresting. Furthermore, it seems that all the teaching was done by one teacher, who may have been more skilful with the phonic than with the look-and-say method.

Few subsequent enquiries have shown so great an advantage for phonic methods. Gates (1927) compared the effects of a phonic method with those of a word recognition method in which the words were taught in meaningful contexts, over a period of about 6 months. The children, who were beginners in reading, were matched for mental age and previous knowledge of words. On the whole, the second group did better than the first; they were 35% better in silent reading for comprehension. They made a general appraisal of words in the light of the context, and analysed them in detail only if they did not seem to fit the context. The first group started with a slow and detailed study of each word, often spending considerable time on unimportant details. With new and isolated words, both groups did about equally well. Gates concluded that although some phonetic analysis of words is desirable, it is inadvisable to give direct teaching of phonetics as a separate study—that is to say, to drill the children in reading and pronouncing lists of phonetic sounds of letters and letter groups not contained in meaningful words.

Sexton and Herron (1928), who found little advantage in phonetic teaching for children when they began to learn, but some advantage after a year's teaching, also concluded that it was preferable to teach phonetic sounds in words, and not to drill them in isolation. Mosher and Newhall (1930) showed that, after two years' teaching, there was no difference in speed of reading, word recognition and performance on reading achievement tests between those taught by look-and-say methods and those who had been given phonic drill. Bond (1935) found that, among backward readers, those who had been taught by phonetic methods showed less ability in the analysis and blending of word sounds than did those who had been taught by look-and-say methods.

Gates and Russell (1938) compared the efficiency of three methods of teaching beginners: (1) with very little word analysis; (2) with informal analysis, especially of confusing words; (3) with large amounts of conventional phonic drill. Group 2 obtained the highest scores on word recognition and comprehension; and group 1 was slightly better than group 3. The differences were greater for moderate and poor readers than for good readers. Work in smaller classes with individual attention and provision for individual differences progressed the best. This result was also obtained by Gates (1937). Gates (1939) also concluded that, with children who were poor at sound blending but relatively good at visual recognition, there should be less phonic and more look-and-say teaching. However, in a later enquiry Russell (1943b) found a definite advantage in the use of phonic teaching. He tested the achievement on the Gates tests of word recognition, naming of letters, spelling and paragraph reading of 116 children aged 6–7 years at the end of their first year at school. About half of them had been taught by methods which used a good deal of phonics and direct teaching of writing; the other half had been taught by informal methods with little or no phonics. The former made a definitely and significantly better performance than the latter. Whether they maintained their advantage at subsequent stages in learning to read was not investigated.

Schonell (1942) stated that intelligent children need comparatively little phonic teaching, presumably because they understand phonetics and the blending of word sounds for themselves. The results of Naesland (1955) supported this view. He studied the reading of eighteen pairs of twins; one twin in each pair was taught by a phonetic method, the other by a sentence method. With the more intelligent children, there was no difference between the reading efficiency produced by the two methods. For the less intelligent, the phonetic method showed a slight advantage. But in all cases, the children taught by the sentence method appeared to find reading more interesting.

Schonell (1945) considered that, if children are showing little progress in reading, the method of instruction should be changed, and the children should be given more writing and tracing, and more systematic phonics. Burt and Lewis (1946) also found with children aged 10–11 years of rather poor intelligence who were still more backward in reading, that a mere change of method was beneficial—but not a change to the phonic method. Possibly these children were too unintelligent to understand formal phonics. Moreover, these results were to some extent controverted by those of Conduct and Ward (1955), who demonstrated the value of phonic teaching with backward readers, aged about 9 years, in their second year in a junior school. These children were given special phonic instruction apart from their ordinary reading of books. By means of 'phonic cards' which show pictures, their names and lists of words containing the same phonetic sounds (and also by means of numerous games and tests with phonetic sounds), they learnt to recognize the phonetic units in words, and how to attack new words. The consequence was that, during a ten-month period of teaching, the reading ages of the forty-four children were increased by 0·8–3·0 years, the average increase being 1·5 years. From a sample set of results of nine children (unfortunately the full results were not given), it appeared that some of the children were almost illiterate at the start. Though they did not attain a normal reading age—several of them were of subnormal I.Q.— they did achieve some degree of literacy. However, Conduct and Ward admitted that the success of the scheme may have been due partly to the enthusiasm and encouragement of the teacher who carried it out (see also Appendix III).

Tate (1937) studied the effect of additional practice in phonics, given for 15 min. a day over a period of 2 months to thirty-seven children aged 6–7 years. They gained the equivalent of 4–6 months over non-phonetically taught controls in word recognition, but slightly less in sentence and paragraph reading. Thus the phonetic teaching did produce some improvement in the mechanics of reading, but less in the understanding of what was read. With older children, too much phonetic teaching may make reading extremely slow; but if none is given, reading may never become accurate. Thus in the Middlesbrough study, some of the reading backwardness was attributed to an excessive reliance on look-and-say methods, and the failure to supplement them, at the appropriate moment, by phonetic analysis. When Agnew (1939), according to Anderson and Dearborn (1952), compared the speed of reading and the number of errors made by eighty-nine children, aged 8–9 years, who had been taught by direct phonic methods, with those of a matched group who had had no direct phonic teaching, he obtained the results shown in Table 41. Clearly the children taught by non-phonic methods read much faster; but this was of no advantage if they were very inaccurate. Agnew concluded that the phonic method did enable the children to read new and unfamiliar words more readily than did the non-phonic method.

Table 41

	Phonics group		Non-phonics group	
	1st test	2nd test	1st test	2nd test
Average reading time (sec.)	73·0	77·5	38·8	52·9
Average number of errors	2·35	7·05	8·79	17·50

We may conclude therefore that a certain amount of *phonetic analysis* is necessary and desirable after the child has received some teaching in the immediate recognition of words by the look-and-say method. There is a danger with the latter method that the child may simply memorize words without really reading them, or will learn to repeat words without knowing what they mean. Analysis is necessary before he can understand how words are built up, and in particular can realize the importance of the correct sequence of letters in the word—since in look-and-say methods he will naturally tend to see words as 'wholes' or identify them by means of a few outstanding letters. Only a limited number of words should be taught by look-and-say before analysis begins. This to some extent precludes the so-called '*experience*' method, in which the child makes up stories about his own ideas and experiences, and then learns to read them. This method may ensure that he uses words the meanings of which he understands. But it is apt to introduce too large a vocabulary and one which includes words which are confusing and difficult to analyse phonetically. Lee (1933), according to Harris (1947), found that this method produced poorer results with six-year-old children than did a more systematic method of teaching. On the other hand, Fernald (1943) claimed that both in teaching beginners and also in remedial teaching of backward readers, children learnt most successfully when the tracing method was accompanied by the writing and subsequent reading of stories which they made up for themselves.

Keir (1951) considered that phonetic drill should begin with familiar words which the children had already learnt to recognize as wholes, by the look-and-say method. Even when new words were introduced, the child should first try to recognize them as wholes. Exercises in writing helped to emphasize the correct order of letters and phonetic units within words. Harris (1947) recommended the teaching of sound blending by the enunciation first of the whole word; then gradually and slowly breaking it up into its separate sounds; and finally fusing these together into the whole word. In some modern teaching methods, analysis is assisted by printing the successive phonetic units in different colours.

It is fairly generally accepted that phonetic teaching should form only a small part of the child's reading activities. Furthermore, the methods should be varied, and some allowance made for individual differences. Thus Gates (1937) found that in a school where methods were varied, and instruction was adapted to the different abilities of the individual children, even those with a mental age as low as 5·0 years could profit by reading instruction. On the other hand, in a school where only stereotyped mass methods of instruction were used, children learnt little until they had reached a mental age of 6½–7 years.

Gates (1930) also pointed out that ease in learning to read depended on the familiarity of the words the children were taught, and the speed at which new words were introduced. The optimum rate for children of normal intelligence was about one new word per sixty old words—though it should be slower for unintelligent children. He was also of opinion that it was better for children to meet new words as far as possible within the text of the reading book, where they would be helped by the context, rather than in isolation or in short sentences. When phonetic analysis became necessary, that also was best carried out with words in context.

A word must be said with respect to some of the *supplementary devices* which are often used to increase interest in reading and stimulate children to attend closely to the shapes and sounds of words. Such devices are: making lists of rhyming words, games of word matching, use of 'flash cards' (exposing words for a short time) and of 'work books' which teach the child to perform a task according to written instructions. Some caution must be observed in the use of these devices, as with the use of phonetic drill in isolated word sounds, lest the child fail to 'transfer' the skill and knowledge acquired by means of the devices to the ordinary reading situation. Particularly, it has been observed that the use of flash cards for rapid recognition of words tends to encourage guessing rather than analysis, and gives no assistance through the relation of meaning to the context. No doubt at some stage the child should be able to recognize words whatever the way in which they are presented. But it may be that in the early stages he should do the major part of his reading from continuous sentences in a reading book as Gates (1930) recommended. The results of Dice (see p. 162) are also apposite to this point.

However, recently a description has been given by Stott (unpublished) of a series of 'games' for special use with backward readers, which are intended to supplement normal courses of reading instruction whether by phonic or look-and-say methods. These games can be played by children among themselves. But in order to succeed, they must learn, first, the connection between speech sounds and printed letters and letter combinations; and secondly, the sounds of syllables and their combinations in words. It is claimed that these games enable the child to develop habits of word analysis and sounding which soon become as automatic as those which the normal reader acquires for himself.

Finally, a comment is necessary on the method advocated by McDade (1937) and Buswell (1945), called the '*non-oral*' method. In this method, children learnt to recognize the printed names of objects, pictures, etc., without speaking them. Oral exercises in word pronunciation were given in separate lesson periods, but were not connected with the reading. The intention was to prevent lip movements and sub-vocal enunciation of words during silent reading. McDade (1937) carried out an experiment in which this method was employed with forty children, of average age 7·0 years and mental age $7\frac{1}{2}$ years, over a period of 9 months. Subsequently reading performance was compared with that of forty children, matched for age and intelligence, taught by phonic drill; and fifty children taught by methods of oral enunciation which did not use direct phonic drill. In the first group, all the children reached the expected level for their age, and 93 % exceeded it by 0·2–1·4 years. In the second group, 25 % fell below the expected level; 45 % exceeded the level in the mechanics of reading, but their comprehension was doubtful. The third group gave an intermediate performance. Test scores of the three groups were 2·65, 2·09 and 2·25 respectively. A subsequent study by Buswell (1945) showed less advantage for the non-oral method. Groups of 465 11-year-old children and 330 8-year-old children who had been taught by the non-oral method were matched for intelligence with children taught by conventional methods. On silent reading tests the older children taught by the non-oral method showed a slight but non-significant superiority to those taught by ordinary methods; but for the younger children there was no difference. Observable lip movements were made by 17 % of the children taught by the non-oral method, as against 21 % of those taught by ordinary methods. The probable conclusion is that the children taught by the non-oral method did in fact enunciate the words sub-vocally, using their phonetic sounds to grasp their meanings. McDade's results do, however, indicate the inferior results obtained by formal phonic drill.

All these results suggest which are the best methods, or the best combination of methods, of teaching children to read in normal school conditions. But they do not show whether unsuitable teaching methods make it so difficult for children to learn to read that they develop a real disability in reading. To obtain some evidence on this point, it is necessary to study actual cases of disability. We may cite first the results of Bond (1935) which showed an association between poor reading and various types of deficient auditory discrimination which appeared more clearly in children taught by phonic than by look-and-say methods. The former obtained poorer scores than the latter on blending speech sounds and on memory for rhythm; and there appeared to be a higher incidence of speech defects among the former than among the latter. Thus the emphasis on phonetics seemed to decrease rather than increase the ability for auditory analysis. But Preston (1939) found that the majority of her 100 cases of reading disability, aged 7–15 years, were taught by look-and-say methods; whereas the majority of her control cases of normal readers were taught by phonetic methods. Durrell (1940) stated that, in 1930, 90% of a group of 100 clinic cases of severe reading difficulty showed the results of too much stress on phonics, and were particularly poor at the rapid recognition of words and the synthesis of word sounds. But in 1936, 90% of another group of cases were suffering from inadequate teaching by look-and-say methods, and were unable to analyse words. Hester (1942) found that 58% of a group of 194 children with reading difficulties appeared to be lacking in a knowledge of the phonetic sounds of words, and of how to blend them. These difficulties were most evident in children of 9–11 years, who should by then have mastered the processes of analysis and blending. Perhaps again the important factor was their inability to analyse words into their phonetic units. Harris (1947) described three cases of severe retardation in reading all of whom were deficient in phonetics, and were unable to analyse words phonetically. One of these said that he had always been taught by visual methods. Anderson and Dearborn (1952), again, quoted the case of a boy of 11 years with a reading age of about 8 years who was still trying to read by word wholes, and constantly confused words with those of similar spelling, and especially with the same initial letters. And Morris (1951) described the case of a boy of 10, taught by look-and-say methods, who had learnt only the shapes of a few words which he could sometimes identify, but no more. After Morris had taught him to begin to recognize letters by means of their sounds, he remarked: 'It's easy to remember words if you take a look at the letters.' Clearly his past five years of teaching had not taught him to do so.

These results seem to show that look-and-say methods alone are inadequate to teach reading, and their exclusive use is liable to result in inability to analyse and read new words. But the inability might also be due not so much to lack of phonetic teaching as to incompetent and unsuitable use of phonetics. A child may be thoroughly confused by phonic drill, and unable to understand its relevance to reading. Preston (1939) showed that 77% of her cases of prolonged reading failure were taught to read satisfactorily, and 13% to read with fair success, by skilful teachers who employed any and every effective method. A good teacher will know just how and when to mix look-and-say and phonetic methods. Thus we cannot conclude that reading disability results from any one particular method of teaching reading. But we may hazard a guess that too prolonged a reliance upon a single method, especially if it is applied in a rigid and stereotyped manner, may prevent children from learning at the normal speed. More experimental investigation is needed to prove or disprove this hypothesis; and also to determine whether such unsuitable teaching can produce permanent and far-reaching disability which cannot be remedied even by more adequate teaching.

(4) CONCLUSIONS

The general conclusion to be drawn from this study of the effects of environmental factors on reading is that they may retard the progress of reading; but that there is no final evidence that the retardation results in a permanent disability.

There is probably little direct effect nowadays of sheer poverty; but the child from the poor and uncultured home may be less intelligent, and may be less interested in learning to read because he receives insufficient encouragement at home. Even then, it is the more advanced stages which are likely to be affected, rather than the acquisition of the mechanics of reading.

As regards the relation to reading of the school environment, it is obvious that inadequate school attendance, caused by frequent absence, and change of school may produce retardation, simply because the child has missed some essential stage in teaching. Clearly such a deficiency should be remedied at the earliest possible moment by ascertaining what the child has missed and seeing that it is made good. It is quite conceivable that, where no attempt is made to do this, either immediately or subsequently, a child who has not covered the earlier stage of reading, and in particular has not learnt to analyse and re-synthesize words, will suffer from a permanent disability.

It is obviously excessively difficult to decide which is the most efficient method of teaching reading, because of (a) the vagaries of fashion in teaching methods, (b) the difficulty of defining exactly what each method includes, (c) the impossibility of assessing exactly the skill of the teachers who employ these methods. All enquiries into the efficacy of educational methods have demonstrated the importance of the third factor; and also that some teachers use one method more efficiently, and other teachers another. Nevertheless, the general run of the evidence from the studies described shows that the first essential is to stimulate the children's interest in the reading process; and that some form of look-and-say method, accompanied by various reading 'games', is the best for the purpose. But after the child has acquired some familiarity with reading material, and has learnt to recognize a certain number of words as wholes, he must proceed to some form of phonetic analysis if he is to acquire an adequate knowledge of the mechanics of reading. There is some divergence of opinion as to the most suitable age at which phonetics should be introduced. Tate (1937) and Agnew (1939) apparently obtained good results by giving some phonetic teaching at 6–7 years, during the first year of learning to read. But the results of Garrison and Heard (1931) and of Dolch (1948) indicated that no useful purpose was served by phonetic teaching below a mental age of 7 years. These apparent contradictions are due probably to the different ways in which the phonetic teaching was given. If it is employed as a stereotyped drill, the younger children cannot apply it to their ordinary reading, and they rapidly become confused and bored. But phonetic analysis carried out with familiar words in context, such that the child can understand the meaning of what he is doing, may be distinctly valuable. It may be assisted also by rhyming and by comparison of words with similar phonetic structures.

Some children appear to be able to develop for themselves the capacity for phonetic analysis and re-synthesis. But the majority require some form of phonetic teaching, and unless they receive this, they will be retarded in reading and perhaps permanently disabled. When it is found that a child is unable to analyse words, it may not always be desirable to begin phonetic teaching immediately, since he may be too confused and resistant to accept it. But the work of Conduct and Ward (1955), and also that of Daniels and Diack (1956), described in Appendix III, showed that it was possible to give special phonetic teaching to backward readers of a kind sufficiently enjoyable to stimulate them to new efforts. Whether a real disability can be completely overcome by suitable remedial teaching will be discussed in the next chapter.

CHAPTER VIII

THE CURE OF READING DISABILITY

A study of the recovery from reading disability, and the methods by which this is achieved, should afford valuable evidence as to whether this disability is in some way inherent, or whether it has been caused by some transitory and remediable defect. Unfortunately, few individual cases have been diagnosed and followed up with sufficient care and skill to demonstrate what was the essential nature of their disability, and whether or not it could be completely removed. Such evidence as there is suggests that severe cases, even if they master the simple mechanics of reading, seldom acquire real facility in it. They tend to remain slow and stumbling, reading word by word, often having to think over the more difficult words before they can understand their meaning. Or they may show persistent disability in spelling. This is a not uncommon complaint among intelligent children in highly educated families, who have managed to overcome their initial disability, but have never attained that complete familiarity with the construction of words which characterizes the normal educated person (see Appendix I, Case I). Such a defect, and the accompanying slow and halting reading, would probably pass almost unnoticed in a child of working-class parents, and would not hinder him from leading a normal life in a manual occupation. For most clerical and professional occupations it is of course prohibitive.

Unfortunately, many studies of remedial reading have not discriminated between the slightly and the severely retarded reader; and have been content to demonstrate a rapid short-term improvement without finding if any real skill is developed. Thus Gates (1922) found that the following method was successful up to a point: a combination of (*a*) careful observation of the printed words while pronouncing the syllables; (*b*) attempts to visualize the word while pronouncing it; (*c*) writing the word while articulating it silently. Moderately retarded readers improved by the equivalent of 2–3 years, on the average, after 4–6 months' training by this method. There were no children in this study who failed altogether to learn to read; but many remained permanently backward. Again, it was stated by McCullough *et al.* (1946) that 90% of a group of illiterates entering the U.S.A. Forces were brought up to the level of reading of the average 9-year-old after 8 weeks' intensive training. They were taught a basic vocabulary of forty-eight words, recognizing them by means of accompanying pictures; the words were related to their experiences in the Army. From this point they could apparently move on to reading simple books and magazines. However, additional help was given individually in cases of special difficulty. In dealing with similar cases in the British Army, Burt (1945) seems to have found phonetic methods useful for the rather more intelligent illiterates. But some men had to be taught their letters first.

However, much the most successful method of teaching the completely illiterate seems to be that of Fernald and Keller (1921). The children they taught were sent to a special clinic school where they worked in small groups, but could be given individual attention whenever they needed it (Fernald, 1943). Each child began by selecting a few words which interested him—sometimes quite long and complicated words. These words were written out for him in large script; he traced them over and over again with the forefinger, while enunciating them, until he could remember them as whole patterns and could write them without looking at the copy. When he had learnt a certain number of words in this way, he began to write down 'stories' of his own invention; unknown words were given him to trace. When his 'story' (which at first might be only a single sentence) had been typed, he read it. After a time he could look at words and say them; but he continued to write all unfamiliar words. Fernald described the progress of two groups of non-readers who were given this treatment:

(1) Twenty-six cases, aged 8–17 years, given an average of 6·9 months' remedial teaching, made an average improvement of 3·8 years in reading age (range, 3–5 years).

(2) Eleven cases, aged 8–14 years, given an average of 10·4

months' remedial teaching, made an average improvement of 4·5 years in reading age (range, 3–7½ years).

These and other cases (sixty-two in all) were followed up subsequently and eventually achieved a normal or superior performance in reading, and also apparently in spelling.

Fernald considered that the individuals who profited by her type of remedial teaching were those who were naturally deficient in visual and auditory imagery, and tended to rely upon tactile and kinaesthetic imagery. It cannot be assumed that all cases of reading disability, whether total or partial, are of this type; and other types might not succeed so well with this form of teaching. Some remedial teachers have found the method extremely slow and laborious. Dearborn (1929) considered that it was too babyish for children over the age of 8 years. Moreover, it might aggravate the difficulties of strongly left-handed children (who apparently were infrequent among Fernald's cases), because of their inability to write easily. Others have stated that the important feature in Fernald's method is not the employment of tactile-kinaesthetic sensation, as Fernald claimed, but the emphasis given by tracing and writing to the order and arrangement of letters and phonetic units in the word (see Gates, 1935; Harris, 1947). Again, the success of the method may have been due in part to the stress on active manipulative behaviour; the child began by making the words with his own hand, instead of assimilating passively the relationship between printed words and word sounds.

Thus teachers who have used methods which included only part of the Fernald technique and not the whole of it have met with very varying success in overcoming reading disability. For instance, Kirk (1933) taught six boys, aged 9–11 years, with I.Q.'s of 63–80, to recognize lists of words, some merely spoken when they were shown, and others traced as well. Though the number of trials taken to learn the words was much the same with both methods, the tracing method produced better recall and speedier re-learning after 24 hours. But these results do not necessarily apply to learning true reading, as distinct from recognizing words from memory.

Monroe (1932) also used tracing among her remedial methods, but she did not stress it to the same extent as did Fernald. Moreover, the children traced the words with a pencil and not with the forefinger, and tried to visualize them while they did so. Certainly the progress of her backward readers did not seem as satisfactory as that of Fernald's cases. There were three groups: *A*, given individual remedial teaching by ordinary teachers, working under close supervision with carefully controlled methods; *B*, given some remedial teaching in groups; *C*, given no special teaching. The results are shown in Table 42. Although the special remedial teaching produced a definite gain in reading age, many of the children were still considerably retarded in reading. Of the children in group *A* 36% were brought up to standard, as against 14% in group *B*. Those who received no remedial teaching showed no improvement in reading age, and their reading indices actually decreased. Subsequent studies by Monroe and Backus (1937) showed that backward readers, aged 6–11 years, given remedial instruction over a period of 21 weeks, improved on the average by only 0·7–0·8 years in reading age; and only about 30% were brought up to standard. However, Monroe and Backus claimed that only 5% of the children showed no improvement.

Table 42

Group	No. in group	Mean age	Mean I.Q.	No. of hours' training	Period of training	Gain in reading age (years)	Final reading index[1]
A	89	10 years	100	27	7 months	1·39	0·723
B	50	11 years 7 months	89	18	7 months	0·79	0·595
C	50	10 years 5 months	91·5	0	—	0·14	0·514

Schonell (1949) studied the effect of four months' remedial teaching in special classes on the reading of twenty-four boys aged 10½–13 years, with I.Q.'s of 72–112. They gained on the average 10 months of reading age, the range being from 5 to 31 months.

[1] The reading index was calculated by dividing the reading performance, expressed in terms of school grades, by the average of the chronological age, mental age and arithmetic performance, also expressed in terms of school grades.

Whereas at the outset 85% of the boys had reading ages below 7 years, at the close 58% had reading ages of 7 and over. This indicates that about half the boys had at least begun to acquire the mechanics of reading, though they were still grossly retarded; and the remainder had not advanced even as far as that. However, four months is a short period, and perhaps no great amount of improvement could be expected in the time.

Distinctly more promising results were obtained from the remedial treatment described by Birch (1949). Seventy-two children aged 9–11 years were sent in groups of twelve, for one quarter of each school day over a period of 6 months, to a coaching centre. There they were first stimulated by various games and activities to take an interest in reading; and they then began to learn it again more or less from the beginning. Informal methods of instruction were used, with much individual activity and work in small groups; and also some attention was given to individual difficulties. The children were tested every three weeks with the Burt Graded Word Reading Test, and their scores were exhibited, in order that they might follow their own improvement. It seems possible that the children may have learnt the words of the Burt test by heart, which somewhat invalidates estimates of their improvement. Birch stated that the results were confirmed by testing with the Schonell Silent Reading Test, but this confirmation does not appear from the results given to have been very exact. We shall return shortly to this question of testing results.

Table 43

	Range in years	Average
Initial reading ages	5·1–9·5	7·2
Initial retardation	3–7	3·6
Improvement	0·8–3·7	1·9

The results, taken at their face value, of the sixty-four children who completed the six-months course are shown in Table 43. A sample set of results for twenty children showed that those of high intelligence attained reading ages which were normal or nearly normal for their chronological ages. Those of average or below average intelligence were still somewhat retarded, but appeared to have acquired at least some of the mechanics of reading.

Conduct and Ward (1955) also obtained good results with moderately retarded readers given specially stimulating teaching (see p. 166). The more severely retarded cases improved to some extent, but did not attain a normal reading age.

A study by Curr and Gourlay (1953) indicated that it is essential to be very careful in measuring the improvement apparently produced by remedial teaching, and to compare it with the increase of test scores in a control group. They studied the effect of individual remedial teaching at a clinic over a period of 15 weeks on the reading of sixty-four children, aged 8–9 years, of normal and above normal intelligence. Half of these were selected by teachers as poor in reading and the other half were shown by tests to be retarded by about $1\frac{1}{2}$ years on the average. The latter group increased their scores on the Schonell Silent Reading Test by 4·7 months in excess of the increase obtained by the control group; but both test and control groups showed about the same amount of improvement on an unstandardized reading test. Thus the gain on a particular test was not apparently transferred to other types of reading performance.

These results have been criticized by Birch (1953) and by Kelimer Pringle and Gulliford (1953), mainly on the grounds that *something* must have occurred to improve the reading of both the experimental and the control groups, which had been so retarded previously. Possibly the ordinary school teachers of the control group were stimulated, more or less unconsciously, to take more interest in their backward readers, and pay more attention to their reading. Also the teachers may have had more time to devote to the remainder of the class once the children given remedial teaching had been removed from it. Neither of these two effects, however, indicate any particular advantage in the remedial teaching itself; some other stimulus to the class teachers might have produced a similar result.

Recently Schonfield (1956) has brought evidence to show that retarded readers, aged 11 years and upwards, showed a blockage or plateau in the improvement produced by remedial teaching round about the reading ages of 8½–9½ years. A certain proportion of the children surmounted this blockage and improved further; but what proportion is not clear from Schonfield's data; certainly a considerable number did not. Schonfield attributed this blockage to the great increase in difficulty of understanding the words encountered at this age. This may have caused the lack of improvement in the actual reading test, but it seems doubtful whether it could have affected reading performance in general. It is more probable that these children had reached the point at which they could progress no further without a thorough grasp of the processes of systematic analysis and re-synthesis which were described in chapter IV, section 5. Thus they were obliged to guess any words they had not memorized, and were unable to tackle new words systematically. Some children were enabled by the remedial teaching to surmount this difficulty, but many were not.

More successful results were, however, obtained by Monroe (1928) by means of *individual remedial teaching* given by herself. The tracing method of Fernald and Keller was used, together with special methods appropriate to the particular defects of each child. These included: ocular defects; deficiencies in auditory discrimination; tendencies to reverse, transpose and substitute words. A group of eight children, aged 7–12 years with I.Q.'s of 82–115, were given this treatment over a period of two months, after which they had improved in reading performance by an average of a little over a year, from a retardation of over three years below their mental ages to one of about two years. Though they were still retarded, they could read sufficiently to carry on normal school work. Another group of eleven children were given a similar period of training. Six children gained an average of three-quarters of a year in reading age, and five gained an average of nine-tenths of a year. A later study (1932) was made of four children of 6–8 years of normal or superior intelligence who could scarcely read at all. Three of these cases were cross-lateral or ambilateral; the fourth was exceptionally clumsy in movement. They were given 9–18 months of intensive remedial teaching, using the tracing method together with drill in the analysis and blending of sounds in words. All achieved normal reading performances for their ages—that is to say, reading indices of 0·94–1·27. Two older children, aged 12 and 13 years, also attained reading performances normal for their ages after 9 months of remedial teaching. A third child of 14 years, who suffered from a severe speech defect as the result of birth palsy, improved only from a reading index of 0·37 to one of 0·56. But it is clear that in general Monroe's methods were effective if applied by a skilled teacher. Indeed, some of the lack of success with group A, described on p. 178, seems to have been due to the unskilfulness of the ordinary school-teachers' remedial teaching; though some of these teachers improved with practice.

Table 44

Group	Average reading age	
	At start	At end
(1)	7 years 3 months	8 years 6 months
(2)	7 years 2 months	7 years 7 months

A study by Schonell (1942) showed that even individual remedial teaching is not always effective. He compared the progress of two groups of backward readers: (1) thirty-one children of average age 9½ years and I.Q. 90, given 15–30 min. individual teaching daily for 3 months by Schonell himself or by teachers instructed by him; and (2) fifty-four children of similar age and intelligence given only ordinary school teaching. The results are shown in Table 44. The range of gains was from 5 to 41 months for group (1), and from 4 to 11 months for group (2). Thus clearly the improvement was only slight for some children; whereas some of those in group (1) learnt to read normally, all of those in group (2) remained below average for their age. Stevenson (1949) studied the improvement in reading made by thirty-five children aged from 8 to 12 years, with intelligence above normal, who were given remedial teaching in a clinic, which included a good deal of individual attention to particular individual difficulties. Of these children, twenty-one made good progress during the year's teaching; but fourteen were still retarded by 2–4 years at the end of the year. The latter showed a considerable amount of emotional maladjustment.

Ellis (1949) studied the improvement made by 100 children varying in age from 7 to 14 years who were referred to a clinic for reading disability. Suitable remedial teaching was recommended by the clinic. It was carried out in their schools over the period of one year, with varying degrees of efficiency ranging from some rather haphazard teaching in class to satisfactory individual tuition. At the end of this period, Ellis found a correlation of 0·62 between improvement in reading and the amount and quality of the remedial teaching. It appeared that with these children, who were not very greatly retarded in reading, but were in some cases emotionally disordered, the care and thoroughness of the remedial teaching constituted the most important factor in producing improvement.

The enquiry of Redmount (1948) indicated that the degree of improvement depended to some extent upon the personality of the children. He studied the effects upon twenty-four children, aged 8–18 years, who went to live for a period of 6 weeks in a special residential school, where they were given much free activity, non-directive play therapy and individual counselling. The Rorschach Test given at the beginning showed that two-thirds of them had some form of personality disturbance. At the end of treatment, 48% had improved in reading scores and 39% in personality adjustment; but 12% had lower reading scores, and 26% showed deterioration in personality adjustment. Twenty-six teachers were employed in this remedial education, and they also were given the Rorschach Test, which indicated that 65% of them had varying degrees of personality maladjustment. The more maladjusted were associated with an absence of change, or with an unfavourable change, in the children they taught. On the other hand, good adjustment in the teacher did not guarantee improvement in the child. However, it is clear that some care must be exercised in choosing teachers who are capable of giving adequate remedial teaching.

Long-term studies of remedial teaching were carried out by

Dearborn (1939) and by Lantz and Liebes (1943). Dearborn found that forty-one cases of severe reading disability, after $3\frac{1}{2}$ years and upwards in good schools, had practically overcome their difficulties in 22% of cases; had partially recovered in 49%; and were still substantially retarded in 29%. In the study by Lantz and Liebes of thirty-three boys living in a cottage orphanage, the length of time devoted to special remedial teaching varied from under 50 hours (in five cases) to over 600 hours, in one case; the average amount was 150 hours. There appeared to be no correlation between the number of hours required and intelligence, or with the number of specific obstacles to reading (poor visual discrimination, poor auditory discrimination, lack of attention, of motivation, etc.). It is true that 28% of these boys had emotional problems of some kind; and the markedly aggressive required more remedial teaching than did the day-dreamers. However, as we have shown in Chapter VI, many backward readers have emotional problems which are contributory to their reading difficulties, or have been set up by them. Thus the children's progress in learning to read is usually slow, and many of them never become really proficient in reading. In some cases, again, the difficulty may persist in an inability to spell correctly.

It is unfortunate that, whereas the number of enthusiastic suggestions and recommendations as to the remedial teaching of backward readers is great, the number of controlled studies of the actual improvement made over any length of time is so small. It seems that mild cases of backwardness are treated comparatively easily, even by class teaching. All they require is some encouragement and some stimulation of the interest they lacked in a rather difficult task. Thus we noted Schonfield's finding (1956) that secondary modern school children who had reached a reading age of $8\frac{1}{2}$ years improved their reading performance substantially when they were given only one period per week for one term of group remedial teaching. But children with lower reading ages did not respond to the same extent.

However, even three to four years of retardation may be considerably reduced by skilled individual remedial teaching, especially if, whenever there is some emotional maladjustment, the child can be relieved of this disorder by therapeutic treatment. But the evidence is extremely conflicting as to the eventual recovery of real cases of disability: children of 8–9 years and over who cannot read at all, or who have learnt merely to memorize a few words. The results of Fernald appear to show that such children can be taught to read normally. But Fernald has not stated her case very clearly or systematically; and few if any other teachers seem to have obtained equally good results, even when employing what they claim to be Fernald's tracing method. It may be that they have not used the method with sufficient care and accuracy; or that the remarkable improvement in Fernald's cases was due in part to other factors, such as the interest and encouragement provided by her clinic school. Or possibly Fernald's were selected cases, of the type which could profit best by her methods; whereas other non-readers suffer from some other form of disability which could not be remedied in this way. It does appear, however, from the other evidence we have, and from the author's own observations, that severe cases of disability seldom or never become completely normal readers. Given suitable treatment, they may acquire the ability to analyse and re-synthesize words in a more or less systematic manner. But they can do this only very slowly; they may have to study each word separately before they can read it; and they may never learn to spell correctly. The fate of such children in an ordinary school is deplorable; they are almost certain to lose all interest in linguistic work, and they may feel permanently resentful or inferior. Certainly a great effort should be made to give them individual remedial teaching, together with psychotherapeutic treatment of the emotional disorders they may have developed, even if they did not possess them originally. But it is probably advisable that they should be directed towards mathematical, scientific or manual work, according to their intelligence, special abilities and interests, and should avoid linguistic subjects.

CHAPTER IX

CONCLUSIONS

We must now summarize some of the data presented in earlier chapters, and attempt to determine what they indicate as to the nature and causes of reading disability. At first sight it appears difficult if not impossible to present any general conclusions. A multitude of factors are associated with reading backwardness in different cases, but there are no factors which appear in all cases. Or rather, the methods of experiment and clinical diagnosis so far employed have failed to isolate any factors which appear universally in all cases of reading backwardness—other than inability to read easily! Neither have the observations made succeeded in eliminating any of these factors altogether from consideration, though they have suggested that certain factors are relatively uncommon or inessential. Furthermore, we are faced with the probability that reading backwardness and reading disability are not single entities, identical in nature and causation in every case. It is also probable that the real disability of the almost totally illiterate child, who does not understand the fundamental processes of reading, and cannot be said to have acquired its mechanics, is quite different in nature from mere backwardness, in which the child just reads slowly and with poor comprehension. This distinction has commonly been overlooked in studies of reading backwardness. Again, there may exist different types of reading disability, produced by different factors, and different complexes of factors, in different cases. The condition is not a simple one, even at the onset, and it is inevitably complicated by the experiences of the child before his disability is detected—his growing sense of confusion and disappointment at his failure.

Thus almost the only fact which appears clearly at first sight is the heterogeneity of cases of reading disability—heterogeneous both in the origin and in the nature of their disability. But there does seem to be one fairly universal characteristic of the disability, namely, the child's general state of doubt and confusion as to the relationship between the printed shapes of words, their sounds and their meanings. This confusion resembles that of a young child who is just beginning to read. He lacks an understanding of the following essentials:

(1) Printed words consist of units, the letters, each of which has a characteristic shape; but this shape can vary in minor details while preserving its universal identity (as, for instance, in different scripts and type faces). Some shapes, however, are extremely similar; in fact they may differ only in spatial orientation. Each word has also a characteristic and invariable structure which is determined by the order of the letters in it.

(2) The enunciation of words in speech is not merely a simple motor activity; but these words have definite connotational significances which correspond with their sound patterns. Each sound pattern, however, consists of a combination of phonetic units possessing certain permanent residual characteristics, although they may also vary greatly in the speech of different people, or even in the same person speaking in different moods. The same phonetic units can be combined in various ways to constitute different word patterns.

(3) When the printed letter units and the spoken phonetic units have been analysed out from the word wholes in which they are combined, they can be associated together in such a manner that visual perception of the letters calls forth certain speech patterns, and hence the corresponding auditory sensations. But the associations, although invariable and consistent for any particular word, are often arbitrary and unsystematic as between different words. Therefore although there are certain rules determining which sounds should be given to certain word and letter shapes, these rules are neither logical nor universally operative.

(4) When the separate phonetic units have been enunciated, they must be combined or blended together in the correct order to produce the total word sound, and hence to indicate its meaning. But frequently the correct enunciation and blending of the phonetic units can be determined only when the total word sound

has been achieved, and this may have to be modified in accordance with the meaning of the word; that is to say, some actually existent word must be selected, and one which fits the meaning of the context.

Now it is clear that these processes are in themselves excessively complicated, and require a considerable degree of intelligence and insight. Thus they demand a certain level of maturity in the child. He can get ready to understand and to learn them by becoming familiar with the sounds and meanings associated with a small number of printed shapes of whole words. In particular, he can learn that printed symbols do represent the words which he uses in speech, just as a pattern of lines on a page represents an object with which he is familiar in his ordinary everyday life. It seems essential that he should reach this stage before trying to proceed further. But it is also certain that he will never learn to read efficiently until he *has* proceeded further. The non-reader and the child with severe reading disability have not progressed any further.

We have no definite evidence as to the incapacity of such cases to perceive and analyse printed words, but it is quite clear that they often fail to recognize that a certain spatial orientation of the letters is essential, and also a particular order and arrangement of the letters within the word (see Chapter IV, section 2). Again, we have no definite evidence that they *cannot* hear the sounds of letters and words, though this may occur in some cases of mild hearing loss and high frequency deafness (see Chapter VI, section 2); but it is probable that many of them do not listen to, and hence do not hear, the separate phonetic units in the total word sound, and do not remember them in their exact order. This may often be due merely to inattention and lack of interest; but sometimes it seems as if they 'are like the deaf adder that stoppeth her ears, which refuseth to hear the voice of the charmer, charm he never so wisely'! The result is that they are unable to associate the visual and auditory units, because they are uncertain which correspond with which. And having failed to understand even the simpler associations, they are naturally more and more confused when they are confronted with the variations and exceptions to the rules of association. Or in some cases it may be that the simpler associations have been learnt but that they are not clearly differentiated from the more complicated and anomalous associations. Thus we may conclude that, rather than suffering from some general defect in visual or auditory perception, imagery or memory, the child with reading disability has broken down at some point, and has failed to learn one or more of the essential processes that we have described. He therefore remains fixed at a particular point and is unable to proceed further.

It might be that the cause of the breakdown was some almost fortuitous circumstance—a period of absence from school, a change of school or of teacher, even a temporary mood of rebelliousness or a lapse of interest and attention. It is of course true that many children are able to surmount such difficulties, because they are given opportunities of repeating the same part of the procedure again and again, with different material, differently presented and applied. Thus if they fail to grasp a process on one occasion, or with one form of instruction, they are able to do so at another. Hence of course the great importance of providing a variety of teaching materials and types of instruction, and of not adhering rigidly to a single stereotyped method. Even when the child misses a whole stage in reading instruction, for instance through prolonged absence from school or through change of school, and his reading becomes moderately retarded, it appears that careful and stimulating teaching covering the missing stage will in many cases enable him to overcome his difficulties, and proceed normally. On the other hand, as with Case V, described in Appendix I, even remedial teaching, if given too late, may sometimes apparently be inadequate to make up for what the child has lost. Again, if he is introduced too early to the difficult processes of systematic analysis and synthesis of word shapes and sounds, he may become so bewildered that he cannot understand what to do next (see Chapter III, section 3). Thus he may be unable to proceed beyond the early stages of recognizing a few words the shapes of which he has memorized. Naturally also if he is not taught specifically, at the appropriate time, how to analyse and synthesize the word shapes and sounds, he may experience great difficulty in carrying out these processes alone and unaided. Thus he also may fail to advance beyond the recognition of a few whole words. But again, the majority of children, if given suitable teaching which directly attacks their difficulties, are able to surmount them and make normal progress.

Why then do certain children fail to recover from a breakdown in learning to perform the succession of processes which constitute reading? We have suggested in Chapter v that some of them belong to a class possessing a congenital disposition towards a set of defects of which reading disability is one. Thus in examining a child who cannot read, or who has extreme difficulty in reading, it is advisable first to ascertain whether his speech is, or has been, in any way defective, or whether he has been unusually slow in speech development; whether he finds difficulty in writing, through left-handedness, ambidextrality or unusually clumsy and inco-ordinated movement; whether he possesses marked temperamental instability. Then if possible his family history should be studied in order to discover if similar defects have appeared in other members of the family. There seems to be sufficient evidence to prove that in certain families these defects are associated, and that one or more of them may appear in many members of the family, particularly the males. What exactly is the nature of the congenital tendency which gives rise to these defects is more doubtful. It may indeed be a lack of maturation in the development of certain areas of the cerebral cortex, and particularly in their differentiation and specialization of function. Or it may be that there is some deficiency in the co-ordination of various parts of the cortex, and especially in the co-ordination of function of the opposite hemi-spheres which underlies hemispherical dominance. Clearly we need much more evidence before we can determine the truth of any one of these theories; and more information still before we can hypothesize as to which mechanisms are responsible for reading disability. But from the practical point of view, we are perhaps justified in concluding that children who themselves show, or whose families show, any of the defects described, are likely to have considerable difficulty in learning to read, write or spell; and that it would be desirable to give them particular care and attention and special teaching. It appears to be the mechanisms by which linguistic tasks are carried out which are affected, rather than the understanding and use of words as such. Thus teaching methods are indicated which stress the meaningful reading of words and the writing of connected sentences; and phonetic methods are contra-indicated. On the other hand, should the child appear to suffer from the condition termed 'auditory imperception' (see p. 63), other methods are probably advisable. But these cases are so rare, and so little is known about them, that it is impossible at present to indicate how they should be treated.

It has been pointed out that we have no evidence as to the frequency of congenital reading disability among backward readers in general; but it is unlikely that they constitute more than a small proportion even of severe cases of reading disability. Certainly not every left-handed backward reader, still less every cross-lateral, should be diagnosed as falling into this category. The frequency and severity of the symptoms described in the child and in his family must be carefully considered before he is labelled as a case of congenital reading disability. Among the remainder of cases, we may next consider those who appear to possess some marked temperamental defect; or some disorder of personality or behaviour which originated before the onset of reading difficulty. Although many of the symptoms of maladjustment observed in cases of reading disability may be due to the reading failure itself, there can be no doubt that there do exist cases in which the maladjustment is primary. Though this does not prove that the maladjustment is *caused* by the reading failure—*post hoc, non propter hoc*—it is at least a reasonable supposition that the two are related. The following appear to be the more characteristic types of personality and behaviour disorder with which reading disability is associated:

We have, first, cases of definite temperamental instability who may perhaps be of the same type as the congenital cases described above. These children are naturally hyper-active, restless, distrac-tible and unable to concentrate. It is not so much that they are unable to understand the successive processes involved in reading, but that they fail through inattention to grasp some essential stage, and lack the application to make good what they have missed. Burt (1937) found a considerable proportion of such children among his generally backward readers. Eleven of Castner's thirteen cases (p. 143) seem to have exhibited some degree of instability, two of them to a marked extent. Such children should, however, be differentiated from those in whom lack of concentration and application to work appears to be due not to an innate defect but to parental indulgence and over-protectiveness. Because they have been spoilt and shielded from all difficulties, they find it very hard to attempt and to perform any task which is arduous and difficult. One of the first of such tasks which they encounter when they go to school is learning to read. They break down, and their failure discourages them still further. Stewart (1950) instanced cases of such children as showing inferiority in reading (p. 141), and Hattwick and Stowell (1936) described their carelessness and their inability to concentrate and to work to their full capacity (p. 141). Despert (1946) showed that speech defects might also occur in such children (p. 132), and these in turn may affect reading. Such children may require constant encouragement and urging from their teacher before they can be induced to tackle and surmount their difficulties. Nevertheless, their prognosis is probably more hopeful than that of cases of marked temperamental instability.

In contrast to the over-protected are those whose parents exert too much pressure upon them to succeed in school. The evidence of Hattwick and Stowell suggests that they also may lack endurance and concentration. But it is possible, as Davis and Kent (1955) indicated, that parental pressure does not produce any harmful effects until the child has begun to lag behind in his school progress (p. 141). Some fortuitous cause may produce failure, such as was described on p. 189. The parents immediately become worried or reproachful, or urge the child to try harder. This makes the child tense and nervous (particularly if he already possesses some degree of emotional instability); the harder he tries, the less successful he is.

Such children require a more relaxed treatment in school. It is no use urging them; they must be helped to succeed, even in some quite minor activity, and praised for their efforts and reassured that they can repeat this success. The good results achieved by Fernald at her clinic seem to have been due in part to the continued assurance produced by a series of small successes.

But there are other cases in which inability to learn to read appears to be a symptom of the child's hostility and aggression towards his parents and towards society, especially the school community. Some of the cases of Stewart (1950), Spache (Robinson, 1953 *b*) and Lantz and Liebes (1943), may have been of this type (pp. 140, 138). The child is already hostile to adult authority when he comes to school. He is therefore indisposed to accept the authority of the teacher who instructs him in reading. Furthermore, his reading failure may constitute a punishment of the parents who have deprived him in the past of care and affection, but who now wish him to succeed. The observations of Spache (1954) seem to indicate that overt expression of this aggression towards adults is often repressed; but it may appear, both in the reading failure, and also in aggressive behaviour to other children (p. 140). In other cases, the reading disability appears to act as a means of attracting the attention of neglectful parents to the child's state of anxiety and insecurity. Again, there are cases in which the child retreats from a hostile world and from his own anxiety into a state of apathy and day-dreaming; thus he does not attempt to accept and understand the instruction he receives in school or to perform the tasks which are given him. And finally there are cases such as those described by Davis and Kent (1955) in which the parents are indifferent to their children and their progress in school, and the children lack the incentive to succeed (p. 141).

In all these cases it is probable that remedial teaching will have little effect unless the original situation of hostility or anxiety is relieved by suitable therapeutic treatment. The same is true of what seem to be mildly obsessional cases, such as those described by Solomon (Robinson, 1953 *a*), who appeared to be rigidly and severely controlled and apt to niggle over unimportant details

(p. 140). Such cases do not seem to have been observed and reported by other experimenters or clinicians, and they may be infrequent. But it is quite possible that such children would fail to perceive the important features in the structure of printed and spoken words, and to differentiate them from unimportant details and variations. This type of failure, however, also appears in the immature child. Thus obsessional characteristics should not be diagnosed unless there is a good deal of corroborative clinical evidence of other kinds.

It should not, however, be assumed that the personality disorders and behaviour maladjustment of these children are in themselves necessary and sufficient causes in every case of reading disability. In some cases, as we have seen, psychotherapeutic treatment which relieves the disorder and produces social adjustment seems also to result in recovery from the disability, and to enable the child to learn to read. Even in cases where reading still proves difficult, it may be that the child has become so bewildered and his thought processes so stultified that great effort is required to disentangle him from his confusion and set him on the right path. But it is also possible that in these cases there has always been something lacking in the child's cognitive capacities—for instance, some immaturity and lack of clarity of thought in associating word shapes and sounds—and that the emotional disability is a predisposing factor, reinforcing and magnifying the cognitive incapacity and making it harder to overcome, rather than actually creating it. Not all maladjusted children fail to learn to read; indeed, as Stewart showed, some of them are superior readers (p. 141). It seems possible that, as so often happens in cases of personality disorder, the emotional inhibitions and conflicts fasten upon some line of weakness, and express themselves in symptoms related to that weakness. We must still therefore retain in mind the possible existence of some inherent cognitive disability, although it has so far been impossible to demonstrate its existence as an independent incapacity.

The same possibility must be borne in mind in considering that residuum of cases which remains after the factors of congenital disability and personality disorder have been eliminated. Here also there may be some innate cognitive incapacity, magnified and focalized by one or more of a multitude of predisposing factors, such as: minor defects of vision and hearing, and other physical defects; unfavourable home circumstances, including lack of cultural support in the home, as well as minor degrees of insecurity or hostility; irregular school attendance; teaching methods unsuitable for children of particular abilities or stage of maturation (including perhaps Fernald's cases with predominantly tactile-kinaesthetic imagery); and lack of interest in the reading situation, or of ability to persist in arduous intellectual tasks and to struggle in overcoming difficulties. It is essential that the particular factors operating in each individual case should be diagnosed at the earliest possible moment, before the disability has become firmly ingrained, and that all of these factors should be remedied as speedily and as effectively as possible in the circumstances. Thus the school medical officer should examine such children in order to discover and treat any physical defects.[1] Some approach to the parents by the teacher, or by a psychiatric social worker, might improve the home situation, for instance, by inviting the parents to encourage and sympathize with the child, rather than to reproach him or punish him, or to be completely indifferent to his difficulties. Where teaching has been inadequate or unsuitable, an immediate attempt should be made to supply what is missing.

But the relief of these conditions will not necessarily by itself produce recovery from the disability—partly because the confusion and sense of failure have become deeply ingrained, and partly also because there may exist some fundamental incapacity which still requires treatment. Thus the child must be given some form of remedial teaching appropriate to the particular form of his disability. Even a change of method, or teaching in a special class, may assist him; though it appears likely that, in the more serious

---

[1] English *et al.* (1939) found that the ordinary school medical inspection did not detect all the cases of visual defect which an ophthalmologist would refer for treatment. Other investigators have shown that reading disability may be associated with binocular imbalance (pp. 117 19), which is not readily apparent from a simple examination for refractive errors.

cases, skilled individual instruction and help are necessary. Several of the studies described in the previous chapter indicated that remedial teaching is more effective if given by a specially trained teacher who is not an ordinary member of the school staff; and in new surroundings which are not associated by the child with the atmosphere of failure and discouragement. It is interesting to note in the *Report of the Committee on Maladjusted Children* (Ministry of Education, 1955) that the London County Council has established a set of part-time special classes, outside the school, to which maladjusted and backward children can be sent for two to five half-days per week. There they work in very small classes under special teachers. Such an arrangement might be profitable for cases of reading disability, though possibly difficult to organize.

Finally, we must hope that further psychological investigation will determine whether in fact reading disability is based upon some fundamental cognitive incapacity, as we have suggested above, and will elucidate the nature of this incapacity. So far the methods of investigation have not been satisfactory. What is required is a detailed experimental and clinical investigation of an adequate number of cases, confined to children who cannot read at all, or can only recognize a few words the shapes of which they have memorized in a vague and inaccurate manner. The first step is then to determine if there are any such cases in which there exist no disorders of personality or physique, and no apparent evidence of inadequate or unsuitable teaching. The enquiry of Schilder (1944) seemed to establish that such cases existed, even when there was no evidence of congenital disposition (see p. 79). The essential procedure then is to investigate these children's thought processes, both in reading and in other tasks. It is not sufficient to give them simple tests of visual and auditory perception, imagery, memory and association. Even when the children appear to be somewhat inefficient in some types of perception and imagery (and this is by no means always the case), the inadequacy may be the result rather than the cause of deficiency in the reasoning processes. Again, little is gained by analysing the child's errors in reading into reversals, substitutions, omissions, etc., or into visual and auditory errors, since it is almost certainly the reasoned combination and manipulation of letter and word shapes and sounds which is at fault. What is required is a study of the ability or inability to analyse various kinds of material into their constituent units in their correct order and arrangement; to generalize the rules of combination of these units; and to re-synthesize them in accordance with the rules. It must be established whether there is a lack of these abilities (*a*) in reading only; (*b*) with linguistic material generally; or (*c*) with other, non-linguistic, material. It may be claimed that whenever the measured I.Q. of cases of reading disability is not subnormal, there can be no deficiency in the reasoning processes. But intelligence tests as a rule cover only certain types of reasoning. It may be that these are not closely related to the complex reasoning processes which must be employed in learning to read. In particular, they do not cover the processes of grasping the systematic arrangement in correct order which is so essential in reading. But all cases must be treated individually before it is possible to generalize in any way from these individual cases. The nature of cognitive incapacity—the particular area of failure in reading—may vary in different cases of disability.

At first sight it may appear that such an investigation is of purely theoretical interest, in establishing the psychological nature and basis of reading disability. But if the exact nature of this disability is more clearly understood, it might be possible to design remedial techniques for treating and eliminating it directly, rather than relying upon the only partially successful hit-or-miss methods which are employed at present. If the Chinese, according to *Elia*, could discover how to roast pork without burning their houses down, it may be possible for us to attack and remedy the fundamental cause of reading disability without applying excessively lengthy and possibly irrelevant remedial procedures.

APPENDIX I

In this appendix is given a description of five cases of reading disability, tested by the author, to illustrate the complexes of factors which can occur in such cases. The first two cases demonstrate the significance of left-handedness and incomplete lateralization. The first gives a clear illustration of a congenital disability in a member of an intelligent and educated family; but the effect of the congenital tendency was probably aggravated by emotional factors. In the second case, there was no evidence of congenital defect; but any effect of incomplete lateralization was greatly reinforced by lack of motivation and home encouragement, and by bad teaching.

Lack of interest and family encouragement seem to have been the main factors in the third case. It is clear, however, that the reading disability could be overcome fairly successfully by good remedial teaching. The same also may be true of the fourth case, if the emotional maladjustment resulting from unfavourable upbringing could be relieved. The fifth case gives an illustration of that puzzling type of disability for which there is no obvious cause. The suggestion is made that this child may have missed some essential stage in learning to read through absence from illness. But it is hard to account for the severity and persistence of his disability.

CASE I

Henry was the 14-year-old eldest son of a father who was a professional engineer. His intelligence was normal, indeed rather above normal, in activities in which he was not handicapped by his linguistic defects. He was retarded by five years in reading (reading age on a comprehension test, 9 years 3 months), and by seven years in spelling. He could read easy prose by guessing the more difficult words; but was incapable of analysing and reading correctly, or spelling, many words in which the letters did not have their simplest phonetic value. Even in easy words he often transposed the order of letters; and he confused the mirror image letters, and some letters of similar form, such as 'm' and 'n'. He was inaccurate and inattentive to detail, which appeared also in his poor arithmetical achievement. His immediate memory, though comparatively normal for visually presented material, was very defective for all forms of orally presented material. He was strongly left-handed, but right-eyed; and his movements in writing were excessively clumsy and cramped. Partly because of his awkward movements, and the fatigue they caused him, and partly because of his inability to spell, he could scarcely write at all. Yet his constructive ability was normal; he could make models and do other manipulative work with skill and dexterity.

His parents appeared to be normal, except that his mother, and her grandfather, were partially left-handed. His early development was normal, but he was frequently in hospital for various complaints between the ages of 5 and 8 years. These periods in hospital seem to have upset him considerably, and he became timid and anxious, clinging to his mother, self-conscious and nervous, and worrying about minor aches and pains. Symptoms of backwardness in school appeared at about 7 years. But he was apparently quite happy at school till he was obliged to move to a new school at the age of 14. In this school he had no craft work, which he enjoyed; and was afraid of the other boys.

He seemed to be a case in whom there was some congenital tendency to incomplete lateralization, motor inco-ordination and temperamental instability. After his periods in hospital, he failed to develop normally, and remained childishly immature. This appeared both in his timidity, and also in his immature syncretist perception, which showed in his inability to analyse words. The reading backwardness was aggravated by writing difficulties, upon which the tendency to motor inco-ordination had become focused. He seemed as it were to have given up the struggle to analyse words properly, and was resigned to a condition in which he could just read, though very inefficiently. He had received no remedial teaching, and appeared by now to be unlikely to profit from it.

CASE II

Robin was 9 years old. His intelligence was normal, including his vocabulary, but his reading age was only about 6½ years. In other words, he could read letters and very simple monosyllables, which he guessed at sight; and in matching words and spelling he showed transpositions in the order of letters, though there was no particular tendency to reversal. He could not read numbers correctly; and his immediate memory for them and for nonsense syllables (presented orally) was poor, although his memory for shapes was normal. He was fairly strongly left-handed and right-eyed, but he could draw well, and his movements were not unduly clumsy.

His family was apparently normal, though his father tended to worry. His own personality was judged normal by the psychiatrist, though he was somewhat timid, and was occasionally bullied by other children. But his mother read with difficulty, and his parents showed little interest in his educational difficulties. At school, he had apparently been put into a backward group, and then more or less completely neglected. The five boys in this group were left to read by themselves, and to help one another with the words they could not read; if they encountered a word which no one knew, they could ask the master who was teaching another class. It was not surprising that Robin's reading was not improving in any way.

His incomplete lateralization may have been a predisposing factor, together with a certain lack of drive and initiative. To learn to read normally, he required the stimulation and encouragement which neither his parents nor his school had given him.

CASE III

Jack was 10 years of age, and of good intelligence—Wechsler Verbal I.Q. 101, Performance I.Q. 116. His reading age was about 6 years; but after two years in a remedial reading class it rose to 8½ years, and subsequently reached approximately normal level. His immediate memory was good; and he could match words presented visually or spoken to him, although he could not read them. He was rather backward in arithmetic.

He was a lively, active, normal boy, completely right-sided. There were said to be several poor readers in his family, though the home was highly respectable. He was somewhat spoilt by his mother.

It appeared that he had little natural interest in school work, and was quite unworried by his backwardness because it was an accepted thing in his family. At first he made little effort in the remedial class to overcome his backwardness; but eventually he was stimulated to do so, possibly by the prospect of going on to the senior school, and apparently learnt to read almost suddenly.

CASE IV

Maurice was 8 years old, of slightly subnormal intelligence (Terman–Merrill I.Q. 82). His reading age was under 6 years; he could read letters, but only very few words which he guessed at sight. He could, however, match a fair number of words and build them from letters. But his immediate memory was poor. He was completely right-sided.

Maurice was an illegitimate child who had had no contact with his mother since infancy, and had been boarded out with a succession of foster-parents; he had been moved eight times. He was aggressive, difficult and destructive. He was now at a children's home, where he clamoured for attention and affection. That he had not learnt to read normally was not surprising in the circumstances. But it is perhaps interesting to note that he was not completely incapable of reading, but did have some understanding of word structure.

CASE V

Edward was 10½ years old, of normal intelligence—Wechsler Verbal I.Q. 94, Performance I.Q. 115. His vocabulary was rather poor, but he was quite good at arithmetic. His reading age was 6 years. His immediate memory was normal, and he could match words presented orally and visually, though he could not read them.

He was a quiet, conscientious, hard-working and apparently quite normal little boy, though right-handed and left-eyed. His parents were rather poor and unintelligent. He had frequently been absent from school with minor illnesses. He made little progress while in the remedial reading class, and could still read only very little when he went on to a secondary school.

There appears to have been no obvious cause for Edward's disability, other than the possibility that he had missed some essential stage in teaching through absence. This had not been detected early enough to be easily remedied; and the disability was now so firmly rooted as to be almost irremediable.

APPENDIX II

In Chapter I of this book, data were given to indicate the frequency of backwardness in reading in various areas of England and Wales, as shown in the Ministry of Education pamphlet, *Reading Ability* (1950); and among a sample of London school-children (Child, 1955) and of Middlesbrough school-children (Middlesbrough Head Teachers' Association, 1953). Since writing this chapter, the author's attention has been drawn to certain other surveys of the incidence of reading backwardness, and particularly to one made in Leeds.[1] In this enquiry, the reading ability of large groups of children was tested, by means of the Schonell Silent Reading Test A, in 1950, 1952 and 1953. The results are shown in Table 45.

Table 45

Year	No. of children	Age in years	Percentage retarded 2 or more years below chronological age	Percentage unable to read	Percentage retarded below mental age by	
					1 year	2 or more years
1950	5000	9–10	19·0	6·9	—	—
1952	1985	11–12	19·0	0·6	—	—
1953	3184	9–10	15·0	—	12·0	8·6

It should be noted that the group of 11–12-year-old children was one drawn from the original 5000, which had been followed up into the secondary modern school. There were no grammar school children among the 11–12-year-olds. The number of non-readers (twelve in all) had become very small. Though the total number retarded had not decreased in 1952, yet by 1953 it was appreciably less. This improvement seems to have resulted from the special teaching given to backward readers, following on the 1950 survey. In particular, special improvement courses for very backward readers were instituted in 1951, to which children were transferred

[1] City of Leeds Education Committee (1953). *Report on a Survey of Reading Ability.*

from neighbouring schools for a period of a year. Among 143 such children, the improvement during this period ranged from 0·2 to 4·4 years of reading age. Thus the treatment appears to have been effective in reducing the overall percentage of backwardness; but some cases proved relatively intractable.

Further data on the distribution of reading backwardness have recently been published by Kellmer Pringle (1956), and are shown in Table 46. These were obtained in the main from various un-named Midland towns, by testing with the Schonell Silent Reading Tests A or B. Unfortunately the numbers of children tested were not given.

Table 46

Midland town	Date	Age of children in years	Percentage frequency	Criterion (years below mental age)
1	1952	7–8	11	2
2	1955	8–9	15	2
3	1955	7–8	19	1½
3	1955	8–9	23	1½
4	1956	8–9	22	1½
5	1956	7–8	15	1½

These data all relate to children younger than those tested in the surveys previously described. These children presumably would have had little opportunity of receiving much special or remedial teaching or reading. Consequently it is impossible to judge whether their backwardness was of the kind which could be remedied fairly easily, or whether it would persist as a real disability. No doubt these figures constitute a challenge to teachers of reading in the ordinary schools. But it is not possible to judge whether they indicate the existence of large numbers of cases of the type of disability which would require thorough and extensive remedial treatment.

APPENDIX III

A recently published study by Daniels and Diack (1956) has described a comparison of the effects of two methods of teaching reading to non-readers: (1) the modified phonic method used in the 'Royal Road' Readers (Daniels and Diack, 1954); and (2) 'mixed' methods, beginning with look-and-say methods, supplemented at some stage by phonic teaching. In method (1), also, the child begins with simple monosyllabic whole words attached to pictures; but he is taught from the earliest stage to notice and recognize the phonetic sounds of the letters from which the words are built up. The words are grouped in such a way as to emphasize their phonetic similarities and differences. But the letter sounds are always taught as parts of whole words and never in isolation. Reading is supplemented by suitable exercises, with word matching cards and the writing of letters and words.

The comparison was made between the word recognition of group A, forty-four children in the first year of the junior school, taught for a year by method (1), and group B, fifty-five similar children taught for a year by (2), mixed methods. These children were equated for age (c. 8 years) and socio-economic status, but not for intelligence. At the beginning of the year in the junior school they were all non-readers, or approximately so. The teacher who taught group A was a fully experienced one, but the teacher who taught group B was judged to be rather more skilled, especially in the teaching of backward readers. She was a firm believer in individual treatment with a great variety of methods and devices.

The tests given at the end of the year were for the ability to pronounce isolated words (Tests 1–4) and words in sentences (Tests 5–6). Some of the words were new to the children, and some had been encountered in their reading books (words in Tests 3 and 5 had been encountered by the group A children, those in Tests 4 and 6 by the group B children). The percentage results are shown in Table 47. The differences are all statistically significant, and indicate a substantial advantage for method (1), even for recognition of words unfamiliar to group A but familiar to group B. The curves of score frequency for Tests 1–4 showed that in every case there were more children in group B than in group A with very low scores, that is to say, children who had apparently learnt little if anything from their year's teaching.

Table 47

	Percentage of words read by	
Test	Group A	Group B
1	85·5	43·1
2	60·5	35·2
3	79·9	47·7
4	73·5	44·9
5	37·5	26·7
6	35·1	26·3

Daniels and Diack analysed the errors made by the children in these tests, and found that the children in group A made fewer errors of every kind except those in which the phonetic value of the word did not reproduce the conventional phonetic value of its constituent letters. For instance, 'answer' was pronounced with a short 'a' as in 'man'. This suggests that children taught by the phonic method might believe that the phonetic values of English words are regular and logical, and might therefore have more difficulty in accepting irregular values than children taught by the less logical and systematic mixed methods. However, at this stage at least the difficulty does not seem to have been very far-reaching.

Another interesting finding was that, whereas the group A children made no response at all to 16·3% of the test words, the group B children made no response to 46%. Thus the phonic method seemed to be more effective than the mixed methods in encouraging the children to try actively and systematically to tackle words with which they were unfamiliar. This suggests that the group A children had acquired a useful tool, the method of phonetic analysis, with which to attempt new words; whereas the group B children did not know how to proceed with unfamiliar words. This less systematic attack of the group B children was also shown in a greater tendency to ignore or mis-read certain letters, particularly those in the middle of words. Mirror reversals were infrequent, and showed no significant difference of incidence in the two groups.

The evidence from this enquiry thus shows quite definitely that the modified phonic method of Daniels and Diack was successful in enabling the majority of the non-readers who were studied to acquire at least the beginnings of the fundamental processes of reading. We do not know how much intelligence these children possessed; but it seems likely that several of them may have been of rather low intelligence, and that this did not prevent them from profiting by this particular method of instruction. Whether it is equally suitable for children beginning reading at a lower age than 8 years is not certain. Nor can we tell if cases of persistent reading disability could be taught to read in this way; though the results of Conduct and Ward (1955) suggest that the method might be valuable in many cases.

Finally, we cannot judge whether other teachers could apply the modified phonic method with the same efficacy. It appears that the teacher who taught group A did so under careful supervision from the investigators. Further study is required with larger numbers of children and with other teachers of varying skill and experience working without expert supervision, before it is possible to decide finally if the modified phonic method is superior in every case to other teaching methods. But this enquiry certainly suggests that it may be valuable, particularly with children who have shown, by the time they reach the junior school, that they have had difficulty in learning to read. The most valuable feature of the method appears to be the teaching of the phonetic values of letters within easy words which the child can first learn to recognize as meaningful wholes, and then analyse in successive stages.

REFERENCES

AGNEW, D. C. (1939). *Duke University Research Studies in Education*, no. 5.

ALDEN, C. L., SULLIVAN, H. B. and DURRELL, D. D. (1941). *Education*, **62**, 32.

AMES, L. B. and ILG, F. L. (1951). *J. Genet. Psychol.* **79**, 29.

ANDERSON, I. H. and DEARBORN, W. F. (1952). *The Psychology of Teaching Reading.* New York: Ronald Press.

AXLINE, V. M. (1947). *J. Consult. Psychol.* **11**, 61.

BAKWIN, R. M. and BAKWIN, H. (1948). *J. Pediat.* **32**, 465.

BALLARD, P. B. (1912). *J. Exp. Pedag.* **1**, 298.

BARTON HALL, S. and BARTON HALL, M. (1931). *J. Neurol. Psychopath.* **11**, 304.

BENDER, L. (1938). *A Visual Motor Gestalt Test and its Clinical Use.* New York: American Orthopsychiatric Association.

BENNETT, A. (1942). *J. Educ. Psychol.* **33**, 25.

BENNETT, C. C. (1938). *Teachers' Coll. Contr. to Educ.* no. 755.

BENNETT, S. M. (1951). *Brit. J. Educ. Psychol.* **21**, 45.

BERGMAN, W. G. and VREELAND, W. (1932). *Elemen. School J.* **32**, 605.

BETTS, E. A. (1934). *Educ. Res. Bull.* **13**, 135 and 163.

BETTS, E. A. (1936). *The Prevention and Correction of Reading Difficulties.* Evanston, Ill.: Row, Peterson.

BILLS, R. E. (1950). *J. Consult. Psychol.* **14**, 140.

BINET, A. and SIMON, J. (1908). *Ann. Psychol.* **14**, 1.

BIRCH, L. B. (1949). *Educ. Rev.* **1**, 107.

BIRCH, L. B. (1953). *Brit. J. Educ. Psychol.* **23**, 56.

BLACK, J. W. (1937). *Arch. Speech*, **2**, 7.

BLANCHARD, P. (1928). *Mental Hygiene*, **12**, 772.

BLANCHARD, P. (1935). *Amer. J. Orthopsychiat.* **5**, 361.

BLANCHARD, P. (1936). *Mental Hygiene*, **20**, 384.

BLIESMER, E. P. (1954). *J. Educ. Psychol.* **45**, 321.

BOND, G. L. (1935). *Teachers' Coll. Contr. to Educ.* no. 657.

BOND, G. L. and FAY, L. C. (1950). *J. Educ. Res.* **43**, 475.

BOND, G. L. and WAGNER, E. B. (1943). *Teaching the Child to Read.* New York: Macmillan.

BONEY, C. de W. and LYNCH, J. E. (1942). *Elemen. Eng. Rev.* **19**, 115.

BOOME, E. J., BAINES, H. M. S. and HARRIES, D. G. (1939). *Abnormal Speech.* London: Methuen.

BOREL-MAISONNY, S. (1950). *Bull. Soc. Odonto-Stomatol. Rhin.* **4**, 1.

BOWDEN, J. H. (1911). *Elemen. School Teacher*, **12**, 21.

BRADFORD, H. F. (1954). *Elemen. School J.* **54**, 354.

BRAIN, W. R. (1945). *Lancet*, **249**, 837.

BRUCKER, SISTER M. D. (1954). *Cathol. Educ. Rev.* **52**, 249.

BRYNGELSON, B. (1926). *A Study of the Articulatory Difficulties of Thirteen Stutterers.* Univ. Iowa, unpublished thesis.

BRYNGELSON, B. (1935). *J. Genet. Psychol.* **47**, 204.

BURGE, I. C. (1952). *Brit. J. Educ. Psychol.* **22**, 45.

BURKE, R. S. and DALLENBACH, K. M. (1924). *Amer. J. Psychol.* **35**, 267.

BURT, C. (1921). *Mental and Scholastic Tests.* London: P. S. King.

BURT, C. (1937). *The Backward Child.* University of London Press.

BURT, C. (1945). *Brit. J. Educ. Psychol.* **15**, 20.

BURT, C. (1952). *The Causes and Treatment of Backwardness.* University of London Press.

BURT, C. and LEWIS, R. B. (1946). *Brit. J. Educ. Psychol.* **16**, 116.

BUSWELL, G. T. (1945). *Suppl. Educ. Monogr.* no. 60.

BUXTON, C. E. and CROSLAND, H. R. (1937). *Amer. J. Psychol.* **49**, 458.

CARMICHAEL, L. and CASHMAN, H. (1932). *J. Gen. Psychol.* **6**, 296.

CARRIGAN, M. D. (1948). *Studies in Reading*, 1. Publications of the Scottish Coun. for Res. in Educ., 26.

CARTER, D. B. (1953). *J. Psychol.* **36**, 299.

CASTNER, B. M. (1935). *Amer. J. Orthopsychiat.* **5**, 375.

CHALLMAN, R. C. (1939). *J. Except. Chil.* **6**, 7.

CHAMBERLAIN, E. (1929). *J. Heredity*, **9**, 557.

CHILD, H. A. T. (1955). In *Univ. of London Inst. of Educ., Stud. in Educ.* no. 7. London: Evans.

CITY OF LEEDS EDUCATION COMMITTEE (1953). *Report on a Survey of Reading Ability.*

CLARK, B. (1935). *J. Educ. Psychol.* **26**, 530.

CLARK, B. (1936). *J. Educ. Psychol.* **27**, 473.

COBB, S. (1943). *Borderlands of Psychiatry.* Harv. Univ. Monogr. Med. Publ. Hlth, no. 4.

COHN, R. (1949). *Clinical Electroencephalography.* New York: McGraw-Hill.

COLEMAN, J. C. (1953). *J. Educ. Psychol.* **44**, 497.

CONDUCT, G. N. and WARD, H. (1955). *Educ. Rev.* **7**, 212.

CONWAY, C. B. (1937). *The Hearing Abilities of Children in Toronto Public Schools.* Ontario Coll. of Educ., Dep. of Educ. Res. Bull. no. 9.

CRIDER, B. (1944). *J. Gen. Psychol.* **31**, 179.

CROSLAND, H. R. (1938). *J. Educ. Res.* **32**, 410.

CROWE, S. J. *et al.* (1942). *Laryngoscope*, **52**, 790.

CUFF, N. B. (1930). *J. Genet. Psychol.* **37**, 530.

CUFF, N. B. (1931). *J. Exp. Psychol.* **14**, 164.

CUMMINGS, J. D. (1944). *Brit. J. Educ. Psychol.* **14**, 151.

CUMMINGS, J. D. (1946). *Brit. J. Educ. Psychol.* **16**, 163.

CURR, W. and GOURLAY, N. (1953). *Brit. J. Educ. Psychol.* **23**, 45.

DALLENBACH, K. M. (1923). *Amer. J. Psychol.* **34**, 282.

DANIELS, J. C. and DIACK, H. (1954). *The Royal Road Readers.* London: Chatto and Windus.

DANIELS, J. C. and DIACK, H. (1956). *Progress in Reading.* University of Nottingham Institute of Education.

DAVIDSON, H. P. (1931). *Genet. Psychol. Monogr.* **9**, 119.
DAVIDSON, H. P. (1934). *J. Genet. Psychol.* **45**, 452.
DAVIS, D. R. and KENT, N. (1955). *Proc. Roy. Soc. Med.* **48**, 993.
DAVIS, E. A. (1937). *Inst. Child Welfare Monogr. Ser.* no. 14.
DAVIS, L. F. (1939). *Suppl. Educ. Monogr.* no. 49.
DAVIS, L. F., ILG, V., SPRINGER, M. K. and HANCK, D. A. (1949). *Perceptual Training of Young Children.* Evanston, Ill.: Row, Peterson.
DAWSON, S. (1936). *Brit. J. Psychol.* **27**, 129.
DEARBORN, W. F. (1929). *Elemen. School J.* **30**, 266.
DEARBORN, W. F. (1933). *Proc. Amer. Ass. for Mental Deficiency,* **38**, 266.
DEARBORN, W. F. (1936). *Psychol. Monogr.* **47**, no. 2, 1.
DEARBORN, W. F. (1939). *Suppl. Educ. Monogr.* no. 49.
DEARBORN, W. F. and ANDERSON, I. H. (1938). *J. Exp. Psychol.* **23**, 559.
DESPERT, J. L. (1943). *Nerv. Child,* **2**, 134.
DESPERT, J. L. (1946). *Amer. J. Orthopsychiat.* **16**, 100.
DICE, L. K. (1942). *J. Educ. Res.* **36**, 535.
DOLCH, E. W. (1934). *J. Educ. Res.* **28**, 271.
DOLCH, E. W. (1948). *Problems in Reading.* Champaign, Ill.: The Garrard Press.
DOLCH, E. W. and BLOOMSTER, M. (1937). *Elemen. School J.* **38**, 201.
DONNELLY, H. E. (1935). *Education,* **56**, 40.
DOUGLASS, L. C. (1943). *J. Exp. Psychol.* **32**, 247.
DOWNEY, J. E. (1927). *Amer. J. Psychol.* **38**, 317.
DURRELL, D. D. (1940). *The Improvement of Basic Reading Abilities.* Yonkers: World Book Co.
DURRELL, D. D. and SULLIVAN, H. B. (1937). *Reading Capacity and Achievement Tests.* Yonkers: World Book Co.
EAMES, T. H. (1932). *J. Educ. Res.* **25**, 211.
EAMES, T. H. (1933). *Amer. J. Ophthal.* **21**, 1370.
EAMES, T. H. (1935). *J. Educ. Res.* **29**, 1.
EAMES, T. H. (1945). *J. Educ. Res.* **38**, 506.
EAMES, T. H. (1948a). *Amer. J. Ophthal.* **31**, 713.
EAMES, T. H. (1948b). *J. Pediat.* **33**, 614.
ELLIS, A. (1949). *J. Consult. Psychol.* **13**, 56.
ENGLISH, B. C., SHMUKLER, B. C. and COWAN, A. (1939). *Arch. Ophthal* **22**, 1068.
ETTLINGER, G. and JACKSON, C. V. (1955). *Proc. Roy. Soc. Med.* **48**, 998.
EUSTIS, R. S. (1947a). *J. Pediat.* **31**, 448.
EUSTIS, R. S. (1947b). *New England Med. J.* **237**, 243.
EVANS, E. G. S. (1953). *Brit. J. Educ. Psychol.* **23**, 127.
EWING, A. W. G. (1930). *Aphasia in Children.* Oxford Medical Publications.
EWING, I. R. and EWING, A. W. G. (1954). *Speech and the Deaf Child.* Manchester University Press.
FABIAN, A. A. (1945). *J. Educ. Psychol.* **36**, 129.
FARRIS, L. P. (1936). *J. Exp. Educ.* **5**, 58.
FENDRICK, P. (1935). *Teachers' Coll. Contr. to Educ.* no. 656.
FENDRICK, P. and BOND, G. (1936). *J. Genet. Psychol.* **48**, 236.

FERNALD, G. M. (1943). *Remedial Techniques in Basic School Subjects.* New York: McGraw-Hill.

FERNALD, G. M. and KELLER, H. (1921). *J. Educ. Res.* **4**, 355.

FILDES, L. G. (1921). *Brain*, **44**, 286.

FITT, A. B. and O'HALLORAN, K. H. (1934). *J. Educ. Psychol.* **25**, 286.

FLEMING, C. M. (1943). *Brit. J. Educ. Psychol.* **13**, 74.

FLESCH, R. (1955). *Why Johnny Can't Read.* New York: Harper.

FLETCHER, H. (1929). *Speech and Hearing.* New York: Van Nostrand.

FLETCHER, H. (1953). *Speech and Hearing in Communication.* New York: Van Nostrand.

FORGAYS, D. G. (1953). *J. Exp. Psychol.* **45**, 165.

FRANK, H. (1935). *Brit. J. Educ. Psychol.* **5**, 41.

FROESCHELS, E. (1944). *Arch. Neurol. Psychiat.* **51**, 544.

GAHAGAN, L. (1933). *J. Gen. Psychol.* **9**, 455.

GALIFRET-GRANJON, N. (1951). *Enfance*, no. 5, 445.

GALIFRET-GRANJON, N. (1953). *Ann. Psychol.* **53**, 503.

GALIFRET-GRANJON, N. (1954). *Enfance*, no. 7, 179.

GALIFRET-GRANJON, N. and AJURIAGUERRA, J. (1951). *L'Encéphale*, no. 3, 385.

GARDNER, D. E. M. (1942). *Testing Results in the Infant School.* London: Methuen.

GARDNER, D. E. M. (1950). *Long Term Results of Infant School Methods.* London: Methuen.

GARRISON, S. C. and HEARD, M. T. (1931). *Peabody J. Educ.* **9**, 9.

GATES, A. I. (1922). *Teachers' Coll. Contr. to Educ.* no. 129.

GATES, A. I. (1926). *J. Educ. Psychol.* **17**, 433.

GATES, A. I. (1927). *J. Educ. Psychol.* **18**, 217.

GATES, A. I. (1930). *Interest and Ability in Reading.* New York: Macmillan.

GATES, A. I. (1935). *The Improvement of Reading.* New York: Macmillan.

GATES, A. I. (1936). *J. Nat. Educ. Ass.* **25**, 205.

GATES, A. I. (1937). *Elemen. School J.* **37**, 497.

GATES, A. I. (1939). *Elemen. School J.* **39**, 497.

GATES, A. I. (1940). *Elemen. School J.* **40**, 577.

GATES, A. I. (1941). *J. Genet. Psychol.* **59**, 77.

GATES, A. I. and BOEKER, E. (1923). *Teachers' Coll. Record*, **24**, 469.

GATES, A. I. and BOND, G. L. (1936). *J. Educ. Psychol.* **27**, 450.

GATES, A. I. and CHASE, E. H. (1926). *J. Educ. Psychol.* **17**, 289.

GATES, A. I. and RUSSELL, D. H. (1938). *Elemen. School J.* **39**, 119.

GATES, A. I. and RUSSELL, D. H. (1939). *J. Educ. Res.* **32**, 321.

GELLERMAN, L. W. (1933). *J. Genet. Psychol.* **42**, 3 and 28.

GESELL, A. and AMATRUDA, C. S. (1941). *Developmental Diagnosis: Normal and Abnormal Child Development.* New York: Hoeber.

GESELL, A. and AMES, L. B. (1946). *J. Genet. Psychol.* **68**, 45.

GESELL, A. and AMES, L. B. (1947). *J. Genet. Psychol.* **70**, 155.

GESELL, A. and ILG, F. L. (1946). *The Child from Five to Ten.* London: Hamish Hamilton.

GESELL, A., ILG, F. L. and BULLIS, G. E. (1949). *Vision: Its Development in Infant and Child.* New York: Harper.

GESELL, A. and LORD, E. E. (1927). *J. Genet. Psychol.* **34**, 339.

GIBBONS, H. (1934). *Proc. Amer. Speech Corr. Ass.* **4**, 7.

GILLE, R., HENRY, L., TABAH, L., SUTTER, J., BERGUES, H., GIRARD, A. and BASTIDE, H. (1954). *Le Niveau Intellectuel des Enfants d'Âge Scolaire.* Paris: Presses Universitaires de France.

GLANVILLE, A. D. and ANTONITIS, J. J. (1955). *J. Exp. Psychol.* **49**, 294.

GRAY, W. S. (1937). *36th Yearbook, Part I, Nat. Soc. for Stud. of Educ.* p. 65. Bloomington, Ill.: Public School Publishing Co.

GRIFFITHS, R. (1954). *The Abilities of Babies.* University of London Press.

HALLGREN, B. (1950). Specific Dyslexia. *Acta Psychiat. Neurol.* Suppl., 65.

HARRIMAN, M. and HARRIMAN, P. L. (1950). *J. Clin. Psychol.* **6**, 175.

HARRIS, A. J. (1947). *How to Increase Reading Ability.* New York: Longmans Green.

HARTMANN, G. W. (1941). *Educational Psychology.* New York: American Book Co.

HATTWICK, B. W. and STOWELL, M. (1936). *J. Educ. Res.* **30**, 169.

HENRY, S. (1947). *J. Genet. Psychol.* **70**, 211; **71**, 3 and 49.

HESTER, K. B. (1942). *Elemen. School J.* **43**, 171.

HILDRETH, G. (1932). *Child Devel.* **3**, 1.

HILDRETH, G. (1934). *J. Educ. Psychol.* **25**, 1.

HILDRETH, G. (1949). *J. Genet. Psychol.* **75**, 197.

HILDRETH, G. (1950). *J. Genet. Psychol.* **76**, 39.

HILL, M. B. (1936). *J. Educ. Res.* **29**, 487.

HILLIARD, G. H. and TROXELL, E. (1937). *Elemen. School J.* **38**, 255.

HINCKS, E. M. (1926). *Harvard Monogr. in Educ.* Ser. I, vol. 2, no. 2.

HINSHELWOOD, J. (1917). *Congenital Word Blindness.* London: H. K. Lewis.

HIRSCH, I. J. (1952). *The Measurement of Hearing.* New York: McGraw-Hill.

HORN, E. (1929). *J. Educ. Psychol.* **20**, 161.

HUNNICUTT, C. W. (1943). *Elemen. School J.* **43**, 530.

ILG, F. L. and AMES, L. B. (1950). *J. Genet. Psychol.* **76**, 291.

JACKSON, J. (1944). *J. Genet. Psychol.* **65**, 113.

JASPER, H. H. and RANEY, E. T. (1937). *Amer. J. Psychol.* **49**, 450.

JASTAK, J. (1939). *J. Appl. Psychol.* **23**, 473.

JENKINS, R. L., BROWN, A. W. and ELMENDORF, L. (1937). *Amer. J. Orthopsychiat.* **7**, 72.

JENSEN, M. B. (1943). *J. Appl. Psychol.* **27**, 535.

JOHNSON, M. S. (1955). *J. Educ. Res.* **48**, 565.

JOHNSON, W. and DUKE, D. (1940). *J. Educ. Psychol.* **31**, 45.

JOHNSON, W. and KING, A. (1942). *J. Exp. Psychol.* **31**, 293.

KARLIN, I. W. (1950). *J. Amer. Med. Ass.* **143**, 732.

KEIR, G. (1951). *Adventures in Reading for Backward Readers: Teachers' Companion.* Oxford University Press.

KELLMER PRINGLE, M. L. (1956). *Times Educational Supplement*, 12 October.

KELLMER PRINGLE, M. L. and GULLIFORD, R. (1953). *Brit. J. Educ. Psychol.* **23**, 196.
KELLY, A. (1954). *Brit. J. Educ. Psychol.* **24**, 49.
KEMP, L. C. D. (1955). *Brit. J. Educ. Psychol.* **25**, 67.
KENDALL, B. S. (1948). *J. Educ. Psychol.* **39**, 370.
KENNEDY, H. (1942). *J. Exp. Educ.* **10**, 238.
KETCHAM, W. A. (1951). *Child Develop.* **22**, 185.
KIRK, S. A. (1933). *J. Educ. Psychol.* **24**, 525.
KNEHR, C. A. (1941). *J. Exp. Psychol.* **29**, 133.
KNOTT, J. R. and TJOSSEM, T. D. (1943). *J. Exp. Psychol.* **32**, 357.
KÖHLER, W. (1939). *Dynamics in Psychology.* London: Faber and Faber.
KOPEL, D. (1942). *Teachers' Coll. J.* **13**, 64.
KOPP, H. (1943). *Nerv. Child,* **2**, 107.
KOVARSKY, V. (1938). *Extraits des Annales Médicopsychologiques,* no. 4.
KRISE, M. (1952). *J. Educ. Psychol.* **43**, 408.
LADD, M. (1933). *Teachers' Coll. Contr. to Educ.* no. 582.
LAGRONE, C. W. and HOLLAND, B. F. (1943). *Amer. J. Psychol.* **56**, 592.
LAGRONE, T. G. (1936). *J. Exp. Educ.* **5**, 40.
LANTZ, B. and LIEBES, G. B. (1943). *J. Educ. Res.* **36**, 604.
LAUTERBACH, C. E. (1933). *J. Genet. Psychol.* **43**, 454.
LEE, J. M. (1933). *Elemen. School J.* **33**, 447.
LICHTENSTEIN, A. (1938). *J. Genet. Psychol.* **52**, 407.
LINCOLN, E. A. (1927). *Sex Differences in the Growth of American Children.* Baltimore: Warwick and York.
LINDER, M. (1951). *Z. Kind-Psychiat.* 18.
LINDSLEY, D. B. (1940). *J. Exp. Psychol.* **26**, 211.
LINE, W. (1931). *Brit. J. Psychol. Monogr.* no. 15.
LORD, E. E., CARMICHAEL, L. and DEARBORN, W. F. (1925). *Harvard Monogr. in Educ.,* Ser. I, vol. 2, no. 1.
LOUTTIT, C. M. (1935). *Clinical Psychology.* New York: Harper.
MACGREGOR, G. (1934). *Achievement Tests in the Primary School.* Publications of the Scottish Coun. for Res. in Educ. 6.
MACLATCHY, J. (1946). *Educ. Res. Bull.* **25**, 141.
MACMEEKEN, M. (1939). *Ocular Dominance in Relation to Developmental Aphasia.* University of London Press.
MACMEEKEN, M. (1942). *Developmental Aphasia in Educationally Retarded Children.* University of London Press.
MCCARTHY, D. (1930). *Inst. Child Welfare,* no. 4.
MCCARTHY, D. (1946). In *Manual of Child Psychology.* Ed. by L. Carmichael. New York: John Wiley.
MCCARTHY, D. (1953). *J. Psychol.* **35**, 155.
MCCLAREN, V. M. (1950). *Studies in Reading,* **2**. Publications of the Scottish Coun. for Res. in Educ. 34.
MCCULLOUGH, C. M., STRANG, R. M. and TRAXLER, A. E. (1946). *Problems in the Improvement of Reading.* New York: McGraw-Hill.
MCDADE, J. E. (1937). *J. Educ. Res.* **30**, 489.
MCFIE, J. (1952). *J. Neurol. Psychiat.* **15**, 194.

McGovney, M. (1930). *Elemen. Eng. Rev.* **7**, 146.

McNemar, Q. (1942). *The Revision of the Stanford-Binet Test.* Boston: Houghton Mifflin.

Madison, L. (1956). *Percept. Motor Skills,* **6**, 21.

Mateer, F. (1935). *Psychol. Bull.* **32**, 736.

Meek, L. M. (1925). *Teachers' Coll. Contr. to Educ.* no. 164.

Mehus, H. (1953). *Amer. J. Orthopsychiat.* **23**, 416.

Meili, R. (1931). *Arch. Psychol.* **23**, 25.

Mellone, M. A. (1942). *Brit. J. Educ. Psychol.* **12**, 128.

Metraux, R. W. (1944). *J. Speech Dis.* **9**, 31.

Middlesbrough Head Teachers' Association (1953). *Report of a Survey of Reading Ability.* Middlesbrough Education Committee.

Midgeley, J. D. (1952). *Report to the Medical Research Council Committee on the Educational Treatment of Deafness.* Unpublished.

Miles, P. W. (1953). *Arch. Ophthal.* **50**, 475.

Miller, G. A. (1951). *Language and Communication.* New York: McGraw-Hill.

Miller, W. A. (1938). *Elemen. School J.,* **39**, 280.

Mills, L. (1925). *Amer. J. Ophthal.* **8**, 933.

Ministry of Education (1950). *Reading Ability.* Pamphlet no. 18. London: H.M. Stationery Office.

Ministry of Education (1955). *Report of the Committee on Maladjusted Children.* London: H.M. Stationery Office.

Mishkin, M. and Forgays, D. G. (1952). *J. Exp. Psychol.* **43**, 43.

Missildine, W. H. (1946). *Nerv. Child,* **5**, 263.

Missildine, W. H. and Glasner, P. J. (1947). *J. Pediat.* **31**, 300.

Monroe, M. (1928). *Genet. Psychol. Monogr.* **4**, nos. 4 and 5.

Monroe, M. (1932). *Children Who Cannot Read.* University of Chicago Press.

Monroe, M. (1951). *Growing into Reading.* Chicago: Scott, Foresman.

Monroe, M. and Backus, B. (1937). *Remedial Reading.* London: Harrap.

Morphett, M. V. and Washburne, C. (1931). *Elemen. School J.* **31**, 496.

Morris, R. (1951). *The Quality of Learning.* London: Methuen.

Mosher, R. M. and Newhall, S. M. (1930). *J. Educ. Psychol.* **21**, 500.

Murray, E. (1932). *Psychol. Monogr.* **43**, no. 1, 218.

Naesland, J. (1955). *Res. Bull. from the Instit. of Educ., Univ. of Stockholm,* no. 4.

Nelson, O. W. (1953). *J. Educ. Res.* **47**, 211.

Newson, E. (1955). The Development of Line Figure Discrimination in Pre-School Children. Unpublished Ph.D. thesis, University of Nottingham.

Nice, M. M. (1918). *Ped. Sem.* **25**, 141.

Nielson, J. M. (1940). *Amer. Neurol. Ass.* **66**, 43.

Oates, D. W. (1929). *Forum Educ.* **7**, 91.

Ojemann, R. H. (1930). *J. Educ. Psychol.* **21**, 597.

Orbach, J. (1952). *Amer. J. Psychol.* **65**, 555.

Orton, S. T. (1928). *J. Amer. Med. Ass.* **90**, 1095.

ORTON, S. T. (1929). *J. Educ. Psychol.* **20**, 135.

ORTON, S. T. (1937). *Reading, Writing and Speech Problems in Children.* London: Chapman and Hall.

OSTERREITH, P. A. (1945). *Arch. de Psychol.* **30**, 205.

PARK, G. E. (1948). *Amer. J. Ophthal.* **31**, 28.

PARK, G. E. (1953). *J. Pediat.* **42**, 120.

PARK, G. E. and BURRI, C. (1943*a*). *J. Educ. Psychol.* **34**, 420.

PARK, G. E. and BURRI, C. (1943*b*). *J. Educ. Psychol.* **34**, 535.

PAYNE, C. S. (1930). *Harvard Monogr. in Educ.* no. 10.

PECK, L. and McGLOTHLIN, L. E. (1940). *J. Educ. Psychol.* **31**, 653.

PETTY, M. C. (1939). *J. Educ. Psychol.* **30**, 215.

PIAGET, J. and INHELDER, B. (1948). *La Représentation de l'Espace chez l'Enfant.* Paris: Presses Universitaires de France.

POSTON, F. and PATRICK, J. R. (1944). *J. Appl. Psychol.* **28**, 142.

POTTER, M. C. (1940). *Teachers' Coll. Contr. to Educ.* no. 939.

PRESTON, M. I. (1939). *Child Develop.* **10**, 173.

PRESTON, M. I. (1940). *Amer. J. Orthopsychiat.* **10**, 239.

PRESTON, R. C. and SCHNEYER, J. W. (1956). *J. Educ. Res.* **49**, 455.

PROVINS, K. A. (1956). *Quart. J. Exp. Psychol.* **8**, 79.

RANEY, E. T. (1938). *J. Exp. Psychol.* **23**, 304.

RANEY, E. T. (1939). *J. Exp. Psychol.* **24**, 21.

REDMOUNT, R. S. (1948). *J. Educ. Psychol.* **39**, 347.

REYNOLDS, M. C. (1953). *J. Educ. Res.* **46**, 439.

RHEINBERGER, M. B., KARLIN, I. W. and BERMAN, A. B. (1943). *Nerv. Child*, **2**, 117.

RICKARD, G. E. (1935). *J. Educ. Res.* **29**, 281.

RILEY, SISTER MARY (1929). Visual Perception in Reading and Spelling. Unpublished Thesis, Catholic University of America.

RIZZO, N. D. (1939). *J. Exp. Educ.* **8**, 208.

ROBIN, G. (1952). *Concours médical*, p. 573.

ROBINSON, H. M. (1946). *Why Pupils Fail in Reading.* University of Chicago Press.

ROBINSON, H. M. (1953*a*). *Suppl. Educ. Monogr.* no. 77.

ROBINSON, H. M. (1953*b*). *Suppl. Educ. Monogr.* no. 79.

ROSSIGNOL, L. J. (1948). *Teachers' Coll. Contr. to Educ.* no. 936.

RUSSELL, D. H. (1937). *Teachers' Coll. Contr. to Educ.* no. 727.

RUSSELL, D. H. (1943*a*). *J. Educ. Psychol.* **34**, 115.

RUSSELL, D. H. (1943*b*). *J. Educ. Res.* **37**, 276.

SCHIEDEMANN, N. V. (1931). *The Psychology of Exceptional Children.* Boston: Houghton Mifflin.

SCHILDER, P. (1944). *J. Genet. Psychol.* **65**, 67.

SCHONELL, F. J. (1940). *Brit. J. Educ. Psychol.* **10**, 227.

SCHONELL, F. J. (1941). *Brit. J. Educ. Psychol.* **11**, 20.

SCHONELL, F. J. (1942). *Backwardness in the Basic Subjects.* Edinburgh: Oliver and Boyd.

SCHONELL, F. J. (1945). *The Psychology and Teaching of Reading.* Edinburgh: Oliver and Boyd.

SCHONELL, F. J. (1949). *Brit. J. Educ. Psychol.* **19**, 82.
SCHONELL, F. J. and SCHONELL, F. E. (1950). *Diagnostic and Attainment Testing.* Edinburgh: Oliver and Boyd.
SCHONFIELD, D. (1956). *Brit. J. Educ. Psychol.* **26**, 39.
SCRIPTURE, M. K., GLOGAN, O. and DE BRA, A. H. (1917). *Laryngoscope,* **27**, 157.
SEASHORE, H. G. (1951). *J. Consult. Psychol.* **15**, 62.
SEGERS, J. F. (1926). *J. de Psychol.* **23**, 608 and 723.
SELZER, C. A. (1933). *Harvard Monogr. in Educ.* no. 12.
SETH, G. and GUTHRIE, D. (1935). *Speech in Childhood.* Oxford University Press.
SEXTON, E. K. and HERRON, J. S. (1928). *Elemen. School J.* **28**, 690.
SHELDON, W. D. and CARRILLO, L. (1952). *Elemen. School J.* **52**, 262.
SHERIDAN, M. D. (1955). *The Child's Hearing for Speech.* London: Methuen.
SHOLTY, M. (1912). *Elemen. School Teacher,* **12**, 272.
SMITH, K. U. (1945). *J. Gen. Psychol.* **32**, 39.
SMITH, L. C. (1950). *J. Exp. Educ.* **18**, 321.
SMITH, M. E. (1926). *Univ. Iowa Stud. in Child Welfare,* **3**, no. 5.
SMITH, M. K. (1941). *Genet. Psychol. Monogr.* **24**, 311.
SMITH, N. B. (1928). *J. Educ. Psychol.* **19**, 560.
SPACHE, G. (1940). *Amer. J. Orthopsychiat.* **10**, 229.
SPACHE, G. (1941). *J. Educ. Res.* **34**, 561.
SPACHE, G. (1944). *J. Educ. Res.* **37**, 616.
SPACHE, G. (1954). *Educ. Psychol. Measurem.* **14**, 186.
SPIEL, W. (1953). *Wien. Z. Nervenheilk.* **7**, 20.
STAMBAK, M. (1951). *Enfance,* no. 5, 480.
STEVENSON, L. P. (1949). *Suppl. Educ. Monogr.* no. 68, 7.
STEWART, R. S. (1950). *Amer. J. Orthopsychiat.* **20**, 410.
STRANG, R. (1943). *Educ. Psychol. Measurem.* **3**, 355.
STROUD, J. B. (1945). *J. Educ. Psychol.* **36**, 487.
SYLVESTER, E. and KUNST, M. S. (1943). *Amer. J. Orthopsychiat.* **13**, 69.
TATE, H. L. (1937). *Elemen. School J.* **37**, 752.
TAYLOR, C. D. (1950). *Studies in Reading,* **2**. Publications of the Scottish Coun. for Res. in Educ., 34.
TAYLOR, E. A. (1937). *Controlled Reading.* University of Chicago Press.
TEEGARDEN, L. (1932). *Child. Educ.* **9**, 82.
TEEGARDEN, L. (1933). *J. Educ. Res.* **27**, 81.
TEMPLIN, M. C. (1954). *J. Educ. Res.* **47**, 441.
TERMAN, L. M. and MERRILL, M. A. (1937). *Measuring Intelligence.* London: Harrap.
TOWNSEND, E. A. (1951). *Genet. Psychol. Monogr.* **43**, 1.
TRAVIS, L. E. (1931). *Speech Pathology.* New York: D. Appleton Co.
TRAVIS, L. E. and RASMUS, B. J. (1931). *Quart. J. Speech Educ.* **17**, 217.
TRAXLER, A. E. (1939). *J. Educ. Res.* **32**, 329.
UTLEY, J. (1944). *J. Speech Dis.* **9**, 103.

VAN RIPER, C. (1935). *J. Exp. Psychol.* **18**, 372.

VERNON, M. D. (1931). *The Experimental Study of Reading.* Cambridge University Press.

VERNON, M. D. (1940). *Brit. J. Psychol.* **30**, 273; **31**, 1.

VERNON, P. E. (1948). *Studies in Reading,* **1**. Publications of the Scottish Coun. for Res. in Educ. 26.

VERNON, P. E., O'GORMAN, M. B. and McLELLAN, A. (1955). *Brit. J. Educ. Psychol.* **25**, 195.

WAGNER, G. W. (1936). *Psychol. Monogr.* **48**, no. 3, 108.

WALL, W. D. (1945). *Brit. J. Educ. Psychol.* **15**, 28.

WALL, W. D. (1946). *Brit. J. Educ. Psychol.* **16**, 133.

WALLIN, J. E. W. (1916). *School and Soc.* **3**, 213.

WALLIN, J. E. W. (1921). *Lancet,* **200**, 890.

WATSON, T. J. (1954). Private communication.

WATTS, A. F. (1944). *The Language and Mental Development of Children.* London: Harrap.

WERNER, H. (1954). *J. Gen. Psychol.* **50**, 181.

WETMORE, R. G. and ESTABROOKS, G. H. (1929). *J. Educ. Psychol.* **20**, 628.

WHEELER, L. R. and WHEELER, V. D. (1954). *J. Educ. Res.* **48**, 103.

WHIPPLE, G. (1944). *Elemen. School J.* **44**, 525.

WHITE, A. M. and DALLENBACH, K. M. (1932). *Amer. J. Psychol.* **44**, 175.

WILE, I. S. (1942). *Arch. Ophthal.* **28**, 780.

WILEY, W. E. (1928). *J. Educ. Res.* **17**, 278.

WILKING, S. V. (1941). *Elemen. School J.* **42**, 268.

WILLIAMS, H. M. (1937). *Univ. Iowa Stud. in Child Welfare,* **13**, no. 2.

WILSON, F. T., BURKE, A. and FLEMMING, C. W. (1939). *J. Educ. Res.* **32**, 570.

WILSON, F. T. and FLEMMING, C. W. (1938). *J. Genet. Psychol.* **53**, 3.

WILSON, F. T. and FLEMMING, C. W. (1939). *J. Psychol.* **8**, 99.

WILSON, F. T. and FLEMMING, C. W. (1940). *J. Educ. Psychol.* **31**, 1.

WINCH, W. H. (1925). *J. Educ. Res. Monog.* no. 8.

WISELEY, W. G. (1930). *Ohio Schools,* p. 144.

WITTY, P. A. and KOPEL, D. (1935). *J. Educ. Res.* **29**, 449.

WITTY, P. A. and KOPEL, D. (1936). *J. Educ. Psychol.* **27**, 119.

WOLFE, L. S. (1939). *Amer. J. Psychol.* **52**, 533.

WOLFE, L. S. (1941). *J. Genet. Psychol.* **58**, 45 and 57.

WOOD, L. and SHULMAN, E. (1940). *J. Educ. Psychol.* **31**, 591.

WOODROW, H. (1945). *J. Educ. Psychol.* **36**, 155.

WOODY, C. and PHILLIPS, A. J. (1934). *J. Educ. Res.* **27**, 651.

WORSTER-DROUGHT, C. and ALLEN, I. M. (1929). *J. Neurol. Psychopath.* **9**, 193.

WORSTER-DROUGHT, C. and ALLEN, I. M. (1930). *J. Neurol. Psychopath.* **10**, 193.

YEDINACK, J. G. (1949). *J. Genet. Psychol.* **74**, 23.

YOUNG, F. M. (1941). *Genet. Psychol. Monogr.* **23**, 3.

YOUNG, R. A. (1938). *Amer. J. Orthopsychiat.* **8**, 230.

ZANGWILL, O. L. (1955). *Advanc. Sci. Lond.,* **12**, 55.

INDEX OF AUTHORS

INDEX OF SUBJECTS

For EU product safety concerns, contact us at Calle de José Abascal, 56–1°, 28003 Madrid, Spain or eugpsr@cambridge.org.

www.ingramcontent.com/pod-product-compliance
Ingram Content Group UK Ltd.
Pitfield, Milton Keynes, MK11 3LW, UK
UKHW010337140625
459647UK00010B/662